California's Spiritual Frontiers

California's Spiritual Frontiers

Religious Alternatives in Anglo-Protestantism, 1850–1910

Sandra Sizer Frankiel

University of California Press

Berkeley / Los Angeles / London

University of California Press
Berkeley and Los Angeles, California

University of California Press, Ltd.
London, England

© 1988 by
The Regents of the University of California

**Library of Congress Cataloging-in-Publication
Data**

Frankiel, Sandra Sizer, 1946–
  California's spiritual frontiers.

  Bibliography: p.
  1. California—Religion.   I. Title.
BL2527.C2F72   1988   291'.09794   87-14301
ISBN 0-520-06120-9 (alk. paper)

Printed in the United States of America

1   2   3   4   5   6   7   8   9

to Hirsch,
who helped me learn to love California

Contents

Preface

By 1848, when the American flag was hoisted over Monterey, the tradition generally known to historians as evangelicalism was enjoying its heyday: it had become the most powerful religious influence—and perhaps the most important single cultural influence—in the United States. Evangelicalism has generally meant, since the work of nineteenth-century historian Robert Baird, the voluntaristic, revivalistic Protestantism that aimed to shape American civilization along moral lines. Denominationally, it embraced the membership of Baptist, Congregational, Disciples of Christ, Methodist, and Presbyterian churches as well as a number of smaller sects; its chief opponent was Roman Catholicism. Evangelicals emphasized a personal relationship with God in Jesus Christ established through prayer, devotion, and (often) a conversion experience; they supported strong churches to educate and fortify their members against the temptations of secular society. Through their educational, organizational, and revivalistic efforts, they made Protestant churches a bulwark of American society during the first third of the nineteenth century. Although evangelical leaders had to battle with secularists who resented religious influence in public affairs, and although they met with increasing resistance from the growing Roman Catholic population, on the whole they were successful in upholding traditional Protestant values as the norm for American society.

Evangelicals maintained their preeminence throughout the middle years of the nineteenth century by means of revivals, reform associations, and the popular media as well as through the churches. They were largely responsible for the great antislavery campaigns, for temperance and prohibition crusades, for maintenance of Sabbath observance in most communities, and for the establishment of private colleges, orphanages, and asylums. Their influence was felt throughout the nation, and they faced relatively few challenges until the 1870s. Then evangelicalism itself began to splinter into liberal

and conservative factions. Still, however, Protestant values governed
American public life and the private lives of most of the citizens.

At least, that is the picture of evangelicalism appearing in American histories if they treat of religion at all.[1] Yet the portrait of a
triumphant evangelical tradition is based primarily on data from east
of the Mississippi. In the Far West developments were taking a different turn. Roman Catholicism was strong in the formerly Spanish
areas, of course; but even in many areas where Anglos dominated,
Protestantism did not fare as well as on earlier frontiers. Census data
from nearly all the states of the Rocky Mountain region and westward suggest a lower level of Protestant church membership than in
other regions. The lack of notable religious movements in the Far
West, judging from the scant historical research thus far, suggests a
lack of religious ferment or a lower level of religious interest than in
the East and Midwest. Did religion die a slow death, even while denominations continued to exist, west of the Rockies? What happened to the great evangelical tradition?

Each area of the West—the Rocky Mountain region, the Pacific
Northwest, the Southwest, and California—had its distinctive kind
of religious development, and each deserves separate study. We will
consider some of the significant developments in California, where
traditional Protestantism evolved so differently that it may not be appropriate to speak of evangelicalism there as a distinctive and coherent system. While we see many examples of an evangelical approach
among ministers and missionaries in the early years of American settlement, it is not long before we find instead a settled denominational
Protestantism, mutually tolerant and seldom fired with the interdenominational zeal of the East's Second Great Awakening, the major
series of revivals that occurred between 1790 and 1835. Because of
the variety of attitudes among the evangelical denominations and the
strong presence alongside them of Episcopalian institutions, we will
use the term *Anglo-Protestantism* to refer to the tradition as it
evolved in California. For in examining Californian Protestantism,
we find ourselves looking at the adjustments to a new culture of one
ethnic group among many, rather than at the transplanting of a
clearly defined tradition. The evangelicals were visible in California
as a vocal, highly significant ethno-religious group, but they no
longer constituted a system that defined regional religious culture.

The research for this work has focused on areas of rapid growth
in northern and southern California before 1910—the mining coun-

try, the San Francisco Bay Area, and early Los Angeles (after 1910 shifts in migration patterns changed the religious scene considerably). In the early period, the mining country and urban areas were chief targets of Protestant ministers and missionaries. Yet by 1906, after nearly sixty years of Anglo domination, barely 14 percent of California's population belonged to any Protestant church. Roman Catholics accounted for 30 percent of the population in 1850, but less than 20 percent in 1906, while by 1906 other small groups comprised 2 to 3 percent of the total. Thus in 1906 nearly 65 percent of California's population was unchurched. Considering the great effort of ministerial talent in California and the wealth of the population as a whole, which could have supported a strong religious establishment, the Anglo-Protestant churches did not fare well.

As we will see, there were several reasons why Californians did not join Protestant churches in as large numbers as their immediate predecessors in the East. One significant factor was the development of a small but significant minority who from the beginning interpreted life in religious terms that, explicitly or implicitly, challenged traditional Protestant interpretations by giving expression to an alternative tradition. This challenge and its effect on Protestantism in California will be the main subject of this book. Before pursuing it, however, we must introduce the main actors in the drama.

First were the leaders of the Anglo-Protestant churches, who viewed themselves as agents of the Protestant civilization that began in the New England towns and extended into the entire American empire. They saw themselves as representing true, mainstream Christianity. Doctrinally, they guarded standard Protestant beliefs in a personal God who saved mankind through the sacrificial acts of his son, Jesus Christ; in reward or punishment after death; in human sinfulness and the necessity of repentance; and in clear standards of morality and justice derived from the Bible and democratic traditions. They considered religion to be both individual and communal: individual in that each person had to develop his or her own relation to God (many, but certainly not all, expected this to include a clear experience of conversion), communal in that the churches provided the moral center and continuing education essential for a solid citizenry. Anglo-Protestants in California generally avoided disputes between denominations, adopting the view that groups might have significant differences, but that it was not appropriate to fight publicly over them. This was more than a live-and-let-live mentality; the various denominations often cooperated on enterprises of joint concern. But they showed no interest in merging. Each denomination had its own clientele, and all together carried the Protestant banner.

Second were the liberals emerging in California, as in the East, throughout the second half of the nineteenth century. While not giving up Protestant doctrines entirely, many softened their views on sin and punishment, or de-emphasized conversion. There was no cohesive, institutionalized liberal movement, but a diffuse California mythology arose, emphasizing the state's uniqueness and offering a liberal religious outlook. Many from traditional backgrounds came to consider themselves religiously tolerant, independent thinkers who transcended denominationalism. In the 1860s a strong and clear liberal voice arrived, that of Unitarian minister Thomas Starr King, the most popular Protestant preacher California has ever known. In the Bay Area, Laurentine Hamilton carried on the liberal tradition in the late 1860s and early 1870s. King's connections to eastern Unitarianism and Universalism and Hamilton's to liberal Presbyterianism exemplify an openness in matters of religion that would become firmly ingrained in the attitudes of many of their Protestant contemporaries. Starr King was more the transcendentalist, a visionary who seemed to know a mystical communion with nature and history; Hamilton more the rationalist, developing an intellectual understanding of the universe as organic and meaningful. Their ideas defined the outer range of liberal Anglo-Protestantism in California. Most leaders connected with the traditional denominations did not go so far, at least not before the end of the century. King the Unitarian and Hamilton the exiled Presbyterian (he was declared a heretic in 1869) were too radical to be comfortable partners with the regular churches.

In northern California, Protestant leaders seemed to be battling secularism and struggling with liberalism almost from the beginning. In southern California, traditional Anglo-Protestants seemed at first to gain a stronger foothold when that region began to develop rapidly after 1880. Yet by 1895 challenges from the even more radical metaphysical religions—Christian Science, New Thought, and Theosophy—had begun to undermine the hegemony of traditional Protestant beliefs. These are the third significant group of actors in the story. Liberals, who had already begun integrating some new ideas (for example, from science) into their beliefs, were most directly affected by the metaphysicians. But traditionalists too were

challenged by the new movements, and even within conservative
Protestantism one can detect evidence of alternative ways of thinking—notably in the leadership of the holiness movement that co-
alesced around the Church of the Nazarene in Los Angeles. In short,
by 1910 Protestantism in southern California had many liberals
within its ranks and had to face a multitude of small, competing religious movements. Most of these were rooted in the same tradition
as the earlier northern liberals, namely New England transcendentalism, Unitarianism, and popular Spiritualism.

The challenging movements together formed a distinctive popular tradition that appeared in various shapes and guises over the decades, achieving a clear institutionalization in the metaphysical religions mentioned above. Before 1900 the main features of this
distinctive tradition had been well articulated: belief in an impersonal divine principle more than in a personal God; a focus on the
individual's inner life developed through study, concentration, or
contemplation; an aim of union with or perfect apprehension of the
divine; little interest in social reform, political activity, or institution
building (except sometimes their own churches); an approach to
spiritual life through rational or transrational perception rather than
emotional religiosity; and a belief in the possibility of continuing
spiritual progress, even after death. A yet more secularized version
of this tradition appeared in a kind of nature-mysticism, drawn from
Emersonian Transcendentalism and exemplified most fully in John
Muir.

The institutionalized segments of this alternative, mystically-
inclined tradition remained small. By 1915 its chief expressions, the
metaphysical religions, were counted as 5 to 6 percent of the Protestant population and less than 2 percent of the population as a
whole. Yet their influence on white Protestants of California was
strong; for decades to come, the many related groups who came to
California would find congenial audiences there, as would religious
missionaries to Americans from Asia. They did not—we should observe here—immediately involve the many ethnically rooted Roman
Catholics, Jews, blacks, Hispanics, or Asians. The struggle between
traditionalists and mystics that we will portray was the history of the
adjustment of one ethnic group, white Protestants of the East and
Midwest, to their new environment. To be sure, Anglo-Protestants
sometimes created mythologies of the others among whom they
lived: they developed a nostalgic memory of Spanish California and

encountered Asian thought in a mythologized form through such movements as Theosophy. Yet, while these myths undoubtedly nourished openness and tolerance in belief, they did not necessarily lead to relationships, religious or social, with Spanish-speaking or Asian neighbors.

Our reconstruction of developments, therefore, stays within the Anglo-Protestant camp. Even there, sources do not always permit us to trace clearly the development of the alternative tradition in relation to the regular denominations. From the nineteenth century there is evidence of a few important figures and debates plus widely scattered hints of the impact of new movements. After the turn of the century we find more systematic presentations, developed arguments, and some relations among individuals and groups that can be traced. In general, however, religious documents have not been so well kept in California as in the eastern states; in addition, popular movements with their less established character often do not leave clear traces. For these reasons the following chapters may seem more a series of essays than the story of a single clear development. Taken together, however, they form a coherent picture of significant religious formations in California.

For each set of materials I have tried to show how the California social situation, questions of religious and regional identity, specific personalities, and national trends interweave to create distinctive religious issues and attitudes in California. I hope this work will serve to suggest the importance in American religious history of locales, regions, and specific ethnic groups as well as national trends. It is precisely by more careful work in specific areas that we can bring forth the kind of comparisons that make national history interesting and meaningful. The writing of the religious history of the regions of the West has hardly begun; yet one day it will undoubtedly contribute new insights to our understanding of American history, American culture, and modern religion itself.

I wish to acknowledge the generosity of the following libraries in granting permission to use their materials: the Bancroft Library of the University of California, Berkeley; the Graduate Theological Union, Berkeley; the San Francisco Theological Seminary Library, San Anselmo; the Graduate Research Library of the University of California, Los Angeles; the Doheny Library of the University of Southern California, Los Angeles; the Point Loma College Library, San Diego; and the State Historical Society Library, Sacramento. I am most grateful to the National Endowment for the Humanities for providing me with a major research fellowship, without which I could not have undertaken this project. My thanks go also to my research assistant, Rhonda Packer; to Catherine Albanese, Eldon Ernst, and Mark Juergensmeyer, who read the manuscript in earlier stages; to Doug Anderson, a fellow worker in California research, who provided me with his unpublished research results and gave me valuable feedback; and to my husband Harry Frankiel, who as always has supported my work and helped me have free time to do it.

1. California Dreams

When the news of the discovery of gold in California reached the East, thousands of young men, singly or in companies, boarded ships for Panama and westward or set out on the arduous cross-country journey. These were the famous Forty-Niners. Not far behind them were Protestant ministers, acting as missionaries to those who had left civilization and religion behind. The young men were starry-eyed about the riches that awaited them in the gold mines; they hoped to make their fortune and return home unbelievably wealthy. The missionaries were starry-eyed too, not so much for wealth (though some did try their hands at mining) as for the opportunity of spreading Christianity and civilization to the far reaches of the continent. Like the circuit riders and the frontier pastors who had been migrating west for decades, the California ministers felt that they carried their treasure—Christianity—with them; and they wanted to make sure that it became firmly established in their new location.

New England ministers cherished the idea of remaking California in the image of their homeland. Their tradition had taught them to see New England as a great Puritan city on a hill, toward which all the world would look for an example of a perfect civilization. By replanting their faith—now a considerably modified version of their ancestors' religion—they hoped to establish California as a center of civilization as well. Joseph A. Benton, the "father of California Congregationalism," expressed the sentiments of many New Englanders:

> We are here, in the Providence of God, to establish and mature . . . the same institutions—to rear and perfect the same fabric of government—to extend the sphere of the same civil rights and social order—to diffuse the blessings of the same benign and holy faith—and to hallow in memory and observe the same secular and religious festivals, as have been the strength, and glory, and beauty of the land of our Fathers and the places of our birth.

Benton envisioned a California cultivated like New England, with marshes drained, farm houses dotting the valleys, and blossoming flowers in what seemed to him the arid waste around San Francisco Bay. When that vision was fulfilled, he believed, then everyone would come to California: "The world's centre will have changed.—This will be the land of pilgrimage, and no man will be thought to have seen the world till he has visited California!"[1] William Pond, another Congregationalist minister, prophesied that "the time was surely coming when not New York but California would be the 'empire state' in our Union—no one with open eyes can doubt it."[2]

Nor were the powerful New England Congregationalists the only ones to have a dramatic vision of California and its future. James Woods, a pioneer Presbyterian of the Old School, echoed Benton's and Pond's perceptions of the significance of California:

> *Unparalleled in the history of the world is the march of progress in California*. . . . Instead of being a remote, and almost unknown, and uncared for portion of the globe, with but a few scattering and degenerate sons of Spain, and a few enterprising adventurers, and a few tribes of wretchedly degraded Indians, it now in the short space of two years has become a central spot of earth, where almost all nations of the world have their representatives congregated.[3]

S. D. Simonds, a Methodist minister, proclaimed that "California is the New World of the Nineteenth Century, and her influence will be lasting as her majestic mountains . . . and more precious than the gold of her quartz and placers."[4] Similarly, Darius Stokes, a leading black minister of the African Methodist Episcopal church, spoke of California as destined to be the next great "world emporium." He warned, however, that the churches must ensure the progress of religion and morals, especially freedom from oppression for blacks, along with the temporal and material achievements of the age.[5] Another Methodist, Lorenzo Waugh, as he settled in Petaluma, extolled California as a new Eden[6]—and quickly set about organizing a temperance crusade.

None of the ministers, of course, saw California as perfect; it had to be made Christian. Many worried about the temptations that stemmed from the focus on gold and wealth and from the fast-paced life of adventurers. Others were concerned about California's cosmopolitanism and the lack of unity among the population.[7] On the whole, however, ministers came to the Golden State with high hopes and a strong drive to make California a fine Christian state. An essay in the *Congregational Quarterly* of 1861 argued that the New England influence would turn the trick:

> A single family of genuine Puritan substance . . . is a germ, around which a whole flood of miscellaneous population will take form. . . . the innate validity of this element molds the rising communities of the West, and unconsciously fashions all after the ideas with which it comes charged.[8]

Laymen also thought it likely that California would be transformed into a replica of the East. A farmer writing to the *American Agriculturist* in 1849 declared, apparently with some ambivalence, that "California will soon be California no longer. The hordes of emigrants and adventurers . . . will speedily convert this wild, cattle-breeding, lasso-throwing, idle, bigoted, bull-baiting race, into an industrious, shrewd, trafficking Protestant set of thorough-going Yankees."[9]

What did it mean for Anglo-Protestants of the nineteenth century to be making California a Christian state like Massachusetts or some other place east of the Mississippi? The ministers possessed a fairly clear image of themselves and their role in such an enterprise: they were shapers of society; the churches were its pillars.[10] Leaders of each denomination saw themselves as cooperating with others, but they did not necessarily view themselves as parts of a grand alliance. The Presbyterians and Congregationalists cooperated most closely, as they had in the eastern states. For seventeen years one major newspaper served them both—the *Pacific*, sponsored by the Congregational churches—which claimed it was "the organ of no Sect or Party."[11] By 1868, however, the Presbyterians had decided to publish their own paper, the *Occident*, which clearly supported their denominational "sentiments and aims" while maintaining harmonious relations with other Christians.[12] The Methodist paper, the *California Christian Advocate*, never wanted to be other than Methodist, stating clearly in its first issue, "We cannot claim to be Union." The Methodists held that each denomination ought to be itself, and believed that differences "in names, and modes, and governments, and beliefs" would not necessarily lead to strife among Christians.[13]

A gentle and courteous denominationalism, rather than a united front, was the implicit rule. Writers for the popular Protestant media did not generally refer to themselves as evangelicals, but simply as Christians. Some of the ministers brought this attitude with them from the East; they knew of the efforts at union and the difficulties that had been encountered. Anglo-Protestant opinion at midcentury generally favored acceptance of differences within the framework of a general common purpose. By 1867, the *California Christian Advocate* could cite with approval Henry Ward Beecher (a Congregationalist) to the effect that harmony among differences was the state most desired.[14] Each denomination had a fairly clear sense of itself. The Methodists' peculiar mission, said Bishop E. Thompson in his speech to the California Conference in 1867, was to awaken spiritual life and lead "to the high places of religious experience" while encouraging a life of self-denial and constant prayer.[15] The Presbyterian *Occident* saw its church's purpose as helping to build society and strengthen the churches.[16] The Baptists saw themselves as enforcing a clear standard of church discipline and doctrine as well as general social morality.[17] Moreover, the situation in California reinforced this attitude. Bishop Thompson summed it up:

> The Pacific coast is the theological equator. As early as the last century, the Latin and Greek churches met in the valley of the Sonoma. . . . Monotheism in its four forms; Judaism, in its orthodox and heterodox schools; Christianity, in its Latin, Greek, and Protestant churches; Deism, . . . from that of the devout and considerate Herbert, to that of the blaspheming Paine; Polytheism, in its different shapes; and defiant Mormonism, with its polygamous practices and cruel spirit, meet here. Hence, we should be especially on our guard, doctrinally. . . . we are in danger of, first, liberalism, then indifferentism, finally skepticism . . . . The Christian faith should be clearly defined; and while its minor points are but little insisted on, its *essential* doctrines and full experience should be steadily, fully, and uncompromisingly, though charitably, maintained.[18]

The pluralism of California made it essential for each denomination to have a clear sense of itself, to oppose "Romanists," Mormons, and other suspect groups, and at the same time to be charitable, as Christians, toward other denominations.

In daily life, the role of the Protestant ministers was to guide the people in devotion and morality. They would raise up churches where the Word would be preached. The people would not only attend services, but also keep Sunday apart as a day of worship. They would pray daily, alone and with their families. The population in general would abstain from vice, especially liquor, gambling, and worse sins. People would respect order and government while guarding against corruption and bad influences. Church members would organize to correct social abuses, help the needy, and support missionaries to bring into the fold those who had not received the gospel. They would be educated in secular knowledge in common schools and religious colleges, which would also inculcate a Christian spirit at all levels.

That kind of society was, of course, an ideal seldom realized even in the East. Anglo-Protestant ministers did not seem daunted, however, by any differences they found in their new environment. They set about creating the institutions and movements that they believed would be pillars of California society as they had been of the eastern branch of the Protestant empire. Churches were the most obvious of these institutions, and the buildings rose rapidly. In 1850, only two years after the great migration began, Protestant churches in California had "sittings," that is, seats in the churches, for twelve thousand people, or 13 percent of the population. San Francisco, though it had the greatest proportion of non-Protestants, boasted twenty-two Protestant churches by 1852, and many of these by 1860 had attracted well-known ministers from the East. Whether church membership matched the growth in buildings and ministers' salaries is another question; unfortunately, membership figures are not available for the early years. Nevertheless the clergy clearly had some support, both for churches and for the other staple of Anglo-Protestant culture, the printed word. Every denomination established one or more newspapers, and by 1860 the largest, the *Pacific*, had a circulation of four thousand, while the *California Christian Advocate* was sent to nearly two thousand in the state.[19]

Other activities soon followed the building of churches. Anglo-Protestant concern for social and moral order found expression in a crusade, beginning in 1851, for a strong state Sabbath law. By 1855 the legislature passed a mild law banning noisy amusements, and by 1858 a stricter law was approved, forbidding businesses to be open on Sunday. Other reform organizations were created to propagandize against liquor, gambling, and prostitution, and to aid sailors and orphans. Temperance was one of the more popular causes: Lorenzo Waugh's Bands of Hope, established to involve young people in the anti-liquor movement, spread throughout the towns of California. Ministers were instrumental in convincing San Franciscans to set up free elementary schools, and they themselves frequently established high schools (the first public high school was not founded until 1875). Denominations founded seminaries—Baptist, Congregational, Methodist, Presbyterian—and eventually some created colleges: the College of California (later the University of California, Berkeley) was founded by New England Congregationalists and Presbyterians, and the University of the Pacific by the Methodists. In all, sixty church-sponsored schools were founded between 1850 and 1874.[20]

Finally, the Anglo-Protestant clergy often appointed themselves watchmen over government. When in 1856 conflict erupted in San Francisco over alleged government corruption, ministers generally supported the Vigilance Committee, a businessmen's organization that took the law into its own hands, claiming to restore order and honest government. Whether support of the vigilantes was the most honorable of causes is debatable, but the alliance with the mercantile community clearly showed that Protestant ministers had become part of the network of social power in early California.[21]

Josiah Royce, a Harvard philosopher and California native, recalled that in those early years community spirit was at least as well represented by the churches as by the saloons. That may say more for the saloons than the churches. But early California has so often been portrayed as wild country, dominated by men lusting for pleasure and wealth, that we should consider the force of Royce's observations. "There was from the first," he wrote, "the characteristic American feeling prevalent that churches were a good and sober element in the social order, and that one wanted them to prosper, whether one took a private and personal interest in any of them or not."[22]

Yet the end of that statement presents the other side of the coin. Royce portrays a society where people wanted churches to support order and community spirit, but did not always take a "private and personal" interest in them. Royce believed, indeed, that many church members who would have been devout back East were quite "cold" in California; they had a "distrust toward enthusiasm." His observations agree with evidence from other sources; enthusiastic religion did not succeed, and people often did not make strong personal commitments to the churches. Camp meetings with their more emotional religious style did not fare as well in California as on earlier frontiers; nor did urban revivalists. Californians participated in the nationwide "lay revival" of 1858, but comment on the movement is infrequent in the annals of the time.[23] Ministers' complaints must be taken with a grain of salt, but many of their comments support this general impression. Presbyterian pastor Albert Williams bemoaned the fact, not that people ignored religion entirely, but that less than half the "professors of religion" (in other words, those who had been converted) would admit it openly.[24] Another minister observed in 1880 that the secular press in California, unlike the Eastern press, seldom reported religious news.[25] People gave freely of their wealth, but expended their personal energy on other things.

Thus even as church membership grew, there was little of what Royce called "enthusiasm." By 1871 the *Pacific Methodist*, the organ of the Southern Methodist church, had acknowledged that "business Christianity"—that is, the support of the church as an institution—was as good as or better than contemplative and joyous camp-meeting Christianity.[26] Such a remark is as startling in its context as the famous turnaround of Lyman Beecher, who, after fighting tooth and nail to keep the Congregational church established, decided after defeat that voluntarism was better. In California, though, society was electing "business Christianity" and condemning enthusiasm. If a prominent person took an unusual religious position, he was open to ridicule. For example, when the well-known editor Mr. Owen of the *San Jose Mercury* joined the Disciples of Christ, the *Petaluma Crescent*, far away at the opposite end of the Bay, declared him a "Campbellite" and heaped scorn on him:

> We expect soon to hear of his cultivating a pig-tail and preaching Confucius and rats, or else advocating Mohammedanism in San Jose. But the world should be lenient with Owen; he is as crazy on religion as a bedbug that has filled itself from the body of a benzine-saturated individual.[27]

We may reasonably suspect some personal animosity between the two editors. Still, if one's neighbors were watching so closely for signs of religious eccentricity, there must have been considerable pressure to be reserved about one's religious interests and commitments.

Ministers often blamed this situation on competition from secular and material pursuits. As Baptist minister O. C. Wheeler wrote, it was extremely difficult "to get a man to look through a lump of gold into eternity."[28] Secular entertainments made matters worse; one minister reported that his revival camp meeting had to compete with a circus. Mexican fiestas and bullfights were often held on Sundays; gambling houses and saloons were often the only places where single men might meet women. Methodist street preacher William Taylor believed that despite people's open and generous temperaments, California was still "the hardest country in the world in which to get sinners converted to God."[29]

Do secularism and materialism provide an adequate explanation for Californians' reluctance to get involved in the churches? California was an unusual society in many ways; gold was not the only factor. The population, for example, in 1850 was made up almost entirely of men (about 90 percent), and most of them were between the ages of twenty and forty years. By 1860 more women had arrived, but it was not until after 1870 that the sexes approached equality in numbers. Most men came to California with the intention of leaving soon; they were called "argonauts," from their eagerness to gather the golden fleece and return home. Few had economic security; many had sold all their possessions to finance the trip west. Some, especially from New England, had come in "companies" that provided temporary economic and social support. But early California in general was not a stable society of householders and their families; rather, it was a collection of independent individuals trying to become self-made men.[30]

Cultural variety was much greater than on earlier frontiers. California already had an established culture, the Spanish-Mexican one that had begun some seventy years before. Native Americans, largely assimilated or dispersed, made up a small part of the population. When the gold rush began, people from many different backgrounds flocked to the region, and not only from the United States. Besides American Jews, Catholics, blacks, and white Protestants, there were men from France, Germany, England, Ireland, and other parts of Europe, plus a large population of Orientals, mostly Chinese. Protestants were a minority, and they did not have the advantages of earlier settlement, a firm attachment to the land, or special connections, which might have made them more resistant to the unsettled life and new wealth of the region. By about 1870 California began to look more like the rest of the country in its ethnic balance, but between 1850 and 1870 the gold region and its cities, including San Francisco, were among the most cosmopolitan areas in the world.[31]

As a state, an organized society, California was barely formed. In contrast to earlier additions to the Union, which tended to grow gradually before being admitted to statehood, California became one of the United States while still in its infancy as a society. Laws of property and juries to settle disputes had to be created on the spot during gold rush times. Mining camps were flourishing towns one year and ghost towns the next. Those who decided to settle on the land were likely to be involved for years in disputes over former Mexican holdings and competing claims to the land. The land and its settlements were unstable; community, law, and tradition had to be created virtually from scratch. That was not the case on earlier frontiers, where families generally traveled west together, where the next frontier adjoined the former, and where there was immediate permanent settlement. Californians, on the contrary, were intensely aware of the distance from their former homes and families and of the difference in the lives they had to live. They were thrown back on their own resources time and again. They gained a reputation for independence and were proud of it.[32]

This was not the sort of society that Anglo-Protestant ministers had grown up in and been trained to serve. As Kenneth Janzen has argued, the New England tradition demanded a culturally homogeneous, theologically versed, responsible body of householders. Kevin Starr has observed, similarly, that the radically new situation of California simply could not be regulated by the forms and procedures of a New England parish[33]—or, we might add, an Ohio village or Virginia plantation. Methodists and Baptists might seem to be better suited, as they were on other frontiers, to a loosely structured society than were the Congregationalists and Presbyterians; they did not require such high standards of theological education, and they were flexible in licensing preachers and serving new congregations. But in place of education they expected higher "enthusiasm." They, too, assumed a society of householders with relatively stable occupations, a society with mutual obligations, interlocking interests, ties of tradition, and bonds of affection.

Even the theologies of the Anglo-Protestant churches presumed the social elements they had left behind in the East. If a minister was conservative, he preached a strongly orthodox doctrine of sin and guilt, which meant that a person had to repent and be forgiven and saved through Christ's sacrificial atonement, or else be damned. This theology was based on a legal model—a sinner was like a guilty criminal—which assumed clear obligations and definitions of right and wrong. But Californians had no commonly accepted obligations: laws were in flux, different groups had different customs, and any moral code could appear to be merely a private opinion.

On the other hand, a more liberal minister might de-emphasize guilt and damnation, preaching instead the love of God in Christ. In the mid-nineteenth century liberal ministers would usually liken Jesus to an intimate friend or loving parent, especially a mother who would give her all in loving self-sacrifice for her child. God's love was like a mother's love; in response, a person should turn to God, or "rest in the arms of Jesus." The model of divine-human relations here is the ideal family, which Californians no longer had. The social context—thousands of independent, striving, mostly single men—was not suited to the theology that was heard even in the more liberal churches.[34]

Anglo-Protestant thought, then, was something of an anomaly; yet in such a structureless society, churches were one of the few sources, or at least reminders, of morality and order. Thus people supported them, though without "enthusiasm."[35] But we still have not explained the lack of susceptibility of Californians to revivalist religion. It may be true that Californians had left home and mother, society and legal traditions; but had they also left behind their emotions? Would we not expect that out of revivalism, which so often prospers in a society in flux, a new tradition of emotional religion might have emerged?

Under other circumstances, that might have happened. But Californians of the 1850–1870 period had learned to associate religious or political enthusiasms with factionalism, sectarianism, divisiveness, and even violence. Most of the men in California had been born in the East or Midwest between 1810 and 1830. They grew up during or shortly after the Second Great Awakening, the greatest period of religious excitement in the United States since colonial times. In its aftermath reform crusades, utopian ideas, and new sects mushroomed all over the Northeast, and religious schisms appeared in the South as well. Religious enthusiasm often resulted in acrimonious debates within and among churches and reformers, or persecution of fringe groups like the Mormons. One of the worst examples within mainstream Protestantism was the debate, which sometimes erupted in mob violence, between radical abolitionists and anti-abolitionists in the North; the abolitionists were directly influenced by revivals and religious enthusiasm.

Politics was also heating up during the same period, with popular heroes like Andrew Jackson and popular issues like the movement against the Bank of the United States creating enormous political excitement. Then, in the 1830s, there emerged the specter of civil war. In 1832 South Carolina precipitated the nullification crisis, which could have led to secession and war. After that, the nation's leaders were preoccupied with the struggle to preserve the Union. By the 1850s many people were advocating stricter social control and were accusing any enthusiasts, whether political or religious, of being extremists or fanatics.

Under any circumstances it would have been natural for men in their twenties and early thirties to rebel against the tendencies of their parents—in this case to turn away from religious enthusiasm. That reaction would be even more pronounced under the threat of war, and still more in a section of society that was highly disorganized. It is in this light that we can understand the slogan of the San Francisco Vigilance Committee of 1856: "No creed. No party. No sectional issues." It meant: no religion, no politics, no war. Unity in the nation and social order in California seemed to depend on controlling factors—especially emotional enthusiasms—that could give rise to factionalism and divisiveness. Furthermore, Californians were familiar with another kind of emotional derangement: one of the early institutions of the state was the insane asylum at Stockton. While many stories about its inhabitants implied that the lust for wealth had driven them crazy, there were occasional accounts of an overzealous religious person or false Messiah who ended up there.[36] In every realm, from the national to the local to the mental, order was too fragile to allow the exploration of deep religious emotions. The lack of religious enthusiasm in Protestant California was an intense response to the sense of fragmentation in American society in the period.[37]

Lower levels of emotionalism went hand in hand with the gentle denominationalism espoused, as we noted earlier, by the clergy. Most denominations showed declining interests in tests of orthodoxy, while their parishioners showed a growing indifference to actual church membership. As we will see in a later chapter, there was a brief spate of heresy trials; but interdenominational fighting among Protestants was rare. By 1869 the Presbyterian *Occident* observed that denominational differences were no longer a reason for churches to attack one another. While criticizing the Unitarians for having no binding creed and the Universalists for abandoning certain biblical doctrines, the *Occident* also declared that soon all the denominations would say simply, "We are Christians."[38] Unity and tolerance were becoming the watchwords of California religious attitudes, and would remain so for many decades to come.

Thus far the religious experience of the Californians whom Anglo-Protestant ministers hoped to reach appears merely negative. There was no enthusiasm, no sectarianism, little commitment to religious institutions. Churches were supported only for instrumental reasons, such as their support of social order; ultimately there was a resigned tolerance, since nothing else was possible. But in fact the immigrants from the East, sons and daughters of old Protestants, were developing their own sense of identity, their own mythology, outside the traditional churches. Clerics saw no unity among the people, no common bonds. (As the Rev. Albert Williams asked, "Can settled, fixed purposes coexist with the manifold interests, aims, and projects of communities without any seeming bond of union?"[39] From his eastern Protestant perspective, the answer would be no.) But Californians considered themselves a unique community despite their diversity. Years later Royce observed, "How swiftly, in that country, the Californians of the early days seized upon every suggestion that could give a sense of the unique importance of their new provincial life." They tended, he said, "to idealize whatever tended to make [their] community, and all its affairs, seem unique, beloved, and deeply founded upon some significant natural basis."[40] Indeed, the attempt to forge an identity out of California experience led eventually to the development, among a significant number of white Protestant Californians, of an alternative to the Anglo-Protestant religious tradition.

Before identifying that alternative, however, we must understand better how ordinary Californians viewed themselves in those first crucial years. One of the unique elements they idealized was their recent social experience—the gold rush itself. In descriptions of those times we find repeatedly an exaltation of democratic values, generosity and sharing during hard times, and noncompetitiveness. We know that in fact there was a great deal of competition, claim-jumping, theft, and outlawry in the mining areas, but people preferred to remember the brighter side. They cherished the fact—which must at first have been a shock—that they could not tell a person's status or occupation by his dress or appearance.[41] People of all backgrounds mingled together: a former attorney and a factory worker, a grocer and a medical doctor, would all be knee-deep in mud, panning gold from the same stream. Further, the ups and downs of gold rush economics meant that people could be enormously wealthy and liberal with handouts, or find themselves struggling to make a meal together. James Woods recalled being overwhelmed by a "donation party" for his family, in which goods were piled high around his home by generous neighbors; while miners remembered sharing bits of food they had scrounged to make a holiday dinner.[42] Such stories helped create images of democratic values, generosity, shared joys and hardships, and generally the plenitude of California itself.

Some Californians also cherished an idealized memory of the pre-Anglo past. Legends of the Californios—the Spanish-Mexican landowners—supported the mythical image of the gold rush. The Californios, it was said, were known far and wide for their generosity and hospitality. They supposedly lived a life of leisure, not unlike the genteel Southern plantation owner, but without the negative side of slavery. Later, white Californians romanticized the mission era, when, it was said, gentle Franciscan fathers tenderly took degraded Indians under their wings. Ultimately California took on the coloring of an exotic Mediterranean country, a perfect Greece or Italy. Such images ignored large chunks of reality: the destruction of Native American cultures, evidence of violence and poverty among Californios, the impact of urban economics on the region after Anglos arrived. But the legends in many ways were more powerful, reinforcing the idea of a society gentle and genteel, open and hospitable, intimately related to the land and the climate. Kevin Starr has suggested that the image of California as Mediterranean "encouraged new attitudes toward work and leisure and what was important to live for. As a metaphor, it stood for a culture anxious to foster an alternative to the industrial ethic."[43] Of course, the very people who created that metaphor were deeply implicated in urban industrial and commerical society. Yet the metaphor indicates that some of them, at least, yearned for a different way of life, even more than did their eastern countrymen.

Together with generosity and gentility went that open-minded tolerance mentioned earlier, which gradually became a universalistic belief that all religions were different aspects of a fundamental truth. Not only other Protestants were tolerated: any tradition could be viewed as a sincere attempt to find God or as a source of universal wisdom. This attitude grew very strong in the latter part of the nineteenth century; but even in the early years it is evident in Protestant attitudes toward Roman Catholics and Asians. There were, of course, many Protestant clerical pronouncements against "Romanism"; but at the popular level there was far less tension between Protestants and Catholics then there had been in the East. Some prejudice emerged in the 1850s during the Vigilante episodes of San Francisco, when mostly Protestant merchants allied against Irish Catholic elements they believed to be corrupt. For generations, too, there was discrimination against Mexicans. The latter, however, was clearly a racial rather than a religious prejudice; although the Catholic church was sometimes criticized for not educating the Spanish-speaking well enough, both Indian and Hispanic Mexicans were generally regarded as lower-class citizens because of racial qualities rather than religious heritage. On the positive side, many Protestants sent their children to Catholic schools, because in the early years they were often far better staffed. This encouraged more positive interaction and lessened the friction between the two groups.

Asians, especially the Chinese, suffered from prejudice and outright persecution, especially during times of economic depression or high rates of immigration. At these times Chinese competed with Americans as a cheap source of labor in the mines or in building the railroads. During intense periods of persecution and legislation against the Chinese, everything about their religion and culture came in for criticism. They were regarded as idol-worshippers and as conceited people who believed their civilization was the highest in the world.[44] Many Protestants, however, while viewing the Chinese as rather strange, also saw them as bearers of a great, ancient tradition. As early as 1852 the *Pacific* announced in a surprised tone that the Chinese were showing themselves to be self-respecting human beings who cared about justice and morality and deserved to be treated justly and humanely.[45] One Protestant clergyman, the Rev. A. W. Loomis, wrote a book on Confucianism that was favorably reviewed by the *Occident* and frequently mentioned in clerical circles with high praise; while the Rev. William Speer expended great efforts to convince California Protestants that the Chinese and American empires could interact to their mutual benefit. Thus the clergy encouraged an openness that never appeared in their writings on Roman Catholicism. Of course, Protestants still regarded Chinese and other Pacific peoples as targets for missionary work;[46] but at least among the educated populace an interest in understanding other peoples sowed the seeds of positive attitudes toward other traditions.

Many white Californians of Anglo-Protestant background were developing a new picture of themselves as expansive, open, social beings, unique in their potential for development, searching for the best and truest as they moved vigorously into the future. They found in their natural environment a reflection of those same traits. The pages of California's magazines for the first half-century and more were filled with glorious descriptions of a wondrous, grand, and healthy environment. The Geysers (a natural hot springs), Yosemite, the Pacific coast, the southern deserts—nature in California seemed unique, and each new scene seemed to demand that a person experience life more fully. Methodists holding their camp meeting conferences in the countryside appreciated that, as S. D. Simonds put it, the meetings could bring together such congenial spirits, "the lovers of God and the lovers of nature."[47] Even New Englanders, on occasion, forgot their urge to remake California into Massachusetts and admired the distinctive beauty of the state. One article in the *New Englander* of 1858 argued against civilizing California too much:

> Culture improves nothing. California was finished as a world of beauty, before civilization appeared. The magnificent valleys opened wide and clean. The scattered oaks stood in majesty, here and there, and took away the nakedness. Civilization comes, cuts down the oaks for firewood, fences off the plains into squares, covers them with grain or stubble, scatters wild mustard over them, it may be, and converts them into a weedy looking desolation. . . . There is never to be a lawn, or a neat grassy slope, as with us, because there is no proper turf.[48]

Some were so awed by the natural wonders that they made the land an allegory for their spiritual understanding. The *Occident* in 1868 printed a sermon, preached by Henry M. Scudder after his vacation in the Sierras, that was essentially a meditation on the life of the soul as like a mountain stream.[49] Even the most conservative churchmen sometimes translated the beauties of California into religious terms—or, one might equally well argue, allowed their religious sensibilities to be transformed by their California experience. One of the most remarkable examples comes from the *California Sketches* of O. P. Fitzgerald, a Southern Methodist pastor. He ends the book with a poem he wrote in the Russian River Valley, describing what was virtually a mystical experience of viewing Mount St. Helen at sunrise. Seeing the light at the top and orange-tinted clouds beneath the summit, he proclaimed its "glory supernal," and went on:

> O glory yet greater! The white, silent mountain,
>   Transfigured with sunrise, flames out in the light
> That beams on its face from its far-distant fountain,
>   And bathes in full splendor its East-looking height.
>
> My soul, in that moment so rapt and so holy,
>   Was transfigured with nature and felt the deep spell;
> My spirit, entranced, bent meekly and lowly
>   With rapture that only an angel could tell.
>
> When the night mists of time around me are flying,
>   When the shadows of death gather round me apace,
> O Jesus, my Sun, shine on me when dying,
>   Transfigure my soul with the light of thy face![50]

Fitzgerald, experiencing nature as transformative, prayed that Jesus might bring such transformation at the moment of death, like a sunrise for the soul on the way to the life beyond the grave. In that kind of experience Fitzgerald, though an orthodox Protestant pastor, was a forerunner of the many Californians who would turn to nature as a spiritual resource and mode of understanding the divine.

Thus many Protestants in California experienced some transformation, through nature or their new society or both. Some saw their society as the epitome of democracy; others felt themselves to be natural aristocrats—without any slaves or oppressed workers. Some saw their new home as a land of plenty, while still others felt transported into other dimensions by the sight of a sunset over the Pacific. All these experiences blended in the popular tradition, as Californians described themselves to each other and to their acquaintances back home. Even while building an urban industrial society, they were creating a myth of their state as a very different kind of society—a leisured, elegant life in glorious natural surroundings, a noncompetitive society without hierarchy, whose people, through the bounty of the land and the generosity of all, were supplied with everything they needed, both physically and spiritually.

However fantastic the myth, in light of reality, it is in striking conflict too with traditional Anglo-Protestant images of the good life. Midcentury Protestants back East were still dedicated to the Puritan ideal of hard work, with economic reward as a blessing from God, not a natural gift of the land. They accepted, implicitly, if not explicitly, the necessity of fair competition and the ideal of material progress. A leisurely society would seem merely a collection of idlers. The Mediterranean image might cause a Yankee to shudder, for it could mean Catholic oppression or Southern decadence. As for nature, the beauties of God's creation were private experiences confirming God's wisdom and goodness; one could not build on them a public consciousness and a sound Christian civilization.[51] Protestant ministers might understand some of the yearnings that were emerging among many new Californians, but they were not likely to sympathize deeply with all the new experiences their fellow statesmen cherished. They offered, with pride, the image of an orderly, morally conscious, democratic society, and invited other Californians to participate in building it. For the most part they could not integrate into this image the unique California dreams that were emerging from the people's reflection on their own experience.

Neither traditional religious enthusiasm nor traditional religious order were at the core of what white Californians from the East now wanted. There were, however, other elements in American religious traditions that could appeal to them. Openness and tolerance, independence in religious thinking, and reflection on the beauties of nature were characteristic of one tradition that had already emerged as a kind of counter-culture to mainstream Protestantism: namely, the New England tradition that led from Unitarianism to Transcendentalism. Early in the American period of California, a minister of that lineage came and captured the hearts of the people: Thomas Starr King. King was a legend in his own time as an orator and political hero; but what we will explore is the deeper basis of his popularity. In his famous speeches that stirred the multitudes during the few brief years he was a Californian, he articulated California dreams. His presence and preaching helped set the tone for the future of alternative religion, as we will see in the next chapter.

2. The Gospel of Unity

The statue of Thomas Starr King (1824–64) stands in Washington, D.C., along with that of Father Junipero Serra, as one of the two outstanding persons in California history. Both, significantly, were men of religious profession. Yet King is best known in California legend and popular history as the man who "saved California for the Union"—who kept the state from seceding during the Civil War. He was remembered as a preacher of Unionism; but deeper than that, as we will see, he was a preacher of unity. Not that the legend is false; there was agitation for secession in California, both by Southerners who wanted the state to join the Confederacy and by others who wanted to form an independent Pacific Republic. Historians generally agree, however, that even without King the secession movement would likely have failed; King himself observed that Union sentiment was strong from the beginning.[1] His political role was to encourage and fortify Union sentiment and to raise funds to support Union efforts.

Starr King had another role, however; he was first of all a minister, the pulpit orator of the First Unitarian Church in San Francisco. Even when he spent much of his time stumping around the state delivering patriotic speeches, he almost always lectured or preached in a church as well. He was spreading Unitarian Christianity—or, as he would have preferred to call it, "spiritual Christianity."[2] The relationship of this part of King's work to emerging California Protestant culture has received little attention from his biographers and other historians; so we must examine it more carefully.

It is remarkable that Starr King has been portrayed as saving California for the Union when in fact he did not, and as performing primarily a political duty when in fact he was a minister, and himself regarded his patriotism and his religion as identical.[3] When we observe such incongruities between historical evidence and historians' interpretations, we must look for the reason behind them. In this case, it is likely that California historians have failed to recognize Starr King's religious impact because King himself did not seem to care about traditional church religion. He did not become a denominational leader or form any organization outside the churches. He refused to enter denominational controversies; he did not care whether people became Unitarians or not. His religious vision was so large that it transcended what most nineteenth-century Christians, and most historians until recently, have considered religious. It has been simpler to view him as an orator, than to delve into his controversial religious beliefs.

In fact, Starr King became a "savior" of California because he, like most charismatic figures, epitomized the highest values of the people to whom he spoke; he articulated the beliefs and feelings of his audiences. There is no doubt of his popularity; he spoke to packed houses in halls and churches all over northern and central California for nearly four years. Sometimes his lectures lasted two or three hours, but he held people spellbound. Of course, oratory was a familiar medium to white northern Protestants in the mid-nineteenth century. Californians recently arrived from the East were eager for a good lecture, and King's were among the best. His mastery of the medium, together with his own presence and the things he stood for, were deeply admired by Protestant Californians.

Moreover, California of the mid 1800s was a region in flux, with high social mobility, heavy immigration, and rapidly changing social and economic patterns. It might have been a site of exceptional religious excitement, but there were compelling reasons for people to resist a highly emotional religion. Starr King offered another alternative: a grand religio-political vision that appeared to be founded on reason rather than emotion. People could see King as an exemplary person, and his vision as a source of order in a time of social disorder; he served as a kind of "prophetic" figure. But since he did not try to found a new church or organization or even mobilize a new movement, and instead supported existing religious and political institutions, it was only his image and his published speeches that survived his death.

Starr King himself was a self-made man. He had worked for a living from his teenage years and was largely self-educated, with the help of tutors, in metaphysics, theology, and classical and modern languages. At the age of twenty-two, without a divinity degree, he was called to his first pulpit, in his father's former church, the Universalist Church in Charlestown, Massachusetts. From there he went to Hollis Street Unitarian Church in Boston. While in Boston, he made a name for himself and was called to lecture frequently in other parts of New England; he was invited to become the permanent minister in churches as far west as Cincinnati. Yet because of his lack of a divinity degree and other status symbols important in the East, some regarded him as belonging to the second rank among the liberal ministers of New England. Popular as he was, he could not command the highest salaries or the most prestigious pulpits; sometimes it was difficult for him to support his family.[4]

Nevertheless he stayed in Boston until, in 1860, he was invited to San Francisco by the struggling Unitarian church there. He intended to take only a leave of absence from Hollis Street, but once in California—he arrived in 1861—he became involved in the life of the region and especially in supporting the Northern cause in the Civil War. He was homesick and spoke often of wanting to return to New England, but felt that California needed him. So he stayed, working harder and harder, until in 1864 he contracted diphtheria and died that spring, at the age of forty. In the meantime he had spoken to thousands in lecture halls and churches in all the cities and most of the substantial towns in California. He had raised contributions for the Sanitary Commission (which aided Northern soldiers) in an amount that exceeded any other state's share. And he had made a name for himself, coming from comparative obscurity in Boston to become one of the great figures of California history.

Starr King was small in stature, with a powerful voice; he had achieved some status in Boston, but he had the potential for greatness. That potential was realized in California. Here he seemed to blossom, to expand in his oratory and personal presence. Californians admired his development; we may guess that they saw in it what they experienced, or hoped for, in themselves. Transplanted New Englanders, now Californians, loved to tell their acquaintances back home that those "who heard him only in New England have not the faintest idea of what King became after he had passed through the Golden Gate."[5] In this respect he mirrored them: it was more the rule than the exception that Californians of white middle-class Protestant background went through many changes in adapting to California life. A young man raised on a farm in upstate New York might become a miner, a temporary government employee, a shipping merchant, and eventually a real estate speculator. Someone from the upper levels of society might do only moderately well on the Pacific coast. Those who survived the early chaos had taken risks and had dedicated a great deal to their new life—just as had Starr King. For that reason he could be a model of what they had become, or what they hoped to be.

Moreover, King shared and articulated the religious attitudes of openness and tolerance that, as we observed in Chapter I, were becoming characteristic of California in the 1860s. He supported all the churches, saying that different church governments and different rituals were suited to different temperaments. It did not matter which denomination one chose so long as it helped bring one closer to God. For that reason he did not enter into denominational controversies. He preached in a wide variety of churches, even one as conservative as Old School Presbyterian. His colleagues in other Protestant denominations disavowed his liberalism, but judged him more nearly orthodox than most eastern Unitarians. (Whether they were right in that judgment is questionable.)[6] His open attitude and his ability to travel freely in all religious circles appealed to Californians who did not want to be tied to a denomination. In that respect, too, he was both a model and someone they could see as similar to themselves.

Starr King offered them even more. In his lectures and sermons he formulated a set of beliefs and attitudes and an imaginative vision that captured the hearts of Californians. His denomination was Unitarian, but he did not preach a doctrinal Unitarianism. Classical Unitarianism, emerging in Boston in the early 1800s, rejected the Trinity for a belief that only God the Father had supreme divinity (hence the name *Unitarian*). It taught the rationality and benevolence of God and emphasized the human side of religion. This classical view had already developed into a diverse movement. By the mid 1830s it had sprouted Transcendentalism in many forms, from the philosophy of Ralph Waldo Emerson to the humanitarianism of abolitionist Theodore Parker. Starr King had immersed himself in the writings of William Ellery Channing, the principal spokesman for the movement in the 1820s, but was also a protégé of Parker. His father, who died when he was fifteen, was a Universalist pastor; from him King may have inherited his belief in the eventual salvation of all, with no one damned to eternal punishment. Clearly, he was a product of a wide-ranging liberal movement.

Following the liberal thought of his day, King's first principle was that true Christianity could not be contained in doctrines and creeds or in any one sect or denomination. Religious truth was a light that illumined everything and everyone, spreading life, grace, beauty, joy, and all good things. In his lecture on "Spiritual Christianity," delivered in the East as the last in a series by different denominational representatives, King declared one could find no unity in Christianity if one looked at dogma, clergy, or institutions—in short, any of the specific forms of religion. Christianity had to be understood rather as "the communication of life to the [human] race from the heavens . . . an unsealing of the treasury of the skies, an overflow into time of the infinite light and grace to illumine and regenerate the world."[7] God's overflowing love and truth, he said, had been disclosed when he poured it first into Jesus Christ, and then into human souls. If a person now would repent and have faith, he too could receive that communication and inflow from God, the "Infinite Spirit" indwelling as the substance of life, illumining the world. The question was not what one believed, the creed to which one subscribed, or the church to which one belonged, but "how near is the man to the Spirit of God?" Grace, King added, did not flow in prescribed channels of ritual and organization, but was, rather, like the rains:

> It falls on the mountain slopes; it collects in rills; it combines into streams and rivers; it hides underground, and bubbles in fountains. Now it floods all its channels; now it leaves the old beds to cut new paths for its leaping music; and it will often burst up in fresh districts to gladden the ground with beauty.[8]

With such images Starr King could appeal to the self-proclaimed tolerance of Californians and reinforce their resistance to organized religion, while still not offending any particular church. But something else appeared in the images King used: a strong mystical element, speaking of the "inflow" of God and Infinite Spirit into human souls and lives and employing metaphors from nature to express the grace of God. Both of these would become important in the religious vision of the alternative tradition among Protestants.

We will return later to the overall character of Starr King's mysticism. First, however, it will be helpful to look at his use of images from nature. The beauties of California were part of the emerging mythology, and few people came so prepared as Starr King to appreciate nature and its potential for defining Californians' identity. In New England, King had spent summers either at the seashore or in the mountains, finally choosing the mountains as best for his health and spirit. His book on the White Hills of Vermont was regarded as a masterpiece of description and travelogue. In California he was drawn to the grandeur of the Sierra Nevada and wrote sermons using his Sierra experiences as a theme.

King's "Living Water from Lake Tahoe" (1863) is perhaps the most eloquent of these pieces. In it he took the lake as an allegory, a lesson by which we should understand God. Essentially, he instructed his audiences in the principles of a Christianity founded on a religion of nature. He argued, from the brilliant colors of the lake and surrounding mountains, that God's message to humanity was above all a message of beauty and joy—those were the central truths of existence. To be sure, nature also showed God's awfulness, power, and rugged justice, but it clothed them in the play of light and color. Lake Tahoe showed that the Creator's holiness was not severe, but like "the purity of a lily's leaf, of a tree's robe of blossoms, of the light of a star, of the sunset radiance on mountain snow."[9] To know God was to know purity, beauty, and joy beyond mere human conception; Christianity, indeed all true religion, was to be founded on these things more than on severity and justice.

King was telling Californians that the glory of nature by which they were surrounded and often entranced was not a distraction from religious duty, but an expression of the essence of religion itself. And, he said, we should regard our institutions and authorities likewise: as sources of inspiration, not literal truth. He even introduced the question of whether the Bible was truly divine by an analogy with nature: he heard in the murmur of the pines around Lake Tahoe, he said, a sound like the Hebrew genius from which Christianity sprang. But we do not know how much of that genius was from God, and how much from man.

> We cannot tell in the forest how much of the tone we hear is of the wind and how much of the tree. Neither can we tell in the great passages of the Bible what proportion of the music is of God and what proportion is of man. . . . We must go to the Bible as to a grove of evergreens, not asking for cold, clear truth, but for sacred influence, for revival to the devout sentiment, for the breath of the Holy Ghost, not as it wanders in pure space, but as it sweeps through cedars and pines.[10]

Here again, he established a basis for Christian liberalism by using analogies from nature.

Finally, King likened Lake Tahoe to another, cosmically significant lake: the Sea of Galilee. Jesus and his followers who traveled there were craftsmen and laborers, and therefore, King said (bowing to miners and other laborers), "not distinguished from those who ply their calling under the shadows of the Sierra." Jesus' healing of demoniacs called to mind the miracles of the Spirit in healing the insane minds of King's own day—in the Stockton asylum. These correspondences between Lake Tahoe and the Sea of Galilee led King to a grand synthesis. The Sea of Galilee, site of many miracles, was a "fountainhead of living water" that has flowed throughout the globe: "The truth that first fell upon its shores has cast a glory, by association, upon all other inland lakes, and indeed has illumined all nature."[11] Such lakes were, in King's view, to be regarded "as realizing a conception or a dream" by God; Tahoe, as one of many mirrors of Galilee, reflected the mind of God:

> He delights in his works. . . . And it is our sovereign privilege that we are called to the possibility of sympathy with his joy. The universe is the home of God. He has lined its walls with beauty. He has invited us into his palace. He offers to us the glory of sympathy with his mind. By love of nature, by joy in the communion with its beauty, by growing insight into the wonders of color, form, and purpose, we enter into fellowship with the Creative art. We go into harmony with God. . . . But the inmost harmony with the Infinite we find only through love, and the reception of his love. Then we are prepared to see the world aright, to find the deepest joy in its pure beauty, and to wait for the hour of translation to the glories of the interior and deeper world.[12]

Beginning with an experience of California's natural beauty, Starr King offered Californians a mystical cosmology that promised communion with God through nature and revealed correspondences between their own experience and Christian mythology. He often based sermons on such analogies between particular experiences and universal truths. He preached, for example, on the comet of 1861; and he had in his repertoire a sermon called "Religious Lessons from Metallurgy" (1863), in which he related the life of miners and the science of mining to the universe as a whole.[13] Although his oratory may seem flowery to twentieth century tastes, it was certainly not so for the 1860s. His images were concrete and clear, his analogies carefully elaborated. He painted a cosmic vision into which Californians could enter because of their experience of nature.

Sermons based on nature, important as they may have been in forming bonds with other Californians, were only a small part of Starr King's repertoire. More prominent and more frequent were his patriotic speeches. These were most famous during the Civil War, but he had often lectured on political subjects before coming to California; he was famous for his lectures on Daniel Webster and George Washington. Starr King, like Theodore Parker and many other activists of the time, saw political issues and patriotic causes as grounded in religion. This was certainly true of King's efforts to assure California's support for the Union cause. His speeches sought to accomplish that end by, again, relating the particular to the universal, California to the destiny of America, and that destiny in turn to God's purposes.

According to Starr King, God had predestined the North American continent, from the Atlantic to the Pacific, to be the possession of one race, the Anglo-Saxon. This was a common theme of the period, the idea of "manifest destiny"—a destiny supposedly obvious to any observer, because indeed Anglo-Saxons were conquering the continent. King argued his point not only from history, however, but also from the aesthetics of geography. God, he claimed in "American Nationality" (1863), had created the American continent exactly the opposite of Europe and Asia. Those continents had mountain ranges radiating out from their centers, so as to scatter and separate the inhabitants into many different peoples. The United States, however, was shaped like a great basin between two coastal ranges, encouraging the formation of one nation instead of many. "The Constitution of American Nationality," he declared, "is written not on parchment but on nature."[14] Therefore no group or section had the right to disrupt the unity of the continent as a whole.

We recognize today, of course, that such concepts as Anglo-Saxon destiny often have racist overtones. King apparently did not intend such a meaning; he came out clearly for equality of the races and for the rights of human beings whatever their skin color or background. Yet he also subscribed to the prevailing philosophies that held that each race had its distinctive traits—Saxon energy, Greek intellect, Hebrew poetic genius. He could uphold the rights of blacks and in the same paragraph make a slur on the Irish bartender, without seeing the self-contradiction; in that respect he was a product of his time, and racist by twentieth-century standards. But he believed that

Anglo-Saxon liberality would uphold human rights and allow all
races to become part of one America, all equally protected by the
law, all speaking the English language.

Beyond this, however, the crucial element in Starr King's nation-
alism was that he wanted each person to be aware of wholes larger
than himself and see himself as part of larger and larger wholes. In
that way unity could be sustained in the midst of diversity. In "The
Privileges and Duties of Patriotism" (1862) he made this point with
powerful images. He argued that we cannot base our actions on
some general love for all humanity, but must love particular people
and communities; then we can develop to the point where we can feel
"a nation's life in our veins." This is the emotion of patriotism, and
it is a privilege of human, as distinguished from animal, nature to be
able to feel it. Again he used an analogy from his beloved mountains:
patriotic feeling is like being a part of a great mountain and knowing
the whole,

> as if each particle of matter that belongs to a mountain, each crystal hid-
> den in its darkness, each grass-blade on its lower slopes, each pebble
> amid its higher desolation, each snow-flake of its cold and tilted fields,
> could be conscious, all the time, of the whole bulk and symmetry and
> majesty and splendor of the pile. . . . as if each could exult in feeling—I
> am part of this organized majesty; I am an element in one flying buttress
> of it, or its firm-posed peak; I contribute to this frosty radiance; I am en-
> nobled by the joy it awakens in every beholder's breast![15]

Patriotism thus understood was a grand, expansive emotion, second
only to divine love; for, like love of God, it involved the individual in
a whole greater than himself.

This preaching of a larger unity was Starr King's constant theme,
whether he spoke of nature and God, the Union and God, or the soul
and God. To Californians in the 1860s, hearing this message was
crucial. Many of the independent farmers, miners, and merchants,
having built a modern society in little more than a decade at great
financial and emotional risk, were considering extending their independence to the political sphere as well, by creating a Pacific Republic. Starr King sensed that California's isolation needed to be
overcome. He appealed therefore to promises of greatness if California continued the course of American destiny, and to fears that if she
chose to separate herself, the United States might end up like Europe,
a group of small, squabbling nations. Such appeals were the right

tactic politically for strengthening Union sentiment. But they also touched Anglo-Protestant Californians at a deeper level. Their modern, wealthy society was a remarkable achievement, but they had not yet struck deep roots in their new land. They were but one among many ethnic and religious groups. They were not sure they belonged to California, let alone where California belonged. This lack of rootedness could have been a temporary social problem; Starr King made it also a religious one. A proper attitude toward the universe, he implied, meant seeing yourself as belonging to larger and larger unities. You are not simply individuals; you are Californians. You are also Americans; you belong to that larger destiny that spreads from Lake Tahoe to the Sea of Galilee; and you are part of a mysterious cosmos that is the reflection of the mind of God.

Thus King honored the California experience and integrated it into God's grand plan. God's providence in forming the American nation was like his ordering of stars and comets or beautifying the earth with lakes and mountains. The apparently unique experiences of Californians—Tahoe and the Sierras, panning for gold in the creekbeds or mingling with the crowds in San Francisco—were linked to the Sea of Galilee and the Himalayas, the carpenter Jesus, the crowds in Jerusalem, and the westward march of humanity. Even the high incidence of insanity called up images of Jesus' healing miracles. The strangeness of it all—the mixture of all races and professions digging side by side for gold—was not condemned, but valued as Californians valued it: for King as for them, it was a culmination of the movement for equality and dignity of labor. The universe was all of a piece, and Starr King tried to show Californians how it fit together. Virtually the only part of California experience or legend that did not appear in Starr King's oratory was a romanticization of Old California, the Spanish and Mexican era—but that would not have been easy to integrate into Anglo-Saxon destiny.

This inspiring image of California's place in the universe would probably be enough to account for Starr King's popularity. But there is one final element of his thought that I want to emphasize, for it is important in understanding some of the directions taken by later religious thinkers in California: namely, Starr King's emphasis on the spiritual reality behind every apparent material reality. This idea—implicit in his notion that nature mirrors the mind of God, or that a larger purpose lies behind every apparent accident, surprising similarity, or correspondence—is not fully elucidated in any of the works we have examined so far; but it appears as the main theme of one of his most popular lectures, "Substance and Show." Originally written in 1851 and slightly revised while King was in California, this, his biographers said, was the most requested of all the speeches and sermons in his repertoire. In it he brought forth clearly the theme of his whole religious perspective: the idea of *substance* over *show*.

Substance is King's term for the forces that lie behind appearances, standing under and supporting what we see; *show* is his term for external facts. Substance is more important; it is the spirit providing motion, force, order, and organization; it "rules, disposes, penetrates, and vivifies matter." What gives iron, glass, diamonds, and crystals their shape and hardness is the force or substance, just as subtle forces such as electricity energize matter. That being so, King suggested, "the prominent lesson of science to men . . . is faith in the intangible and invisible."[16]

King argued, further, that ideas are powerful, substantial entities. Indeed, the whole universe is an image of thought—it is, he said, citing Jonathan Edwards as his authority, "the continuous image of the Creator's constant thought." Here we see the deeper vision of the world that was echoed in the Lake Tahoe sermon. King went on in a similar vein to say that to delight in the material universe and the beauty of nature, and to receive it deeply into one's soul, is to be in touch with "the world of Divine Substance." To refuse deeper communion with nature is to live only in a superficial world of show.[17]

Not only is love of nature fundamentally religious, but also, the lecture went on, national spirit is substance, as is the cultivation of individual spirit. All the concrete realities, or show, of social life—from brick buildings to whole nations—are manifestations of ideas, affections, spiritual forces. History, our heritage, is a substantial and real influence. The unique character of the American people, like a grand rock formation, is matter held together by the cohesive force of all the spiritual influences of centuries past. Ultimately, what keeps people alive individually and collectively are their ideas and emotions, their attachment and dedication to ideals. "Character," King concluded, "is the culminating substance of nature." Without it a person would be a mere ghost. To build character—to build spirits, to shape great souls—is humanity's great task, for "the stuff a great soul is made of is the most real and unwasting material of the universe."[18]

The popularity of this lecture rested not only on Starr King's use, as always, of compelling imagery and excellent rhetorical structure, but on the force of his point: the world is not the way you see it. The aim of the piece, he once wrote, was to reverse people's usual perceptions of the world—to exchange their reliance on external sense perception for a recognition of inner realities and forces. To see the substance behind the show, the spirit behind the matter, was to see everything in a totally different way. His audiences appear to have gotten the message, or at least to have been intrigued by it. Indeed, they wanted to hear it again and again.

The perspective of "Substance and Show" was novel and significant for Californians. Novel, because many of them felt thoroughly immersed in the material world of wealth and technical progress, building houses and stores and towns, forming corporations, and competing for rewards. Traditional Anglo-Protestants offered pictures of rather alien worlds—of sinners facing judgment and damnation, or of long-lost wanderers coming home to mother and Jesus. To think of spiritual reality in their own midst, undergirding those very stores, towns, and corporations was at the very least an interesting shift in perspective. It suggested still more than that: King held that there was an organizing force behind all the disparate elements, behind all the apparent chaos of a new society. There was a purpose behind the fast-paced lives that people lived. In a society where most institutions had been constructed ad hoc, order and purpose seemed a slow and often distant achievement. In his patriotic speeches, King had tied California to a larger national purpose; in "Substance and Show" he declared order and purpose to be present even when invisible and unnameable.

This was a religious approach to which Californians could respond warmly, whether or not they could grasp the entire philosophy that Starr King was elaborating. They could not name the purpose behind their experience and their continuing work. It did not fit into categories of religious doctrine; it was not like anything they knew from their home states; it was not based on an "ism" or creed or political platform. Nevertheless, the California experience was formative and the makers of the state wanted to believe it was purposeful and meaningful. King's ideas implied that it was more than that: it was "substantial"—just as real as the material reality of California, perhaps more so.

This emphasis on spirit over matter, on a religious perspective that transcended all concrete forms and was different from and more powerful than the forms themselves, was destined to remain a part of California's religious heritage. Starr King influenced some liberal thinkers in California to espouse similar points of view. For example, David Starr Jordan, an Eastern liberal who became the first president of Stanford University, was so impressed by King's work that he took "Starr" as his middle name. Joseph Pomeroy Widney, an influential Southern California minister, spoke of Starr King as one of the few great and broad-minded spirits of the church.[19] In the Bay Area, Laurentine Hamilton was somewhat influenced by King and kept the liberal tradition alive in the years immediately following King's death.

But the traces of King as a direct influence on the life of religious intellectuals are few and far between—generally because most of them were trained in the East, where King always remained a lesser light. We may suspect that something of his ideas or the spirit behind them was transmitted by the people who remembered him, and they and their children would be attracted by people who brought similar ideas. California Unitarians honored him by naming their Berkeley seminary after him. But the memory of Starr King rises up in much stranger places. We find, for example, a brief record of a Mrs. E. P. Thorndyke, a spiritualist and health resort owner who held gatherings of spiritualists at her home in southern California.[20] Mrs. Thorndyke, the memoir tells us, was visited in 1906 on her deathbed by the spirit of Thomas Starr King, who spoke through her lips. The spirit urged everyone to patriotism on the one hand and devotion to the spirit world on the other—themes which, while somewhat distorted in the context of spiritualism, we can see in Starr King's actual messages.

We can say with confidence that Starr King laid a foundation for liberal Christianity in California tradition. His style of liberalism was laced with a Transcendental mysticism and a grounding in love of nature, which recur frequently in California religiosity. His brand of Christianity affected orthodox Protestantism in the long run, as liberal ideas took their different courses through different transmitters of religious traditions. In the short run, however, liberalism came under attack—not while King was alive, because he was careful to avoid controversy among Christians, and his popularity made him almost invulnerable. But soon after his death, some ideas similar to King's appeared in the sermons of the Rev. Laurentine Hamilton, an

Oakland minister who was becoming one of the more prestigious preachers in the Bay Area.[21] Hamilton, however, was a Presbyterian, not a Unitarian. His liberal tendencies eventually brought him into a conflict with his denomination that disturbed churchpeople throughout the Bay Area. In the next chapter, we will look closely at the nature and context of Hamilton's trial for heresy.

3. Issues of Death and Life

Not long after the death of Starr King, unorthodox beliefs were appearing among many northern Californians. By the late 1860s the largely unarticulated popular tradition that we saw in Chapter 1 was being developed by organized groups and spokespersons offering various alternatives to orthodoxy for the Anglo-Protestant population. Spiritualists, for example, who had been present in California since the 1850s publicizing their séances, experienced a resurgence of interest after the Civil War. In 1867 they were able to start their own newspaper, which announced itself as an exponent of liberal religion while denouncing revivalism and all dogmas and creeds.[1] Seventh-day Adventists, preaching the imminent end of the world and espousing unusual theories about the life after death, began a vigorous California missionary campaign in 1868.[2]

Even within the traditional denominations there were dissidents, three of whom were tried as heretics. The first heresy trial was that of S. D. Simonds, who since 1851 had been editor of the *California Christian Advocate*, the major Methodist newspaper. Simonds questioned the doctrine of the Trinity and favored a unified view of God understood through the figure of Christ.[3] It is clear from his columns in the *Advocate* that he always had a strong interest in science and modern thought and in resolving the conflicts between the Bible and secular critics; eventually he was led in a more liberal direction. Simonds was tried for heresy in 1864 but maintained his connection with the church, which reinstated him on grounds of his good character in 1868. Another trial, more serious in its consequences, occurred in 1868–69 among the Presbyterians, when the Rev. Laurentine Hamilton questioned received doctrines about the life after death, or the "future state" as it was euphemistically called. Hamilton was disbarred from the ministry in 1869 and started his own independent church. In 1874 the Methodists again had to deal with a liberal, D. A. Dryden, who was, like Simonds, a highly respected minister from pioneer times. Dryden was excluded from the ministry and went to work for the U.S. government's Indian Bureau.[4] Thus as liberal beliefs, made more respectable by Thomas Starr King, appeared among Anglo-Protestant leaders, traditional ministers tightened their defenses by insisting on heresy trials. It may seem strange that California ministers would resort to arguing over abstruse points of doctrine only a few years after people had warmly supported the open and expansive religiosity of Starr King. Indeed, it seemed strange to many Californians at the time. Perhaps it was true, as King had once written privately to a friend, that in California there was "the tightest orthodoxy [among ministers], in connection with a noble large-heartedness among the people."[5]

Yet heresy trials are not held merely for the sake of intellectual argument. Heresy, as George Shriver has written, is the dislocation of an entire scheme of the universe by the denial of some crucial element within it.[6] That dislocation is precisely what was happening in California between 1865 and 1875. The crucial element denied by at least two of the heretics and many dissidents was the orthodox view of life after death. Spiritualists held that people continued to develop and progress to different levels even after they died; there was no steady state of heavenly bliss or hellish punishment. Adventists denied the eternal punishment of the wicked, and in addition believed that the soul did not live in a heaven after the body died: instead it "slept" till the final resurrection, when it would awaken along with the body. The two ministers who were permanently excluded from their denominations, Hamilton and Dryden, also questioned the punishment of the wicked and developed unusual views of the afterlife. Simonds, who was reinstated, had chosen another, apparently less offensive, point of quarrel. We can hardly doubt that the afterlife was the heart of the problem that traditionalists had with dissidents. As the conservative *Pacific Methodist* observed in 1869, the doctrine of eternal punishment of the wicked was one of the most questioned beliefs of the day,[7] and related issues about the afterlife were being raised on all sides.

Such questions were not new. Unitarians and Universalists had asked—and, in their own ways, answered—them some fifty years before.[8] But after the Civil War this issue came sharply into popular consciousness, not only in California but all across the nation. In the Northeast and Midwest, which dominated national Protestantism, new ideas about the afterlife came to the fore mainly through popular books and hymns. The novels of Elizabeth Stuart Phelps, beginning with her best-selling *The Gates Ajar* (1868), questioned orthodox belief and portrayed the life after death as a pleasant New England town, filled with friends, families, and cultural events such as concerts by Beethoven. Even crotchety agnostics got into heaven, and the punishment of the wicked was virtually dismissed as an issue for outmoded theologians.[9] Theologians paid little attention to Phelps's books, but these and similar works reflected popular consciousness about the issues at hand.

Americans after the Civil War—if we include the Spiritualists, after 1850—wove new fantasies about the life after death. These ideas were, in part, transmutations of utopian and millenarian hopes that had influenced American Protestantism in the North from 1830 to 1850. As utopianism and millennialism faded and society moved toward consolidation and control, visions of the future came to rest in images of the afterlife—which, after all, were more malleable than the world here below.[10] Like utopias, these visions developed out of hope for the spiritual completion of the human being. Thus Phelps developed the ideal of the New England community in heaven, and the Spiritualists imagined a spirit world peopled with family, friends, and heroes.

Harmless as such fantasies might seem, they were dangerous to Protestant orthodoxy in California. Traditional views of a stable heavenly society with eternal bliss for the righteous and eternal punishment for the wicked encouraged belief in the possibility of a clear social and moral order on earth. Questioning the standard views of reward and punishment would cast doubt on the entire divine order of things, established in heaven for all eternity, and would call into question Anglo-Protestant aims of establishing a moral society. If heaven was not ordered as they had believed, how could they say that the order they proposed on earth was according to a divine plan? Thus heresy about the afterlife could be connected to disturbing ideas about society and human destiny in life.

This will become clearer from a specific example. The most illuminating case is that of Laurentine Hamilton, for we have a full record of his heresy and we can reconstruct with considerable confidence its social context. Then we can return briefly to other examples to shed further light on the relation between images of the afterlife and the social reality of northern California white Protestants.

Beginning on Easter Sunday in 1868, Laurentine Hamilton, pastor of Oakland's First Presbyterian Church, preached a series of four sermons on immortality. These sermons must have been the talk of the town, for he was soon asked to publish them. When they appeared in print he achieved immediate notoriety throughout the Bay Area: he was called before the Presbytery of San Jose to defend himself against charges of heresy. The action was shocking because Hamilton was one of the respected ministers of the region. A graduate of Auburn Seminary in New York, he had years of California service behind him, having spent two years in the small town of Columbia (Tuolumne County) and eight years in San Jose before coming to Oakland in 1865. First Presbyterian was a prestigious appointment, probably the wealthiest church in Oakland after First Congregational. Hamilton was not a great orator, but he had become known for his thoughtful sermons and sympathetic manner.[11] He was well enough respected in clerical circles to have had a sermon published recently in the *Occident* (April 1868). The paper's stated policy was to publish only noncontroversial sermons, all of which were by well-known ministers; Hamilton's was a mildly liberal but totally inoffensive defense of the Christian Sabbath.

His series on immortality, however, was quite controversial, especially the second sermon, entitled "Future Punishment," which examined the fate of the wicked after death.[12] In it he argued that if God was truly good and merciful, he would not punish sinners forever. It was more reasonable to suppose that he would either stop the punishment at some point, or arrange matters so that it would come naturally to an end. In fact, Hamilton suggested, the church had misinterpreted the notion of eternal punishment. The biblical adjective translated "eternal" was in Greek *aionios*, from the noun *aion*, which really meant a "dispensation"—a "certain period or flow of time during which one connected series of events and changes runs its course and ends in some consummation."[13] Thus the punishment of the wicked might be for some given period or periods, but it would not truly be eternal in the sense of "endless."

That notion led Hamilton to an entirely different conception of the afterlife. He urged his audience not to imagine our eternal lives as static, "an eternal monotony of psalm-singing or aimless, effortless ecstasies;" that would be "cushions of idleness, misnamed rest." Instead, we should think of our lives after death as going through beginnings, culminations, transformations, and new beginnings through eon after eon. Heavenly life was "the starting forth on a new career of progress . . . a new goal of attainment . . . guided anew for another stretch of the onward and upward advance, all progress still depending on effort."[14] His reinterpretation of the term "eternal" thus undergirded a different conception of the afterlife as progressive and changing.

Conversely, Hamilton argued, we should not imagine the punishment of the wicked as entailing their screaming in pain in eternal flames. Rather, the wicked would suffer a gradual decline, the reverse of progress and advance. Their punishment was a "fearing, shrinking sense of his [God's] being which feels him without knowing him . . . a growing blindness that is ever closing in on the soul in thicker darkness." Hamilton declined to say whether the diminishing light of the soul was ever finally snuffed out. But, via an unusual metaphor, he suggested that it was not: "This dying life is the spiritual counterpart to that line in mathematics which forever approaches but never touches a curve—the spiritual asymptote of annihilation." We may even believe, he suggested, that Christ's atonement was so powerful that salvation could be offered, on the other side of death, to those whose powers were withering.[15]

Punishment, then, could not be said to be eternal, for the suffering of the wicked would actually decrease as their sensitivity declined. The greater their distance from God, the less they could feel. And for all practical purposes, Hamilton believed, wickedness could be said simply to die out. Therefore it did not make sense to urge people to come to God because otherwise they would "burn" forever. Instead, Christians should appeal to their inner sense that "the divine powers of life in them are dying." Spiritually, the wicked suffer not pain but loss—the loss of their own vital powers of feeling and knowing.[16]

Hamilton offered a utopian fantasy of the afterlife that contrasted sharply with orthodox views of heaven and hell. In asking people to imagine a life beyond the grave where they would continue to change and progress, he projected the increasingly popular image of nineteenth-century society as a civilization of growth and progress, where independent individuals set goals and achieved them, gaining a sense of accomplishment and fullness of life. Unlike real society, however, there was no competition in the afterlife, nor were there any wicked people trampling on the efforts of the good. They, because of their lack of sensitivity and devotion to God, were becoming weaker and weaker and were being left far behind.

Interestingly, neither the good nor the evil side of the world beyond was characterized by great emotion or passion. The good were essentially followers of the work ethic, planning and carrying out, learning and accomplishing; but Hamilton said nothing of a growing intimacy, either between a soul and God or among the souls of the dead themselves. We might assume that, unlike the wicked, they retained capacity for feeling; but that was not important in Hamilton's portrayal. Their reward was not intimacy or ecstasy, but accomplishment. The wicked were dying on all counts, in feeling as well as in capacity to know and do; but they did not cry out or suffer agonies at their loss, nor were they demoniacal creatures raging in anger at God. Rather, they grew cold. Hamilton's utopia contained neither joy nor bliss, his dystopia neither pain nor sorrow.

That vision was in tune with Hamilton's general attitude toward emotionality in religion. In the first and third of his sermons on immortality, "The Knowledge of God Eternal Life" and "Fear the Foe of Love," he criticized revivalistic religion for appealing to people's fears, working them up and then letting them down. That, he said, kept people bouncing back and forth between hope and despair, leading not to love of God but to frustration and disbelief. When he was called before the Presbytery to justify the stance taken in his sermons, he launched an attack on two giants of tradition: Jonathan Edwards, father of American evangelicalism, and Charles Spurgeon, recognized as one of the greatest preachers in nineteenth-century Britain. He declared that their views of the gruesome torments of hell were "boundless absurdities." In general, he said, the old views of heaven and hell were based on "an over-strained horror or fear which . . . is essentially hardening and unhealthful, and positively diseasing to the moral sensibility."[17]

Such statements were unlikely to persuade the old guard. They had probably been raised on emotional, revivalistic religion and did not find it hardening or unhealthy. Over the previous two years a major revivalist, A. B. Earle, had been touring the northern part of the state at the invitation of orthodox ministers of many denominations; they were promoting "old-time religion" just at the moment that Hamilton was attacking it. Moreover, liberal religious groups like the Unitarians and Spiritualists were drawing many people away from orthodoxy already, and the Methodists had declared one of their own leaders heretical. In such a situation the Presbyterian ministers must have agreed with Methodist Bishop Thompson's belief that, precisely because of the mixture of views in California, it was necessary to preserve orthodoxy from too much "rational" religion.[18] The Presbytery voted to exclude Hamilton from the ministry. The one dissenting vote was cast by an intellectual from the College of California, Professor Henry Durant, who defended Hamilton when the latter did not appear for trial.

Unfortunately for the public image of the Presbyterians, Hamilton did not quietly fade from view. The Sunday before the final verdict was announced, he gathered with his congregation and announced his impending separation from the Presbyterian church. He and about one-half of his parishioners decided to form their own church.[19] The secular papers rallied around Hamilton, declaring that the trial reminded them of the days of the Inquisition, and pleading for liberty of conscience. The denominational papers quietly supported the Presbytery's stance, but without saying too much directly on the issue. Undoubtedly, they did not wish to raise too many questions within their own ranks. Meanwhile, Hamilton remained prominent in Oakland. A year after his declaration of independence, the Oakland Directory in its church listings gave him and his church two-thirds of a page of description, a highly positive advertisement. In contrast, it described the First Presbyterian Church—the other half of his former congregation—in the briefest possible fashion, giving merely the bare facts of its location, its size, and its new pastor.[20] Over the years Hamilton continued to be recognized as a leader of liberal Christianity, even though his congregation declined in size.

Hamilton attracted many of the elite and upwardly mobile of Oakland. He took with him, when the church split, not only Professor Durant but also a judge, S. B. McKee; Rev. D. McClure, the principal of Oakland Military Academy; and J. S. Emery, the Bay Area contractor after whom Emeryville was named. Educators and real estate men seem to have been prominent in his church, suggesting that those with intellectual leanings and those with an eye to expansive growth (and to connecting with others who had money to buy) were attracted to Hamilton.[21] Oakland itself was a boom town at the time. Northern California in general was in the midst of its first great expansion since the gold rush, because people were expecting the completion of the transcontinental railroad (finished in 1869). In Oakland land values were exploding and there were plenty of opportunities to make money in business or speculation. But this meant that it was also a time of great uncertainty, with frequent change of status and careers and high social mobility.

Those most deeply involved in the economic fortunes of society—the wealthy, the upwardly mobile, the speculators—belonged to either First Presbyterian or First Congregational in Oakland. A significant number of these people were so attracted to Hamilton's utopian vision of the future life that they were willing to leave the stability of their home church and risk a different religious venture. To them Hamilton's views seemed more rational and "progressive." Their own lives were dedicated to progress in the material sphere; as Californians, they would likely have faced many alternative choices and changed careers more than once.[22] The general instability of home life, land ownership, and legal institutions was still an important feature of California life. In that context a clear division between the righteous and the wicked would be difficult to imagine, let alone accept. For men who made daily choices in an atmosphere of economic and moral uncertainty, wagering the security of their families on the next turn in the real estate market, the prospect of clearly identifying good and evil must have seemed dim indeed. It was better to think of each choice as something from which one could learn, gradually correcting one's errors and accomplishing a little at each stage. And that, in essence, was what Hamilton's vision of the future life offered. Orthodoxy, in contrast, believed in objective good and evil that could be objectively rewarded or punished. There were no gradations, no second chances. It was an awesome system—too awesome for the uncertainties of California social life. An opportunistic decision might result in a man's being condemned to the flames of hell for eternity; the torment of that thought would, for some people, be unacceptable, given already the uncertainties of their daily lives. Hamilton's version of the afterlife was highly reassuring.

His attacks on emotional religion would be appealing for similar reasons. It was indispensable, in many situations, to suppress one's emotional responses to events in order to deal with economic uncertainties; this would be especially true of businessmen and speculators who were deeply dependent on the fortunes of the market. Revivals could conceivably have offered an outlet for some of those suppressed feelings. But California lacked the continuing social supports—small churches with intimate relations between parishioners and minister, the structures of town or farm life—that had been part of the context of earlier revivalism. Without these it was best to avoid emotionalism, with its risk of arousing fears and anxieties that were already plentiful.

Hamilton's vision of the afterlife, then, suggested moral relativism as opposed to religious and moral objectivity, continual change and growth rather than stable order, "rationality" (that is, congruence with the emerging social order) over emotionality. While Hamilton's following was small, his reputation was large, and his followers were among the most respectable members of society. Moreover, his views bore just enough similarity to those of other dissenters (primarily Unitarians and Spiritualists) to make ministers, and undoubtedly the religious population at large, wonder whether these dissenting minorities were harbingers of the future. We will consider some of these other dissenters briefly to show more clearly how they together reflected a growing sense of the disparity between traditional doctrine and the world in which California Protestants lived, worked, and dreamed.

Closest to Hamilton among his contemporaries were the Spiritualists. So far as we know, Hamilton had no interest in their communication with the spirits of the dead. We would expect him to class that practice as superstition, in league with the mysticism and pietism he rejected. But if we exclude that feature of spiritualism, there were many similarities to his own doctrine. Like Hamilton, the Spiritualists believed that the soul progressed in the life beyond. Most held, following the teachings of Emanuel Swedenborg and Andrew Jackson Davis,[23] that there were a number of cycles or spirals of existence beyond this world, and the soul would have repeated chances to rise higher in the levels of being, moving toward God. Most rejected all orthodoxy because it insisted on dogmas and creeds, and criticized revivalism. Spiritualists, as R. Laurence Moore has shown, wished to be recognized as rational and believed that ultimately their beliefs would be proven empirically by modern science.[24] Blind faith or emotion had nothing to do with the truth of religion.

As we observed earlier, Spiritualism was enjoying a resurgence in California around the time of Hamilton's trial, and its popularity would continue into the 1870s and beyond. Judging from the California organ of Spiritualism, *The Banner of Progress*, these groups were building their popularity primarily on the two features of their doctrine that were most similar to Hamilton's approach: emphasis on progress and development in the afterlife and rejection of orthodoxy with its creeds and revivalistic tendencies. We have no direct information on California Spiritualists that would tell us what sorts of people were attracted to the movement. Nationally, the prominent and well educated were drawn to it, and the style and advertisements in the *Banner of Progress* suggest a highly literate and even intellectual audience. However, no firm conclusions can be drawn from this, since the prominent denominational papers of the time also carried many articles demanding a considerable intellectual ability. Nevertheless it is clear that Spiritualism represented a diffuse but real challenge springing from the same sources as Hamilton's heresy: a dissatisfaction with the orthodox view of the future life and a new image of the universe presided over by a good and rational deity.

A somewhat different deviation from strict orthodoxy appeared in the case of D. A. Dryden, who was tried for heresy by the Methodists in 1874. We can reconstruct but little of the development of his thought, as we have only his brief account of the controversy and an occasional newspaper communication, the latter being not particularly revealing. From his account it appears that he was less radical than Hamilton but shared some similar viewpoints. Dryden held on the one hand to the pietism of early-nineteenth-century Methodism; he held that true doctrines were better expressed in Methodism's comforting hymns than in its creed. The truth of the church lay in its emphasis on living a life of love.[25] Thus, while Dryden saw the center of Christianity as a personal relationship with Jesus, he wished to reject the beliefs expressed in the creeds: the traditional attempt to describe God, Christ, and man rationally. He focused on the issue of life after death because the sharp separation between good and evil implied in traditional beliefs about heaven and hell was no longer acceptable to him, as it had not been to Hamilton. Dryden saw the life after death as a continuous process of growth in spiritual consciousness. There would be no battle between good and evil powers; there was no time of judgment in which the righteous were eternally divided from the wicked. Like Hamilton, Dryden emphasized continual change, progress, and growth, and denied a once-for-all, objective decision about good or evil.

Dryden wrote that he had come to these views gradually, as a result of his own study over a period of several years. During that time, he was preaching all over the northern part of the state, either with a regular church appointment or as an itinerant. His contributions to Methodism must have been substantial, for he and his wife were remembered as a great pioneer Methodist couple in California.[26] During that period of intense activity he was developing and preaching alternative views of the afterlife that emphasized progress and denied harsh judgments, but without, in his case, rejecting emotional religion with its yearning for intimacy with God. In short, a good number of Methodists in the 1860s and early 1870s must have heard Dryden express his heterodox views.

California Protestants in these years, then, included a broad range of liberals, from reforming Methodists like Dryden to the influential elite supporting Hamilton to the radical Spiritualists. They were certainly not dominant; even if we added earlier liberals such as Unitarians and Universalists, they still would have constituted a small minority. But given the high rate of secularism in the area, there were enough of them to be threatening—especially when secular papers added their voices to the fray, encouraging breaks with tradition under the label of "liberty of conscience." The vocal presence of dissidents and heretics was a reaffirmation of California Protestants' independent thinking, in which they took such pride. Moreover, the dissidents viewed themselves as part of the vanguard of progress, and in that respect too they reinforced many Californians' image of themselves as building a great modern society out of their own resources.[27]

The growth of liberal dissent continually undermined Anglo-Protestant traditions. California social patterns, among whites at least, did not support either legalistic or sentimental religiosity; the utopias of the afterlife offered by Hamilton, Dryden, or the Spiritualists were more directly related to life patterns familiar to Californians. They were, above all, utopias of change and development, oriented toward the individual's progress, free of moral judgment and social expectations. At the same time, they were not mere reflections of social life as it was. The utopias ensured continual growth rather than ups and downs; and they promised that the evildoers, the thoroughly selfish or harmful, would be left far behind. One may well ask, however, if these pictures of the afterlife were so clearly suited to Californians—their self-image, their way of thinking, their hopes and dreams—why did the dissident movements not sweep the state? Why did orthodoxy survive these attacks? Were there hidden weaknesses in the new liberalism?

We can best approach these questions by comparing the liberalism of the late 1860s and 1870s to that of Thomas Starr King. King captured the hearts of thousands of Californians with his liberal version of Christianity, but he left the church institutions strictly alone. He did not even attempt to campaign for his own denomination, because he saw true spirituality as flowing through all channels, inside and outside the churches. One may imagine that if he had developed a religious institution, he could have been a great threat to the established denominations. For he did have a social vision: a rich image of the individual in the social order, of California in the nation, of the social order and the national identity as connected to the natural order. All of these were connected in a mystical way with the plan of God for the whole world, and all could be felt by the individual who developed his spiritual sense. King evoked, in the individual heart and mind, expansive feelings and a sense both of participating in a great dream and of belonging to a social and natural community.

Later liberals adopted the mild anti-institutionalism that we find in Starr King (and in earlier American liberal thinkers); they, like he, believed that spirituality did not flow only in organized channels of belief and ritual. But they lacked the larger social vision, the sense of interlocking destinies and of belonging to communities.[28] Far more than Starr King's, Hamilton's vision of the future was individualistic. Dryden's preference for the "life of love" portrayed in Methodist hymns suggests a potential interest in religious community, but it is more likely that, like most pietists, Dryden was concerned more with the inner life and one's relation to Jesus. The Spiritualists for their part offered a vision and a present experience of community— through communion with the departed. One could reestablish a relation with one's relatives, or with great heroes as models of humanity, even while living here on earth. But Spiritualists did not usually transfer that sense of connectedness to the earthly plane, to building community in a strong sense among fellow believers. Generally they fragmented into small groups with no central leadership, and spiritual development itself remained individualistic.

The one strength of orthodoxy, in contrast, was the church as an institution. Traditional Protestantism offered strong fellowship and a variety of community-building activities, both inside and outside the churches. The dissidents, we might say, offered great hopes for the future, but left people too much alone in the present. The traditional Anglo-Protestants, focusing more and more on everyday reality—on "business Christianity"—maintained the allegiance of the majority of Protestants who wanted a church attachment at all. As long as their liberal challengers remained individualistic, anti-institutional, or both, their success was limited.

We should consider one exception to the patterns we are discussing. Among the dissenters on the issue of the afterlife during this period was a group new to California, the Seventh-day Adventists. They were not liberal by any means. But they did question some basic tenets of orthodoxy: they denied that the soul lived on after death, and they denied the eternal punishment of the wicked. The Adventists held that the soul "slept" while the body lay in the grave, and that both soul and body would awaken at the final resurrection, when all people would be judged. Then the good would reign forever and the wicked be destroyed. There would be no punishment in the flames of hell[29]—that feature of the orthodox view that so horrified liberal thinkers.

Clearly the Adventists were like the orthodox in their insistence on judgment, with a clear division between the righteous and the wicked. They could hold this position consistently because they had a clear moral code, much like traditional Protestantism with the addition of certain distinctive commands and practices—observing Saturday as the Sabbath and vegetarianism, for example. Yet they denied the prevailing theories of the immortality of the soul, especially the idea of heaven and hell as residences of spiritual beings. This meant a denial of the utopian vision, or rather a delay of it, since utopia would come when Christ returned (a time they believed was not so far distant). The denial of heaven and hell discouraged people from thinking of reunion with their families, companionship with angels, ethereal pleasures, or any of the other familiar fantasies of heaven. The point was to live a life of obedience to God now; the results would appear at some distant time.

Despite the simplicity of this vision, which cut through the many speculations about the afterlife, it was not attractive to many Californians. By 1906 the Adventists' membership numbered about 6,400, less than one-half of 1 percent of the population. That was not a bad showing for a small sect (the Unitarians, for example, numbered only about three thousand), but it was not enough to make the Adventists highly influential. This reminds us that beliefs by themselves, however "rational" or straightforward, are not convincing without the accompanying satisfaction of a congruent social reality. Adventist practice required a strong relationship to a community, to be sure, and that may have been attractive to some Californians cut loose from other social bonds; but it also required submission to authority. In a society of supposedly independent thinkers, it was easier to be socially respected by being a secularist or agnostic than an Adventist. In other ways, too, Adventism required a degree of separation from the general society that was undoubtedly too difficult for many.

Thus, despite challenges on all sides, the Anglo-Protestants of the center held their ground, largely on the basis of their institutional reality, the churches themselves. Moreover, they still held out the hope that California would be remade in the image of Massachusetts and society would achieve its goal of a divinely modeled moral order; when that happened, the familiar visions of heaven and hell would make more sense too. In the meantime they disparaged or ignored the dissidents and held firmly to traditional doctrines. The *Pacific Methodist* simply insisted that the orthodox position on the future life and eternal punishment had to be believed, whatever our "tender sympathies." The *Evangelist*, a Disciples of Christ paper, decried the "remote speculations" with which people were occupying themselves. Instead, the editors said, we should concern ourselves only about the simple gospel truths contained in Scripture. If "THE HUMAN MIND IS LEFT ALONE WITH THE WORD OF GOD," they declared, if "it is brought into direct contact with the divine law and testimony," all arguments over the future state would cease.[30] Of course, the so-called heretics believed that they were doing exactly what the *Evangelist* prescribed: interpreting the scriptural word of God with their own human minds.

Still, the orthodox remained on the defensive. Sermons of the 1870s show that Anglo-Protestant ministers increasingly had to defend their religion against challenges from outside. Throughout the 1850s and most of the 1860s they could, using their churches as a base, encourage their audiences to bring traditional morality to California, educate young men properly, understand current events as the providence of God, and learn and teach Christian doctrine more thoroughly—in general, to work at building a Christian civilization. Occasionally they used their sermons as opportunities to criticize Roman Catholics or Mormons as well. In the 1870s and later, however, they had to spend their time defending the very idea of the Christian Sabbath. They had to reply to Spiritualists, Rosicrucians,

Adventists, "freethinkers," and critics from scientific circles, as well as deal with issues raised by Mormons, Catholics, Chinese, and Jews.[31] Pluralism became a more pressing problem than any other; the social reality of California was growing ever more distant from the traditional view of an ordered, homogeneous society. Varieties of liberalism continued to sprout, never becoming strongly enough institutionalized to counter the churches, but continually challenging their authority and the visions of the good life that they cherished.

In the 1870s Anglo-Protestant leaders pinned their hopes on two especially important features of traditional American Protestant life. One was the temperance movement, the symbol of morality in outward personal behavior. The other, more significant in California at this time, was observance of the Sabbath, the symbol of traditional community life. When these two practices were undermined and proved impossible even as hopes (they were never dominant social realities), Protestants were left with nothing but church membership and the vagaries of private belief. In addition, therefore, to Protestant controversies over belief, we must understand their conflicts over practice. In the next chapter we will look at the most significant of these conflicts: the question of the Sabbath.

4. Sacred Time and Holy Community

For midcentury Anglo-Protestants the Sabbath was as much a part of a righteous Christian life as temperance, chastity, and education. While ministers were attempting to establish schools, discourage prostitution, and control the liquor trade, they were simultaneously campaigning for a Sunday law for the state of California. All the states east of the Mississippi had such laws, and in the 1850s they were still generally enforced (with some laxity in the large cities). There, Sunday was quietly and devoutly observed. Businesses were closed; most types of recreation were forbidden because they diverted people from the true purpose of the day, the worship of God. People traveled little, spending the day at home after going to church, or at most visiting nearby friends or relatives; ideally, they spent the day in rest, prayer, and discussion of the morning sermon. From the Anglo-Protestant perspective, such an observance was essential not only to religion but to civilization itself. Without it, men would turn into mere beasts of burden or make their day of rest a day for light-heartedness and wild behavior.[1]

California had never had any such Sabbath. Before the Anglo conquest the Roman Catholic priests had of course conducted services on Sunday, but the Spanish and Mexican traditions did not forbid other activities. Sunday in California was often celebrated with a rodeo or feast, with much dancing and carousing.[2] In mining times Sunday grew even farther from the Anglo-Protestant ideal: besides the Mexican celebrations, the miners gathered in the larger towns for a day of trade and recreation after six days out in the gold fields. Stores were open, political rallies were held, people went on river excursions or watched grizzly bears pitted against bulls. Often on Saturday night and Sunday, entertainers would provide music or theater for the miners.[3] Among these attractions, the quiet and devout worship of God struggled for a place.

From almost the moment they arrived, ministers began calling for a statewide Sunday law. The first serious attempt, in 1853, did not pass the legislature, probably indicating the lack of popular sentiment for it. In 1855, however, lawmakers after considerable debate approved a law barring noisy amusements on Sunday. In 1858 a more stringent law was approved forbidding businesses to be open on that day. Clearly the forces of order were swinging in the direction of Sabbath observance, probably in part because of the upheavals surrounding the Vigilance Committees of San Francisco in 1856. But almost immediately the law was challenged in the State Supreme Court in *ex parte Newman*. Newman, a Sacramento Jew, had been convicted in a lower court of selling clothes on Sunday. The three-man Supreme Court, led by Chief Justice David Terry, overturned his conviction on the grounds that Sunday legislation violated the religious freedom provision of the state constitution. The single dissenter was Justice Stephen Fields, who was soon to become Chief Justice himself, when Terry resigned to fight a duel with David Broderick.

The legislature, following the trend of public opinion, passed another Sunday law in 1861, similar to the 1858 law. This time, when the law was challenged in the Supreme Court (*ex parte Andrews*), Justice Fields was in charge and the conviction was upheld. The Sunday law stood on the books and withstood other challenges for the next two decades.[4] Anglo-Protestant leaders seemed to have achieved a victory for Christianity and civilization in California.

The situation did not remain stable, however. The clergy may have breathed a sigh of relief in 1861, but only seven years later they faced one of the strongest challenges to Sunday observance—not from businessmen who wanted to stay open, but from the Seventh-day Adventists. In 1868 two missionaries, Elders J. N. Loughborough and D. T. Bourdeau, arrived from the Adventists' first General Conference. They met briefly with a small Adventist group in San Francisco, but their course was changed when they encountered a Petaluma man, Mr. C. A. Hough. Hough was one of the leaders of a religious group calling themselves Independents. Led by a dream reported to him by a member of this group, Hough had come to San Francisco to meet these two missionaries from afar. He persuaded Loughborough and Bourdeau to come and preach in Petaluma. They agreed, and began there a round of religious meetings that would stir up the small towns of northern California on the Sabbath issue much as Hamilton's heresy trial aroused religious people in the Bay Area.

The two Adventists held meetings in Petaluma from mid August into the fall, then moved on to Windsor, Santa Rosa, and Healdsburg by the summer of 1869. Before they left Petaluma, however, their teachings had already stirred considerable opposition. Local ministers spoke out against Adventism in their congregations and lectured on the proper observance of the Sabbath and other points of doctrine. Public debates were held in March and September of 1869, attracting hundreds of listeners. The missionaries worked in the counties north and east of the Bay over the next few years, stirring excitement everywhere. They moved into the cities in 1874, holding a tent meeting in Oakland and attracting large crowds with their willing support for the local temperance movement.[5] In the same year they held a great debate with Spiritualists in San Jose. Over the next ten years and more, almost every minister had to deal with the Adventist challenge. Virtually every minister whose works are extant had at least one sermon on the Sabbath in his repertoire, and many gave major series of lectures on the question. Laymen and even non-church members wrote on the issue.[6] The Adventists had managed to stir up issues at the heart of the religious concerns of many Protestant Californians.

The Adventists were an unusual group with an unusual message. Centered around their visionary leader, Ellen G. White and her husband James, who was a major writer on belief and doctrine for the movement, they had adopted distinctive practices, notably vegetarianism and the seventh-day Sabbath. They believed in the imminence of the Second Coming of Christ and in some respects sounded like revivalists with their message of repentance and conversion before it became too late.[7] On the Sabbath issue, however, they differed from other Protestants, on fundamental grounds. The Adventists argued that the New Testament era, from Jesus's time to the present, did not necessarily inaugurate a new code of behavior; some Old Testament laws, and certainly the Ten Commandments, were still valid. As James White put it, when a person is united with Christ the Son, that "does not separate him from the Father and his moral code."[8] Most Protestant groups, while claiming to hold to the Ten Commandments, preached that the Gospel freed men from Old Testament law, "fulfilling the law" by going beyond it to a new spiritual condition; the Adventists insisted that the Law and the Gospel were in total harmony.

On the Sabbath issue, the Adventists argued that the Christian church had long ago fallen into error on the proper day of observance. Sunday observance had its roots, as James White recognized, in the practice of celebrating the Resurrection, which, according to tradition, occurred on a Sunday. But, he said, we should not celebrate the Resurrection as though it represented the completion of redemption, for Christ had yet to return in glory and finish his work. Most Christians, according to White, were one dispensation ahead of God.[9] We might be commanded to celebrate Sunday when Christ returns, but in the meantime people should live under God's law as revealed to date. Since Jesus did not change the day of the Sabbath, the seventh day should still be observed as set forth in the Ten Commandments.

On strictly biblical grounds, the Adventists were right. God had ordained the seventh day as the Sabbath according to Genesis 1, and again in the Ten Commandments as given in Exodus 20, among other places. Christians supposedly retained the Ten Commandments, yet they had changed their observance of a weekly holy day to the first day of the week, commemorating the Resurrection. This change was not authorized by Jesus; it had evolved as the Christian sect had grown away from Judaism. Adventists argued that Protestants, who usually claimed to model their churches on the New Testament church, had in this case accepted a Roman Catholic tradition and adopted a Roman Catholic principle in allowing tradition to take priority over the Bible. The Roman church had rejected the Ten Commandments, supposedly the only thing that God gave in person: that was their great "treason" against Christ.[10] Protestants, by following Catholics in observing Sunday as the Sabbath, were guilty of the same treason. This argument, by comparing traditional Protestants to their great nineteenth-century enemies, the Roman Catholics, was designed to hit where it would hurt most.

Protestant ministers replied in various ways to these charges. One of Loughborough's early opponents reaffirmed the distinction between the Law and the Gospel, arguing that Jesus did in fact nullify the Ten Commandments, and Christians are to live by the "law of love" instead. Loughborough replied that we are not at liberty to steal or commit adultery or murder in the name of the "law of love," so why should we be able to break God's commandment concerning the Sabbath? Another tried an elaborate hedge, suggesting that the "Sabbath" in Genesis 1 was not an ordinary day, because the Bible did not say it had an evening and a morning like the other days. Per haps it was a thousand-year day, or some other unusual period of time. The Adventists' answer was that God would hardly have commanded us to keep the Sabbath if that were the model of it.[11]

The more learned of the Protestant ministers recognized the truth in the Adventist charges and constructed more elaborate arguments. A favorite approach was to trace the pre-Christian and pre-Israelite history of the idea of a Sabbath or rest day—a "primeval Sabbath," as it was sometimes called, which supposedly went back to Adam and Eve—and then to argue that Sunday, the Christian Sabbath, was the perfect observance of God's original intention, untainted by idolatry. For example, M. C. Briggs, a Methodist minister and leading crusader, argued that the original Sabbath established in Genesis was a Sunday, but idolaters later perverted it into a day of sun-worship. So the Jews were given the 15th of Aviv (the first Hebrew month, now called Nisan) as a Sabbath, a reminder of Passover. That day fell on a Saturday in the first year of its observance, and thus the Hebrew Sabbath was distinguished from the Egyptian day of sun-worship, Sunday. With the coming of Jesus, Briggs said, the Jewish Sabbath was superseded and Christians returned to the observance of the original Sabbath of creation (he did not say who authorized the change). [12]

An interesting feature of such arguments was their use of very recent scholarship on the ancient civilizations of the Near East and Egypt, including archeological discoveries and the decoding of previously untranslatable texts. That scholarship was highly fragmentary at the time, however, and much of it would be considered historically unreliable today. Of course, the same scholarship could be used to support either side of the argument. Some claimed, for example, that since Sunday had been proven to be a relic of the days of sun-worship it should be avoided today.[13]

The debate produced many novel uses of the Bible and history, indicating, at the very least, that the protagonists were challenged to use their imaginations and intellects. But it is not for us to judge the merits of the arguments. What is important is that the Adventists successfully challenged a Protestant tradition of biblical interpretation and religious practice on a particularly vulnerable point. It was exceedingly rare in those times for ordinary ministers to resort to nonbiblical evidence—let alone evidence of pre-Israelite practices—to uphold a Christian doctrine. Those who delved into new scholarship on the ancient civilizations were forced to rechart their historical maps of Judaism and Christianity, which undoubtedly had a long-term effect on clerical attitudes toward the Bible and history. More important for California, it had an immediate effect on the Adventists' large audiences. One listener at their Oakland tent meetings in 1874 wrote to the city's newspaper as follows:

> The Elders there are upsetting my theology on some points which I had supposed were impregnable, and I find this to be the case of the majority who attend. Either these preachers have a very plausible way of presenting their theories, or we do not know what good evidence is, if their positions are not true. They give the Bible, chapter and verse, for everything they affirm, and back it up with testimony from eminent authors. They do not seem to shun investigation, but give liberty for questions and objections which they readily answer.[14]

Of course, the Adventists wanted above all to establish the authority of the Bible. But by questioning the dominant interpretations on so basic a matter as Sabbath observance, they contributed to the undermining of religious authority in general. As another listener at the tent meetings said, "The authority of tradition, creed, or party is growing less each year."[15]

Californians had already been exposed to questioning of religious authority, most notably in the tolerant, openhearted liberalism of Thomas Starr King. Concurrently with the Adventists' missionary campaign, Bay Area Californians were reading about Laurentine Hamilton's fight over Presbyterian doctrine. Sabbath observance in particular had other opponents besides the Adventists—Spiritualists, for example,[16] as well as many nonreligious people. But unlike the others, the Adventists could not be dismissed as anti-Christian; they were as devoted to the Bible and its authority as any traditional minister. Their questioning of established Protestant interpretations had a greater impact than that produced by religious liberals who interpreted the Bible freely.

The debate raged throughout the 1870s. Meanwhile, secular forces were gaining ground, and petitions for repeal of the Sunday law came regularly before the legislature. In 1870 a mild law permitting theater performances on Sunday but prohibiting the sale of alcohol was passed. Anglo-Protestant churchmen became concerned about gradual erosion of the law through lack of enforcement. Apparently there was good reason to be concerned; at least in the larger cities, there was some popular demand for grocers to be open on

Sunday. Saloon keepers and tobacconists often opposed the law. The Adventists joined the campaign for repeal on the ground of religious liberty; but just as their approach to the Bible, intended to establish their interpretation as absolute authority, had undermined all authority, so their attacks on the Sunday law, based on a fine principle, undermined the weight of custom and the social authority of the clergy.

By the early 1880s, the *Occident* was complaining loudly about the growing sentiment against the Sunday law. The popular California magazine, the *Argonaut*, had come out openly against Sunday observances, saying they were "unreasonable, unprofitable, and tedious." The *Atlantic*, with its national readership, had claimed that popular sentiment demanded at least some recreation on Sunday.[17] In an effort to stem the tide, the San Francisco Ministerial Union and other religious bodies began to call for enforcement of the law by public officials. They seemed ready for a confrontation; perhaps the traditionalists felt stronger as a result of the Moody revivals of 1881. In any case, they were strong enough to get their way in the election year of 1882. As a result, over 1600 arrests were made between March and June of that year, mostly of Seventh-day Adventists and Jews, with some Chinese. Among the more notable figures arrested was the editor of the Pacific Press Publishing Association, the state's largest publishing firm and the fount of all Seventh-day Adventist literature. Nearly all those arrested demanded a jury trial, thereby flooding the courts. Juries all over the state consistently refused to convict.[18]

Had the arrests focused on the saloonkeepers, public opinion might have been different. But the 1861 law was written so as not to discriminate among types of business that could be open, so that wholesale enforcement meant wholesale arrests. The Adventists in particular had finally forced the hand of their opponents, with the result that large numbers of upright, prosperous, and otherwise lawabiding citizens were being jailed and tried for a serious crime. Popular furor over these developments influenced the political campaigns of 1882. The Democratic platform committee, headed by none other than David Terry, who had overturned the 1858 law, wrote a strong plank demanding repeal of the Sunday law. The delegates to the convention hesitated to endorse it because they feared losing churchpeople's votes. But Mr. Grady of Fresno, the District Attorney of Fresno County and himself a Southern Methodist, spoke up, saying that he had nearly ruined his own reputation and bank-rupted the county by spending four or five thousand dollars trying violators of the Sunday law. In his county, known as one of the most religious areas of the state, he had been unable to get a single con-viction. Grady's conclusion was that even the religious people of his county did not want the Sunday law. After hearing his testimony, the Democrats adopted Terry's platform.[19]

The Republicans were in trouble in 1882, although they had gained a majority of twenty thousand votes in the last election and generally had an edge on the Democrats in the state. Their party had become clearly associated with the railroad interests at a time when anti-monopoly sentiments were on the rise. Although they tried to salvage something by adopting a mild anti-monopoly plank (shock-ing the railroad moguls) and an anti-Chinese statement, the Demo-crats had taken much stronger stands on both those issues. Repub-licans decided to go for the church votes by supporting the existing Sunday law; but even on that they vacillated, saying they did not wish "to force any class of our citizens to spend that day in any man-ner."[20] Their stand mattered little. The Democrats turned the tables, counting a majority of more than twenty thousand votes on their side. One of the first acts of the 1883 legislature was to repeal the Sunday law.[21]

Historians have generally not focused on the Sunday issue, treat-ing the railroad monopoly and the anti-Chinese agitation as the cru-cial issues. The big-city papers would tend to support that interpre-tation. The *San Francisco Examiner* claimed that "the day of rest is no more an issue in this campaign than is the man in the moon," while the *Oakland Times* said Sunday was merely a political foot-ball. But the *Examiner* also reported that newspapers in the inland cities were devoting whole columns to the Sunday question. The *Los Angeles Times*—then still a small-city paper in a heavily Protestant area—had declared that Sunday would be *the* issue of the cam-paign.[22] In cosmopolitan San Francisco, religion had already been squeezed off of center stage, but inland and in the newly emerging southern part of the state, it could not be so easily discounted.

This evidence suggests that the people of the inland cities and towns (we will examine the south later) were formulating new reli-gious attitudes. It is no coincidence that Adventists had worked ac-tively in small towns like Healdsburg, Napa, and Fresno, preaching their distinctive gospel and campaigning strongly for religious liberty. They never became a large denomination: in 1873, after five years of work, they could claim only about three hundred Sabbath-keepers in the state; thirty-five years later they still had only about 6400 members in California.²³ But they had convinced people that their beliefs and way of life deserved respect and that the religious liberty clause of the Constitution should protect them from having to observe Sunday in any way. That is why juries would not convict Sabbath-breakers even in Fresno County, and why many traditional Republicans voted Democratic in 1882.

California never had a Sunday law again. The heavily urbanized states of New York and Massachusetts relaxed their statutes at roughly the same time (1883 and 1887 respectively), but California was the first state to repeal its Sunday regulations entirely. The 1882 election in California marked a permanent victory for openness and tolerance, many years ahead of the rest of the nation.²⁴ Yet something was lost in the process. Protestants were not simply trying to force dissident minorities to conform to their standards; they believed that preserving the Sabbath would promote social order, morality, and a devout populace. We can note also that a community that shares the same temporal rhythms, the same calendar and clock, has a funda-mental unity, which the common Sunday observance might have provided. Looking back on the events from our present standpoint, we can see that the defeat of the Sabbath was a blow to community-building in California. In Chapter 1 we noted Joseph Benton's hope that in California there would be established "the same secular and religious festivals, as have been the strength, and glory, and beauty of the land of our Fathers and the places of our birth"; the Sunday Sabbath was one of those traditions that ministers hoped would make California an extension of Protestant Christian America. In 1882, by their actions in juries and by their ballots, Californians re-jected that bond with traditional Protestant culture in favor of a more open and diverse society.

The large vote against the Sunday law did not signal a grand ex-odus from the traditional churches any more than it did a mass con-version to Adventism. The churches continued to prosper in Cali-fornia, although they were never as strong there as east of the Mississippi.²⁵ Despite their defeat on this issue, Anglo-Protestants by the end of the decade were, according to historian Douglas Ander-son, self-confident and optimistic. Their weekly audiences in the churches were small, but people supported revivals led by Dwight

Moody, Sam Jones, and many lesser lights.[26] Yet in more subtle ways they had to accept, by the 1880s if not before, that their position in California culture was not and could not be dominant. Newspapers were likely to report church events and revivals in one column, and quote with approval the famous agnostic Robert Ingersoll in the next.[27] Californians simply were not committed to traditional religion, or to any one religion; they continued to pride themselves on their tolerance. As the *San Francisco Chronicle* proclaimed in 1889, part of the region's culture was its openness in religion:

> The truth is that there is as much interest in religion, art, literature, and charity here as at the East, but that we make no display of it. All the creeds are represented, and the bitterness of sectarianism, which is so often found in Eastern communities, is absent here, because we are more cosmopolitan, and therefore more tolerant of all beliefs.[28]

Anglo-Protestants in California had to accept that tolerance and fairly genial support without occupying center stage for the culture at large.

That situation was unlikely to change over the next decade or so. Sometimes the Protestant mood seemed overwhelmingly despairing, as ministers worried about the problems of urban life. At the end of the century the *Occident* frequently indulged in clerical self-flagellation: ministers had not preached pure enough doctrine, or the reality of sin; they had let the people lapse from Sabbath observance; they had not explained the truth about the end of the world or about what holiness meant in Christianity. As a result families had collapsed, suicide rates were high, and the church in general was weak.[29] Yet the reality was not too different then from more optimistic times when churchpeople still hoped for a true Christian Sabbath in California, or when revivals stirred the hearts of whole communities. In 1900 as in 1870, membership was small, attendance even smaller; many Christians showed only a weak commitment, while the population as a whole was generally open and tolerant toward many forms of religion.

By the 1880s and 1890s, of course, California was not alone in facing such a situation. In the 1860s there were few places in the nation where people flocked to hear a charismatic Unitarian minister, where respected Methodists and Presbyterians were tried for heresy, and where strange sects like Adventists and Spiritualists required a great deal of attention from the mainstream clergy.[30] But in the late

1870s through the 1890s, heretics abounded in the East. A national battle over the Sabbath began in the 1880s, shortly after California's had ended. Pluralism and ethnic diversity were making themselves felt in all the nation's cities, while labor unrest was common from the 1870s onward. The rest of the nation, at least in the major cities, had caught up with California. Anglo-Protestants in California were now in tune with their counterparts elsewhere: they built larger churches for their wealthy congregations; they worried about urban problems; some began to speak of the Social Gospel; and they supported foreign missions.

One can imagine the Protestant clergy of northern California breathing a collective sigh of relief at the discovery that they could once again feel united with their brothers at the other end of the continent. California might not be so unique; San Francisco was a city like other cities; and Californians could be reached (or not reached) by the gospel taught in seminaries, like Americans elsewhere. But were Californians now going to ignore the distinctive qualities that had shaped early California culture and led them to embrace Starr King's grand vision of nature and spirit, or induced them to become interested in religious viewpoints offering the hope of eternal spiritual progress? Ministers had fought these tendencies and thus far had neither defeated them nor integrated them into Protestantism itself. Would church building and social improvement now force the alternative traditions out of the public eye?

In fact, on the popular level, the alternatives continued to grow. For example, even after the Sabbath question was settled publicly, some dissidents continued to address the issue. One example is found in an unusual manuscript by a layman, Hiram Plank of Gilroy, written (judging from internal evidence) in the late 1880s or a little later. His basic argument about the Sabbath is that no external observance of it is binding on any Christian. Neither the "Jewish" Sabbath (Saturday) nor the "Papal" one (Sunday) is the true Sabbath; the true one is internal, a matter of spirit, and therefore has to be observed by the individual in his heart.[31] That attitude reflects the independence and individualism characteristic of many Protestants in California; moreover, it reveals that even in tiny towns like Gilroy (south of San Jose), some people were thinking about religious matters in a highly internalized way. Anglo-Protestant leaders in California, in contrast, had emphasized the social aspect of religion. They wanted private piety, to be sure, but their great concern in California was to influence morality, law, and social life. Hiram Plank's idea of internalizing the Sabbath moved far in the opposite direction.

This popular tradition of interior religion grew stronger in the last two decades of the nineteenth century in northern California. Occultist and Spiritualist groups appeared, especially in San Francisco, as did strange-sounding cults such as the Delsarte Conservatory of Esthetic Gymnastics and Gnostic School of Psychic and Physical Culture.[32] Although such groups attracted members in the north, the momentum of religious change during these years shifted to the rapidly developing southern half of the state, especially the area around Los Angeles. Since the dissident movements that were to affect the north most strongly by the turn of the century were clearly centered in the south, we must shift our focus to that region in order to understand the new developments. In the sunny southland, as we will see, another strong branch of white Protestant California culture was emerging, together with some disturbing metaphysical religions.

5. Metaphysics in the Southland

In the 1860s and 1870s, when the cosmopolitan north was excited about Adventists, Spiritualists, and heretics, southern California was still a collection of small towns and villages. A minor building boom occurred after 1869 when people began to anticipate a southern extension of the transcontinental railroad, but no extension was actually built at that time. The real beginnings of southern California as we know it came after 1880; from 1882, building and land speculation began in earnest, and after the Santa Fe railroad was completed there was an enormous real estate boom (1886–87). Over one hundred towns were platted in Los Angeles County alone, and the railroads extensively promoted the region for settlement. After 1888, when the balloon had deflated, the Los Angeles Chamber of Commerce, led by Harrison Gray Otis of the *Los Angeles Times*, took on the task of promoting the region.[1] Using descriptions of California such as that written by the famous journalist Charles Nordhoff in 1873, entrepreneurs published pamphlets extolling the rich land, fine climate, and irrigation possibilities. Sometimes their claims were rather extravagant. One promoter, writing in *California as It Is* (1882), described how some regarded the region as the original Eden:

> We have a tradition which points, indeed, to the vicinity of Los Angeles, the City of the Angels, as the site of the very Paradise, and the graves are actually shown of Adam and Eve, father and mother of man, and (through some error, doubtless, since it is disputed that he died) of the serpent also.[2]

Whether they believed the propaganda or not, thousands came to southern California to become businessmen or farmers or to improve their health. Health and wealth, it was said, were the grand attractions of the region.

Among the early settlers were some religious groups. A colony of

German settlers, strongly Presbyterian, founded Anaheim. Mormons settled in San Bernardino. Presbyterians and Methodists joined together to form the Indiana Colony, which settled Pasadena as a temperance town. Perhaps most influential were the large number of Methodists who made their homes in Long Beach. Originally laid out as Willmore City in 1882, Long Beach was publicized (via a familiar railroad device, the excursion train) as a beautiful place for settlement and a temperance area as well. In 1884 investors, including some leading Methodists, built there a hotel, summer camp, and Chautauqua. Long Beach was for many years the Methodists' camp-meeting site, until they moved to Huntington Beach in 1906. Meanwhile many summer campers decided to settle and buy homes there, ensuring a strong Protestant influence in the area.[3]

The Methodists also exerted a strong influence through the first major university in the south, the University of Southern California. Planned principally by Judge Robert Maclay Widney and the Rev. John R. Tansey, the school opened its doors in 1880. Built on land donated by a Protestant, a Catholic, and a Jew (Orzo Childs, John Downey, and Isaias Hellman), it became a celebrated example of interfaith cooperation. Most importantly, it became a symbol for Anglo-Protestants of their mission to the whole community. They saw the university as playing the role in the south that Berkeley's College of California played in the north: a center of religious influence to help make southern California in the image of familiar white Protestant communities.[4]

Not all those who came were committed to traditional Protestantism, of course. A considerable portion of the immigrants of Protestant background—especially those who were wealthy—came to California because of their poor health. They patronized the hotels and resorts that sprang up from Santa Barbara to San Diego, then gradually settled down and bought homes. Like the Forty-Niners in the north, many came only for a visit but stayed the rest of their lives. The propaganda for health was as energetic as the promotion of agriculture.[5] Even many who were not so wealthy could, if they could work a little, afford to come to California for health, pleasure, and residence. Especially after 1896, when agricultural prices rose in the Midwest, many former farmers had the financial means to move west. The well-to-do then chose the new beach towns like Hermosa Beach (1902) and Venice (1905), while the middle classes spread throughout Los Angeles.

Overall, the migrations gradually produced a population in Los Angeles that was significantly weighted toward traditional Anglo-Protestantism. A considerable proportion of immigrants were from midwestern states where the evangelical tradition was strong—Ohio, Illinois, Missouri, Iowa, Pennsylvania, Indiana—while another large segment came from New York. Unlike the gold rush migrants, these newcomers were families and, occasionally, groups of families who came for permanent settlement. Most of them hoped to reestablish in southern California the kind of traditional community that was rapidly vanishing from their home states under pressures of urbanization and industrialization. Gregory H. Singleton has shown, in his superb *Religion in the City of Angels*, that in many ways they did manage to replicate the structures and patterns of the Protestant-dominated towns and small cities of the mid nineteenth century.[6]

Singleton argues that in fact Los Angeles was largely controlled by what he calls the "voluntaristic" Protestants (he includes Episcopalians among these) for forty years, from 1880 to 1920. Certainly the nature of the immigration and the evidence from Protestant churches and other institutions supports that argument. Although the promotional emphasis changed during this period from a focus on agriculture and transportation (targeted at farmers and businessmen) to an emphasis on an exotic landscape with attractive, familiar houses (targeted at retirees and those seeking a leisurely life), similar groups, ethnically and geographically, responded: midwesterners and some easterners with marketable skills or some financial means, mostly middle-aged white Anglos. Increasingly, they came not so much to farm as to enjoy the newly created suburban lifestyle and invest in the expanding economy. After the Spanish-American War in 1898, Hawaii and the Philippines provided additional markets and an important raison d'être for Los Angeles as a shipping point. Meanwhile the new entrepreneurs and investors, from the middle class upward, thrived on the prosperity of the region. It was these people, as Singleton has shown, who supported churches and interdenominational activities such as the Y.M.C.A. and the W.C.T.U. while they gained control over the Chamber of Commerce and eventually most city offices.[7]

Yet, despite the control exercised by the Protestant leaders, the immigration to Southern California was enormously diverse. By 1920 the region's population had grown to 530 percent of the 1890 figure (in the same period the population of the United States rose by 140 percent).[8] Large numbers of East Asians, especially Japanese, and blacks arrived after the turn of the century, while Mexicans always constituted a good proportion of the region's population. The white Protestants generally neglected or discriminated against these groups, considering them targets for missions but seldom interacting with them. Most importantly, few members of these minority ethnic groups reached the higher echelons of power in the community; their effects, if any, on the white Protestant lifestyle were indirect.

Even if we discount the influence of Anglo-Protestants among the ethnic minorities, however, it is debatable how complete their domination was even among the whites, some of whom did not quite fit into the culture of traditional Protestantism. They came from states where Protestant liberalism was strong; if the proportion of southerners had been greater we would expect fewer liberals. In other ways, too, they had been exposed to religious ferment: for example, even conservative Protestants in the Northeast had been disturbed by the holiness movement. Thus even while traditionalists maintained institutional and political control throughout most of the first two decades of the new century, there was fragmentation within the Anglo-Protestant tradition and the population it served. On the conservative side there was the holiness movement, which in California had certain peculiarities that we will consider in a later chapter; on the other side there were liberal and eclectic movements—Theosophy, New Thought, and Christian Science—that had abandoned much of traditional Christian doctrine and were making their presence felt in southern California from about 1890.

Singleton virtually ignores both the conservative and the liberal defectors, and as a result his picture of voluntaristic domination of Los Angeles is somewhat distorted.[9] The defectors were certainly minorities, who had their roots elsewhere in the nation and carried little political weight in California. But they are important to an understanding of the development of southern California Protestantism, for they illustrate some of the factors that made the region distinctive and ultimately affected Protestants in both north and south. In this chapter, then, we will examine the liberal movements in the larger context of the social development of the region.

Theosophy, New Thought, and Christian Science have sometimes been grouped together under the heading of "metaphysical reli-

gions"—that is, religions that focus on broad philosophical principles describing the nature of the universe. One could argue about the
appropriateness of the label, but I will use it here for convenience.
The smallest of these movements was Theosophy. The first Theosophical Society was founded in New York in 1875 by Helena P. Blavatsky (1831–91), a recent Russian immigrant; Henry S. Olcott
(1832–1907); and William Q. Judge (1851–96). Blavatsky and Olcott originally met at a Spiritualist gathering—an indication of their
religious tendencies from the first. Their new organization was dedicated both to occult research, aiming at the discovery of secret
knowledge about the universe, the Divine, and the Self; and to the
brotherhood of man that could emerge from this knowledge. Blavatsky, in her writings *Isis Unveiled* (1877) and *The Secret Doctrine*
(1888), claimed to reveal the inner truth behind all the world's religions and philosophies. She had been taught, she said, by members
of a select brotherhood of advanced human beings who made their
home in the Himalayas, but the teachings were the same truth that
had been taught by all the world's great masters. According to this
teaching, pure impersonal Being was the source of all existing beings; human beings moved through many reincarnations in gaining
spiritual advancement; and ultimately all beings are united in the
One.

Blavatsky died in 1891 and was succeeded by Annie Besant, who
headed the Society until her own death in 1933. There was also a
split in the movement: William Judge left in 1895 to form an independent group, the Theosophical Society of America. A woman
named Kathryn Tingley became in effect the prophetess for Judge's
organization. Tingley, the "Purple Mother," headed a grand new
venture in California: the Point Loma Theosophical Community,
founded in 1897 near San Diego. The community stressed the principle of a Universal Brotherhood of Humanity as well as the study of
Oriental wisdom and occult and psychical knowledge. The other
faction of Theosophists, followers of Besant, later had their representatives in California also. Led by Albert Powell Warrington, a
group settled in 1911 in Krotona, now the center of Hollywood.
Later they moved to the Ojai Valley, where Annie Besant came to live
with the famous Krishnamurti, whom she had "discovered" in India
and displayed as the Messiah of this era (a title that Krishnamurti
later rejected).[10] A smaller faction from Syracuse, New York, started
a colony and sanitorium near Pismo Beach in 1903.

The Theosophists were few in number: the Point Loma community at its height in 1910 had about five hundred residents, including at least 150 to 200 children; we have no estimates of the number of followers who did not reside at the community. The other factions seem to have numbered some fifty to two hundred committed members. Nevertheless their influence was far larger than their numbers would suggest. Point Loma became known for its educational enterprises, taking in immigrants, especially children from the Caribbean islands, as well as educating the offspring of the middle-class Theosophists themselves. They emphasized the fine arts, especially music and theater, and many residents from the San Diego area attended the community's presentations. The Greek Theater, the only original structure still standing, was the site of many cultural events and religious pageants well publicized throughout the region. Even when Theosophists received negative attention from the press—as they did consistently from the *Los Angeles Times*—the papers helped to attract interest in their philosophy and activities. Especially after Tingley won a libel suit against the *Times* in 1903, her group received more positive notice. Southern Californians, therefore, were likely to have been touched by Theosophical influences even though few of them joined the available groups. Theosophy's belief in the spiritual unity of mankind and the oneness of all beings and all religious wisdom, and its humanitarianism combined with mystical thought, became part of the popular religious currency of the region.[11]

A second important movement, New Thought, was less cohesive and less inclined toward the occult. It grew originally from the practical methods devised by the Maine healer Phineas Quimby (1802–66) for curing diseases by the power of the mind. Quimby, after experimenting with mesmerism, had come to believe that disease was caused primarily by erroneous belief. By changing their own inner attitudes and ways of thinking, people could cure themselves. One of Quimby's patients, Warren Felt Evans (1814–1889), developed this practice into an entire system of thought. In numerous works, beginning with *The Mental Cure* (1869), he expounded a philosophy grounded on unity with the One, which he usually called the Christ Principle Within; unity with that Principle or divine spark in the self brought healing and continued personal power. In particular, Evans developed the idea of the power of suggestion—either from a doctor or healer, or from the patient himself ("autosuggestion"). By the use of conscious "affirmations," as they were called, the patient could induce himself to think positively and thus contribute greatly to his improvement. A person troubled by constant worry might repeat to himself, "I am one with the Infinite Spirit," or "I am at peace with myself." Eventually this practice of "positive thinking" came to be used not only for physical and mental health but also as a method of achieving success in business, society, and romance.

Through study groups, beginning with the Metaphysical Club in Boston (founded 1895), congresses and interlocking organizations such as the International Metaphysical League, and most importantly through popular literature, New Thought ideas spread throughout the country. The movement itself was not tightly organized. New Thought groups were not so much churches as study groups and disseminators of information. Members read and distributed literature and discussed it among themselves, usually at Sunday evening meetings; privately, they practiced meditations and affirmations for their own spiritual growth and self-improvement. One could belong to a traditional church and simultaneously become deeply involved in New Thought. Some might join a New Thought church—the Unity School of Christianity headquartered in Kansas City, the Church of Divine Science in Denver and San Francisco, or the Church of Religious Science in Los Angeles (from 1917)—but it was never necessary to give up any other religious practice in order to become part of the New Thought movement.

New Thought had none of the elaborateness of Theosophy—no Oriental literature, no Greek pageants or Purple Mothers. Its first focus was health, physical and mental. As Ralph Waldo Trine put it in his popular book on the subject, *In Tune With the Infinite*—which sold two million copies shortly after its publication in 1897—people could have "Fullness of Peace, Power, and Plenty" from this new system of thought and practice. What Trine and other New Thoughters had in common with Theosophy was their emphasis on spiritual unity, on discovering the oneness of the self with the Divine. Trine wrote:

> In the degree . . . that you come into a vital realization of your oneness with the Infinite Spirit of Life, whence all life in individual form has come and is continually coming, and in the degree that . . . you open yourself to its divine inflow, do you set into operation forces that will sooner or later bring even the physical body into a state of abounding health and strength.[12]

In realizing Oneness, the individual was acting in accordance with the inner law of the universe. One had to discipline one's mind to banish fears, overcome negative feelings like anger and sorrow, and in general maintain a calm, quiet attitude. Once achieved, that state of mind would stabilize and guide an individual in all the vicissitudes of life. This practical emphasis had a much broader appeal than Theosophy's quest for the inner, esoteric secrets, especially among the many health seekers in southern California, yet the two movements were akin in their metaphysical foundations. The Divine Self within and oneness with the Infinite Spirit were variations on the same theme: an invisible principle was the source of all knowledge and well-being, and one could grasp that principle with one's mind.

The most prominent of the three new movements, the one that produced the most powerful organization, was the Church of Christ, Scientist, often called Christian Science. The church was formally chartered in 1879 under the leadership of Mary Baker Eddy (1821–1910), its founder and ultimate living authority. Eddy, like Warren Evans, had been helped in her illnesses by the healing skills of Phineas Quimby. When Quimby died in 1866 Eddy struggled through a difficult period, then developed and wrote down a philosophy of health and healing. Her ideas were based partly on Quimby's, though Eddy was more explicitly Christian in orientation; she and her followers denied her work was derivative.[13] In 1875 she published the great crystallization of her work, *Science and Health*, the basic Christian Science textbook that Eddy revised frequently until her death. Within the movement it ranked beside the Bible as a kind of scripture, for it was the key through which the Bible itself could be understood.

Eddy gathered students around her from 1868 on, eventually establishing her headquarters in Boston in 1882. She taught a truth that she claimed would lead to perfect health, having been revealed in Jesus Christ in the New Testament. Jesus had shown the way to realizing one's perfect spiritual character as a human being. Most of us, Eddy said, are misled into thinking that we are material, when in fact we are immortal and perfect. When one truly realizes this fact—a recognition involving a radical transformation in one's thoughts and attitudes—one can achieve wholeness and health.

Health, in Eddy's view, was the sign of a proper relation to God. God was the Divine Principle, Infinite Mind, and Infinite Love—often named in this impersonal way, but sometimes also as Father-Mother God. God could be thought of as personal if one did not think of personality as involving corporeality or any other kind of limitation. The aim of Christian Science practice was to enter into a full relationship with this God. Eddy held that one did not actually unite with God; there was a distinction between creature and creator, spiritual man (who indeed was pure spirit) and Infinite Spirit. Rather, one could come to apprehend reality as God sees it—to see the universe as good and know one's own perfect being as God created it. Because Christian Science was based on the deepest laws of the universe, its practice led straight to God. Any other science was crass materialism, based on wrong belief in the existence of the material world; one had to give up that belief to begin the process of perfection that would lead to health. This process was also true Christianity, for Jesus exemplified human wholeness and perfect apprehension of the divine.

As Eddy spread her message, she maintained control over the movement. Unlike New Thought, which developed many independent organizations, the Church of Christ, Scientist remained one. At first Scientists' meetings allowed time for personal testimonies, but Eddy soon prohibited them. The churches' leaders were "readers," not preachers, who read prescribed selections from the Bible and *Science and Health* without injecting their own interpretations. Those who wished to become healers or "practitioners," as they were called, studied only Eddy's writings. She believed it was dangerous to entrust the teaching of her discoveries to people still infected with the errors of "mortal mind," that is, ordinary ways of thinking; it was important that each new student connect to a pure source.

Reading and study, the primary practices of Christian Science, led to a mental discipline that cleared the mind of error. The healer, having attained this clarity, could see the client's illness and the false beliefs that gave rise to it, and instruct the client how to rethink his way to health. The aim, for oneself or another, was to think only pure, positive thoughts focused on the perfect spiritual reality. One should not talk about disease, or even name it, because that gave it reality in one's mind. One had to learn to see the world as God saw it, and to see disease, evil, and all material things as illusions. That was the Christian Science equivalent of regeneration, a spiritual rebirth. One could and should also use prayer in this process, but not in the traditional sense of requesting God to give things. Prayer should be silent communion with God, contemplation of his omnipresence and love, and resolution to conform one's will to the divine. This inner work was necessary on the path to perfection.[14]

The parallels between Christian Science and New Thought are clear, as one might expect, given their common derivation from Quimby's mental healing practice. Both emphasized changing the mind and attitudes in order to heal disease; both believed in the possibility of human perfection in approaching the divine. Both believed in a law beyond the material laws of nature, a spiritual law and order governing the physical, mental, and spiritual life. Both emphasized reading, focused study, and certain kinds of meditation to erase old attitudes and create new, positive ones. The two movements differed in certain respects. New Thought's loose conglomeration of groups and its many writers, teachers, and versions of doctrine contrast strongly with Mrs. Eddy's tight control of Christian Science. New Thought drew eclectically on many sources, while Christian Science was tied to the Bible and the revelation of Jesus. Further, Mrs. Eddy insisted on a clear distinction between the human and divine, whereas many New Thought writers ignored or blurred the distinction. Still, their overall orientations and many of their practical methods were similar.

Both movements enjoyed great success in California, first in the southern portion but soon in the north as well. Christian Scientists came to California with the great waves of migration to the Los Angeles area in the late 1880s; so did New Thought followers. One student of Mrs. Eddy's wrote home in 1886, referring to the New Thought people, that "Babel is already in California. . . . we, as Christian Scientists, are denounced for having our jacket too straight [*sic*]."[15] The first known Christian Science church in California was founded at Riverside in 1887 by a practitioner named Emma S. Davis. It grew from ten members in 1890 to two hundred in 1901, and a similar mushrooming soon occurred in other southern cities. Los Angeles proper had its first church by 1893; in 1910–11 the Los Angeles directory listed over one hundred Christian Science practitioners (most of them women). At the time there were only about 350 nurses in the city. Obviously Christian Science had become a major alternative resource for health seekers. In 1890 California had the third-largest Christian Science membership of any state, nearly one-tenth of the total for the entire nation.[16] Moreover, the members tended to be middle class or wealthier and contributed generously to the churches. By 1912 the striking modern architecture of many new Christian Science churches was attracting considerable attention.[17]

If Christian Scientists were the orderly, disciplined group among the new metaphysical religions, we may imagine that New Thought, with its loosely defined membership and wide-ranging literature, attracted many more at least to its periphery. We know that New Thoughters of the Unity School of Christianity were strong enough to build a church in Los Angeles in 1893, suggesting that they may have been on an equal footing with the Scientists, who also had one church (the size of each is unknown). Gail Thain Parker has estimated for New England that New Thought groups had at least as many followers as Christian Science, while probably twice as many more read New Thought literature while remaining members of a traditional church.[18] That estimate is probably conservative, but even so we can use it to reconstruct the probable size of the metaphysical movements.

On the basis of census figures and what we know of the sizes of buildings the Christian Scientists were erecting, it seems likely that the city of Los Angeles had twelve to fifteen hundred Scientists in 1906. Unity School people, usually meeting under the auspices of a "Home of Truth," had three centers in the city by 1909. No estimates are available for other New Thought groups, but following Parker we can estimate that all together, including Unity, they may have equaled the Scientists' total. Theosophists were fewer; those connected with the Judge-Tingley group and those belonging to Besant's organization probably totaled no more than three hundred in Los Angeles. A safe assumption, therefore, is that all the metaphysical movements together had some three thousand members. Following again Parker's estimates, we would assume that at least three thousand were reading in the metaphysical literature while remaining members of a traditional church. The consequences for traditional religion are apparent. At that time membership in the Anglo-Protestant churches was about twenty-five thousand; a competing set of movements at least three thousand strong, with another three thousand potential defectors in the churches themselves, could hardly be ignored. Moreover, the new movements were growing in reputation as well as in numbers. In 1893 Christian Science attracted considerable attention at the much-talked-about World's Parliament of Religions in Chicago. In 1915, at the Panama-Pacific Exposition in San Francisco, an entire day was given over to New Thought.[19]

The new metaphysical religions were shocking to the traditional churches not only because they were growing rapidly, but also because of their teachings. First, Christian Science, New Thought, and

Theosophy were all suggesting a different way of thinking and speaking about God: "he" was the Divine, the Infinite Principle, not a personal Father or Judge (although Christian Science retained the idea of fatherhood). Second, although Christian Science and New Thought claimed to keep Jesus at the center of faith, none of the movements accepted the basic theology of orthodox Christianity: that Jesus had died in atonement for human sins. None, in fact, believed strongly in sin; they admitted only temporary imperfections.

Third, all three movements focused on individual improvement, whether in health, success, or spiritual quest. Only Theosophists had much interest in social issues, and that was limited primarily to educating children. They had briefly supported the political movement of (Bellamy) Nationalist Clubs in the 1890s, but that alliance had soon died. None of the metaphysical movements otherwise was strongly oriented toward politics or social reform. All three believed in the gradual progress of the individual on a spiritual plane, leading to greater powers and deeper connection with the divine. Ultimately, they believed, perfection was possible, either by realizing the divine within oneself or, in Christian Science, by realizing one's perfect being as it exists in the mind of God. The true destiny of human beings was spiritual and divine, turning away from the material. Mrs. Eddy went farther than the others in actually denying the reality of matter; while Malinda Cramer of Divine Science claimed to have had a revelation showing the fundamental principle of creation, the emergence of matter from spirit.[20] But in all cases the metaphysicians valued the inner life over any interaction with the material world. They were regarded as mystics, and in many ways were just that. This was unnerving to Protestants, who were grounded in the reality of both matter and spirit.

Fourth and finally, the practices of the metaphysical movements turned inward, toward mental reality. They practiced study, meditation, affirmations, focused concentration. These became much more important than the traditional Christian way of relating to the divine, namely through prayer addressed to a personal God. Thought and study eliminated the address, the pleas or complaints, the surrender, sympathy, agony, and bliss associated with intense prayer. In that way the metaphysical movements replaced emotional experience with mental comprehension or, more accurately, intellectual-spiritual apprehension providing clarity and a sense of wholeness, harmony, or oneness at a level above ordinary human religious emotions. This too was strange and uncomfortable to most Anglo-Protestants.

Yet there are some strains here that sound familiar in light of our previous examination of trends in northern California. When the metaphysical movements speak of an inner spiritual law, more powerful than material facts, that governs the universe, we may be reminded of Thomas Starr King's lecture "Substance and Show." The rational, mental approach to religion recalls Laurentine Hamilton's rationalism, while the tendency to deny or ignore evil and the expectation of gradually rising to perfection recall his vision of the life after death. Despite these similarities, there were no direct ties between the organized southern California movements and that earlier northern branch of the tradition. But all traced their roots ultimately to the same or related sources: Unitarianism, Transcendentalism (both Theosophists and New Thoughters recognized Ralph Waldo Emerson as one of their forerunners), Spiritualism. Mrs. Eddy denied any precursors, but through Quimby she was related to the same tradition; and her thought has been recognized as having certain similarities to Emerson's.[21] The liberal movements in the north and the metaphysical movements in the south were variations on a mythology recurrently influential in California: a mythology of spiritual unity, of true reality existing in the inmost recesses of one's being, of deep knowledge gained through inward perception, of progress toward spiritual perfection.

But it is not at all obvious why southern Californians should respond to the same family of religions as northerners had. We have shown how the reception and development of that popular tradition was conditioned by the situation in northern California: the independent self-image promoted by the gold rush; the pride northern Californians took in being open and tolerant; the unsettled character of the region for nearly two decades; the lack of stable family and institutional life; the need for unity and the rejection of factionalist politics and religion; the avoidance of emotional expressiveness because of the specific experience of the gold rush generation and the instability of society in general. Southern California was different; it was settled by families and an older population more than by young adventurers, by people with financial means or skills more than by risk-takers. If Singleton's portrayal is correct, these people had a strong commitment to traditional Protestantism and its doctrines, rather than the rebelliousness and independence of the young northerners; for Singleton insists that the settlers of Los Angeles were attempting to preserve the Protestantism of their home towns (presumably the traditions dominant between 1840 and 1880, when they were growing up and establishing families), not to experiment with new fads in doctrine or practice. But that picture leaves us with no explanation for the metaphysical movements at all.

We mentioned that the regions from which most immigrants came had more liberals in the Protestant churches than, for example, the South. The same regions were seeing the greatest increase in the metaphysical religions. In the north central region, from Ohio to Kansas and north to Wisconsin, which was the chief source of southern California's immigrants (in 1910 over 23 percent of all American-born Californians were from there), Christian Science was growing rapidly; Illinois led with fifty-four churches and about 5700 members. New Thought groups had established centers also: Divine Science in Chicago, Topeka (Kansas), and Waterloo (Iowa); Unity School of Christianity in Unity Village, Missouri. Some southern Californians were likely to have known of these movements before they arrived; a number were probably already members. Yet that does not fully explain the movements' successes in California. Even in Illinois, where it was strongest, Christian Science attracted less than one-half of 1 percent of the non-Catholic population, while in California a full 1 percent of that population became Scientists.[22] Moreover, aside from actual membership, the metaphysical religions became part of the cultural ambience in California to a degree that they never did in the Midwest.

We must examine, therefore, the patterns of life that led stable, family-oriented, Protestant folk to beome interested in metaphysical religions. Our best clue comes from the fact that these religions were mushrooming just when the style of development and the style of promotional literature were changing in southern California. Previously, in the 1880s, developers had laid out towns around commercial centers (for example, Long Beach or Pasadena) and sold lots there, while also selling land for farms or ranches; promotions emphasized agriculture, transportation, and business. By the turn of the century we find builders creating landscaped developments like Palos Verdes Estates, the true suburban dream. Such developments were supposed to recapture the village in the midst of the city, but in fact they were not villages. They had no commercial centers, nor any sites for communal activities except a small park for strolling and a children's playground. People who moved there were choosing their residence on some basis other than proximity to work, extended family, or church.[23] From 1910 on, the automobile contributed to this change; but even before, Los Angeles residents moved frequently as more options became open to them. Eventually, the choice of residence was based primarily on aesthetic and social considerations: the style of the home, the beauty of the surroundings, the reputation of the neighborhood—the only limitation being one's pocketbook. The neighborhood's relation to traditional institutions like business or church mattered less and less.[24] As a result, churches followed after settlement patterns rather than being an integral part of them.

This shifting relationship among institutions is a clue to a larger phenomenon. White immigrants until about 1915 were ethnically and geographically from the same groups, but there was a subtle difference between those who came to Los Angeles before (roughly) 1895 and those who came between (roughly) 1895 and 1915. The later arrivals were the next generation, with different values than their earlier relatives. Raised with the rising expectations of the Gilded Age, they had nevertheless experienced a great deal of turmoil, from the Civil War in their early youth to the rapidly changing social and economic conditions in their home states. Their search for peace, stability, and comfort rather than for better business opportunities was symbolized by the planned suburban home. They had watched their cities turn into collections of immigrant neighborhoods, full of people they believed to be unassimilable aliens. Even farmers had begun in the late 1880s and 1890s to suffer from the pressures of bureaucratic capitalism, culminating in the panic of 1893, the worst depression in twenty years. Many California immigrants had survived that era and, when recovery began in 1896, sold out to come west. They were, far more self-consciously than their predecessors, retirees. Instead of hoping to rebuild familiar communities and work well into their old age, according to the old American dream, they were following the new dream offered by the real estate promoters: to reap the benefits of leisure and make the money they needed in investment or speculation.

Yet if the newcomers hoped the transition would be easy, they were mistaken. The suburbs were not like idealized villages. The natural environment was strange; the landscape, weather patterns, and vegetation were exotic and unfamiliar. Carey McWilliams observed that California seemed to Easterners a "paradoxical land with a tricky environment." One visitor from Cincinnati wrote:

> There is a variety in the evenness of the weather, and a strange evenness in this variety, which throws an unreality around life. . . . All alike walk and work in a dream. For something beguiles, deludes, plays falsely with the senses. . . . There is no awareness of the passage of the day.[25]

The climate was unusual, and all kinds of disturbances were attributed to it. Many Easterners believed that it would produce idleness and placidity, or "enervation," as it was called.[26] Charles Nordhoff had warned that a man must "keep his Eastern habits of industry, and beware of the curse of California—idleness and unthrift—to which no doubt the mild climate predisposes men."[27] Nathaniel West believed that the California lifestyle, with its tendency to encourage leisure, would eventually lead to riots and violence in the region because humans were incapable of dealing with such leisure.[28] Whether the climate had an independent effect or not, we may guess that many of those arriving in the 1890s and after were eager to give up their "Eastern habits of industry" and enjoy a bit of idleness. If the climate was distracting, they were open to being distracted. At the same time their change in lifestyle and the change in environment produced a subtle sense of disorientation evident throughout the immigrant literature.[29]

The search for stability and for points of orientation in a new life goes back to the 1880s, and it is clear that the traditional religious communities, the churches, did not provide all that the new immigrants needed. The earlier immigrants had formed, for example, the famous State Societies—organizations of immigrants from the various states of the union, beginning with the Pennsylvania State Society in 1882. These groups gathered at monthly meetings in public places such as cafeterias. Part of their purpose, as the All State Society of Long Beach put it, was to "keep alive the ties and friendships affiliated with the Home State."[30] But they did not gather in small groups or in friendly home surroundings; instead they sought impersonal territory and large meetings to establish rather distant connections, much like a high school reunion. Such gatherings were enormously popular, especially the annual picnics and parades. Fifteen to twenty thousand people attended the two yearly Iowa picnics (one in Los Angeles, one in Long Beach). The State Societies' politi-

cal rallies, church socials, and Thanksgiving celebrations were great
southern California social events.

What stands out most clearly in the descriptions of the State Societies is the combination of nostalgic reminiscences of life "back
home" and extravagant eulogies of California. The prize-winning
float at one Fourth of July parade was a portrayal of a Christmas
scene back home complete with imitation snow—itself a poignant
expression of disorientation. Another expression of longing for the
familiar and over-praise of the new was the humorous 1886 "creed"
of the Illinois Association:

> WHEREAS we . . . having endured the tortures inseparably connected with
> life in a region of ice and snow, and having fled from our beloved state to
> this favored land; therefore be it
> RESOLVED, that we deeply sympathize with our friends and former fellow
> citizens, . . .
> RESOLVED, that we have the tallest mountains, the biggest trees, the
> crookedest railroads, the dryest rivers, the loveliest flowers, the smooth-
> est ocean, the finest fruits, the mildest lives, the softest breezes, the purest
> air, the heaviest pumpkins, the best schools, the most numerous stars, the
> most bashful real estate agents, the brightest skies, and the most genial
> sunshine to be found anywhere . . . in North America. . . .
> RESOLVED, that we heartily welcome other refugees from Illinois, and
> will do all in our power to make them realize that they are sojourning in
> a "City of the Angels" where their hearts will be irrigated by living waters
> flowing from the perennial fountains of health, happiness, and
> longevity.[31]

The former citizens of Illinois glorified and parodied the myth of
California as paradise at the same time that they were trying to
strengthen themselves by numbers of familiar ties and friendly faces.
Singleton suggests that the State Societies were evidence of strong
commitment to traditional midwestern values.[32] They were; but they
also reflect people losing hold of those values and attempting to embrace a new land. Moreover, even the way they reaffirmed their common values was different from the way they had done it back in the
Midwest. Picnics and parades were familiar enough, but the great
anonymity of California gatherings was itself an innovation.

Another example of the search for an orientation was the romanticization of the Old California heritage. We mentioned that some of
this had occurred among newcomers in the north during gold rush
days and after. It developed more fully in the south, however, many

years after the disappearance of most of the Californios. After 1875, popular books about California Indians, the old Franciscan missions, and the Spanish and Mexican traditions began to appear. Around the turn of the century, architects borrowed or invented "Mediterranean" styles for California homes, while public buildings copied the missions with tiled roofs and fake adobe walls. The real-life Mexicans who lived nearby in the barrios were generally ignored if not despised, but "rodeos" and "fiestas" became popular entertainment for newcomers seeking some kind of cultural integrity. Each year at the local fiestas, Chamber of Commerce members donned sombreros and perched on horses as "caballeros," while they elected an Anglo maiden as queen of the Mexican celebration. The anomalies and the distortion are obvious.[33] But clearly that extreme sort of romanticizing indicates that it was not easy for midwesterners to feel at home in California. Even if, as Singleton argues, those who arrived after 1880 were committed to replicating their lost society and culture, they also were acting out a need to connect with the new lifestyle and different culture of California.

The State Societies and Mexican fiestas continued to thrive for decades; moreover, traditional churches provided stability for a significant percentage of the population. One famous churchwoman, Clara Burdette (wife of Robert Burdette of Temple Baptist Church), wrote in the early 1900s that California was an "asylum for every new 'ology' in medicine or religion under the sun." Yet, she said, "earnest, sane men and women" kept working beneath all the restlessness. For her, God seemed to be giving the world "the 'new earth' if not the 'new heaven'" via the work of her church in Los Angeles.[34] But despite the success of the church and other religious institutions in establishing themselves in Los Angeles, despite the auxiliary social ties and entertainments provided by State Societies, fiestas and rodeos, religious restlessness was growing, more so after 1895. Many new immigrants of Protestant background did not join a church; many who joined did not attend; and many, whether churchgoers or not, became involved in one of the metaphysical religions.[35]

The new movements achieved their success and contributed to southern California culture not because of any collapse of the churches or other institutions, but simply because the traditional forms fit inadequately, for many people, with the evolving social and natural environment of California. As in the north, they were transplants that continued to serve some functions but did not take root strongly—hence the supplements of State Societies and Mexican romanticism providing two different kinds of roots. The churches supported a small-town orientation and dedication to a busy, industrious life, with a consciousness of building a society under God's rule. Southern California Protestants shared those values, but by the turn of the century a significant number were living in new residential areas providing a quite different social context. Churches followed them there, but now they included Churches of Christ, Scientist, and a variety of small New Thought groups.[36] At the same time, people were willing to give up some of their orientation toward working and building in order to create another kind of life.

The metaphysical movements, it could be argued, were not necessarily much better at integrating all these new elements; if they had been, people would have flocked to them in much greater numbers. New Thinkers, Christian Scientists, and Theosophists largely ignored southern Californians' experience of nature and climate, their suburban environment, and their economic situation and new lifestyle. Unlike their Protestant counterparts they did not rely for their power on external relations to society or nature. They depended on the individual's personal sense of satisfaction: first, that in some way a practice or belief works or feels helpful; and second, that a person feels as if he or she is contacting deeper knowledge or a deeper level of self.

The metaphysical religions appealed especially to the immigrants' desires for a full life, a "fullness of peace, power, and plenty." If the new southern Californians were escaping the disturbances of the 1880s and 1890s in the Midwest, if they were disoriented in their adjustment to the new region, if they felt "enervated" or unhealthy (which would be natural in the aftermath of their "culture shock"), the metaphysicians showed them a way to calmness, confidence, and physical health. They taught mental focus, release from strain, disciplined reading and study, and ways to achieve a sense of spiritual elevation and create a private retreat from external confusion. They taught, in short, a new form of order. As Malinda Cramer, founder of Divine Science, put it, "we believe in perfect action and perfect thinking . . . in perfect breathing and perfect circulation, perfect digestion and perfect generation, perfect voice and perfect speaking. This is law and order everywhere."[37]

If this portrayal of the white Protestants of southern California is correct—if amid the bustle of establishing and maintaining a strong church-centered culture, there was also considerable disorientation and a search for stability and peace, and if the metaphysical religions were as important culturally as I am suggesting—then we ought to observe some evidence of it in the Protestant denominations. We saw that in the north the presence of people advocating related ideas brought forth denunciation and heresy trials. In the south, too, we would expect ministers or church organizers to respond, either by attacking the challengers or by changing their own religious priorities to take account of the new needs of the people they served. Such responses did occur, and at the time we would expect, namely in the period after the turn of the century, when the metaphysical religions were growing most rapidly. In the next chapter we will examine a few of the most notable responses.

6. Mainstream Churches and the New Mysticism

Anglo-Protestants first responded to the new metaphysical religions by attacking them. Just as in northern California most Protestants had attacked Spiritualists and Adventists a few decades before, so now in both southern and northern California church leaders criticized Christian Scientists, Theosophists, and various mind-cure movements. As early as 1889 the *Occident* expressed concern about the new messages of mental healing. The Committee on the State of Religion, reporting to the Synod of the Pacific, pointed out that there was now "a question that is agitating the church from ocean to ocean, the relation of health to a life hid with Christ in God." The Committee recommended that the truths of Christian Science and mental science be admitted, while their errors should be met by a stronger philosophy and psychology.[1] From that time on, articles questioning or criticizing Christian Science and related movements appeared regularly in the *Occident*. The more secular-minded of New Thought literature, making claims for mental science without reference to religious belief, usually received critical but essentially neutral reviews.[2] Mrs. Eddy's movement, because it claimed to be Christian, came in for the heaviest attacks.

Theosophy received its share of negative responses as well, especially in the south. In 1901 twenty clergymen in San Diego, including some Roman Catholics, published a statement denouncing Theosophy as "destructive alike of aspiration and hope" and "diametrically opposed to the Gospel of Christ."[3] Harrison Gray Otis of the *Los Angeles Times*, a self-appointed crusader against all cults and strong supporter of the city's Anglo-Protestant culture, constantly inveighed against the Point Loma Theosophical Community and similar groups. Religious periodicals regularly warned against false gods and paganism, including Theosophy, Buddhism, and Hinduism.[4]

Some commentators lumped together all the movements trying to bring a new perspective on spirituality and religion. The Rev. Robert J. Burdette, a former humorist who had become minister of Temple Baptist Church in Los Angeles, shrugged off the new metaphysics together with modern art, ridiculing them all as trying to claim that "'Whatever is, isn't,' and conversely, 'Whatever isn't, is.'"[5]

Most ministers saw the crucial issues, the ones that really drew people away from the churches, as being health and healing. Mrs. Eddy's criticism of the traditional churches for having abandoned the healing practices of Jesus and his disciples certainly stung the ministers. Moreover, they were well aware that faith healing had sprung up in some dissident movements in the late nineteenth century—in some branches of the holiness movement within Methodism, for example, and in the popular movement led by healer John Dowie, who made a well-publicized tour of California.[6] To ignore the question would be deliberately obtuse, especially in southern California, where health-seekers abounded. But simply to attack the movements on doctrinal grounds was not entirely satisfactory. William Pond, a long-time Congregationalist minister in California, observed in 1920 that he had advised in 1900 that it was crucial for churchmen to "fight or flank" Christian Science. But the more they fought it, the more it grew.[7]

Some ministers, therefore, eventually sought a reconciliation with the new metaphysical movements. They delved deeper into the philosophical issues instead of focusing only on the issue of healing, and they abandoned direct attacks in order to bring out some of the truths they felt were there. Of ministers who chose this course, some ended up going over to the opponents.[8] Most stayed in the churches, however, and attempted to bring some new light into Christianity. These were unique individuals; there was no general agreement or united response. Those who attempted mediation tended to be liberals rather than conservatives in the denominations, and in this we can see one of the unique characteristics of Anglo-Protestantism in California: liberalism tended less toward the Social Gospel and activism than toward the inner life and mysticism.

We will see this range of development as we examine the thought of five ministers who responded in different ways to the challenge of the metaphysical religions: Dr. Charles Edward Locke, who criticized Christian Science and represents the stance of traditional Protestantism toward these movements; Charles Reynolds Brown, who tackled Christian Science on the health issue; James M. Campbell, who authored books on Christian Science, New Thought, and mysticism; Benjamin Fay Mills, a nationally known evangelist turned liberal, who was deeply affected by the new ideas while in Oakland and Los Angeles; and Joseph Pomeroy Widney, perhaps the most distinctively and eccentrically Californian of the five. The thought of these men will give us a glimpse into the changing contours of California Protestantism in relation to the metaphysical religions.

Dr. Charles Edward Locke represented, probably more than anyone else in southern California, the center of traditional Protestantism imported from the eastern states. He was nationally connected, having spoken at the funeral of the famous revival hymnist Ira D. Sankey. A Methodist, he was neither extremely liberal nor extremely conservative. In an era when discrimination was rampant, he wrote a strong defense of the Negro race; he wrote on social issues only one other time, however, in a pamphlet against prostitution. Neither tract was "social gospel" in tone. On the subject of Christian Science, however, he was no moderate; in a vituperative series of articles entitled "Eddyism" he summarized virtually all the criticisms that had been and would be made of Christian Science.[9]

Locke's arguments ranged from ad hominem invectives directed at Eddy herself to polemics on the deeper religious and intellectual issues. He claimed that Christian Science aimed ultimately at abolishing marriage, since it urged women to some vague role higher than motherhood. He accused Christian Science practitioners of being in practice to earn easy money. Mrs. Eddy, in his view, was a tyrant and a plagiarist, having borrowed heavily from Quimby. She encouraged lying, since she insisted that people deny their pain or illness; and she discouraged the use of intellect, since she forbade her followers to read anything but her own works. Despite these immoralities, he believed Christian Science would probably survive a little while, for it had in it "a touch of 'the eternal feminine.'" He lamented (including Theosophy in his sweep):

> Oh, "this eternal feminine!" What has America done that it must endure at one time Emma Goldman, Anna [sic] Besant, Katherine Tingley, and Mary Baker Patterson Glover Eddy, all hysterical high priestesses of preposterous nonsense?[10]

Locke may not have been a racist in his time, but he was certainly not a feminist, either.

Locke's more fundamental argument, however, was that Christian Science was neither scientific nor Christian. Since it was not subject to experimental verification, the only possible ground on which it might turn out to be scientific was that it used the "therapeutic value of suggestion," the latest fad in the medical marketplace. Suggestion at least had "rebuked the 'orgies of drugging'" to which many had become addicted, "and given some folks something better to think about." It may have even cured some people of "certain imaginary and functional diseases."[11] But that was a psychological fact, and a minor one, not a great truth of science.

Religiously, Christian Science was not Christianity but pantheism, "bald and pagan." Its doctrine claimed that there was no personal God and no separate self. God was Mind; humans were merely manifestations of that Mind. Jesus was not truly God, but simply represented the Divine Idea of Christ. As a result, Locke suggested in an anti-Semitic aside, "many Jews and other enemies of Jesus" had readily turned to this new religion. Eddy denied the meaning of the Incarnation, the Resurrection, and the Atonement of Christ, asserting instead that Christian Science was itself the Holy Ghost and the Second Coming of Christ. She had made her book supersede the Bible and had declared the Bible itself not inspired. For her, sin was an illusion, prayer to a personal God a hindrance, and human sympathy no help at all. Eddy made harmony of mind the only way to heaven, denying any validity to the means of grace offered in the practices and beliefs of the traditional churches. On no count, therefore, was Christian Science truly Christian.

Locke's attack clearly reflects the basic issues differentiating the metaphysical religions from traditional Protestantism. The two sides represent quite different concepts of what is essential in the relation between human beings and the divine. For Anglo-Protestants, God was personal; Jesus was a divine personality performing specific saving acts: dying and sacrificing himself, rising from the dead, atoning for human sins. Sin and judgment were real; human emotions and sympathy were important. For Eddy, the divine was better understood as the Infinite, a generalized principle, "personal" only in the broadest sense. Human beings had the capacity to transcend emotion and concrete action in order to apprehend the unity behind all diversity, and thus go beyond any idea of evil or sin. Psychologically it might work, but from Locke's perspective, it was no form of Christianity he could recognize.

Locke's position was characteristic of the Protestant center in being a flat rejection of Mrs. Eddy as a religious thinker and of Christian Science as an authentic and valuable practice. Locke did not attempt any subtle distinctions among the various ideas of the Science, let alone try to find common ground with it. He set up criteria for what constituted science and Christianity, and Mrs. Eddy's system failed both tests. For him the issue was finished; all that was left was to persuade back into the fold those misguided souls who were tempted to follow her. Locke was true to his beliefs; yet he failed to appreciate that the "fad" of Christian Science and similar systems represented a genuine discovery, or rediscovery, of certain human mental powers. Because many people, including Mary Baker Eddy, believed these powers came from a divine source, the whole issue of mental science raised serious questions for Christianity. It was left for other thinkers than Locke to address those questions more carefully.

Charles Reynolds Brown (1862–1950), pastor of First Congregational Church in Oakland from 1896 to 1911, had moved gradually and modestly toward liberalism. Raised a Methodist and trained at Boston School of Theology, he became a Congregationalist in 1892;[12] he would become dean of Yale Divinity School after leaving California. Brown was oriented toward practical theology and committed to traditional doctrines, while recognizing, in liberal fashion, that they had to be restated for modern listeners.[13] Many of his writings indicate his interest in explaining, in laypeople's language, the essentials of the Christian gospel: for example, *The Main Points* (1899), *The Modern Man's Religion* (1911), and *The Religion of a Layman* (1920). Thus it is not surprising that he would write on a specific contemporary issue such as the metaphysical religions. Moreover, although his main interest was the Social Gospel, he also had an interest in psychology, particularly in William James and pragmatism. Brown believed that the metaphysical movements, understood in practical psychological terms, might have kernels of truth that could be incorporated into the main body of Christian practice. He did not, however, believe these systems could be reconciled with Protestant belief.

In a pamphlet, *The Gospel of Good Health*, and later in the more elaborate *Faith and Health* (1910), Brown took it upon himself to address directly the popularity of Christian Science and other mind-cure systems. In this area he was no novice: he had taken, in 1887, a course in Christian Science in Boston under two officers of Mrs. Eddy's "Mother Church," and had obtained a license to practice as a healer; he had even heard lectures by Mrs. Eddy herself. He had long been interested in health issues because of his own poor health in his youth. After completing the Christian Science course, however, he gave up the practice; we do not know exactly when. He wrote in 1910 that "some twenty years ago" he had learned how to be stronger and healthier, and since then had never had to miss a day of work or an appointment because of illness.

That was not, Brown said, because of his Christian Science training. By 1910 he had little good to say about the movement. Its practitioners emphasized money-making too much; Mrs. Eddy was authoritarian; and her attempts to make people disbelieve in ordinary reality were ridiculous. Here he was referring to her doctrine that all disease, and the whole material world, were but figments of the mortal mind, so that one need not pay attention either to science or to common sense in dealing with illness. If such beliefs were carried to their logical conclusion, Brown said, arsenic could be legalized as food, children could drink stagnant water teeming with typhoid germs, and people could stop bathing and exercising. Therefore, in his view, Christian Science was metaphysically nonsensical and potentially harmful, "a piece of cruel and wicked humbug."[14]

Nevertheless Brown admitted that the system had helped some people by improving their spirits, curing imaginary or functional diseases, and getting apathetic people interested in God and religion.[15] Therefore, he suggested, Christian Science and New Thought had some kernel of insight: they were hunches possibly preparing the way for a science to come, as astrology and alchemy had been precursors of modern astronomy and chemistry. Physicians, scientists, and churchpeople had to sort out the falsehood from the truth within these systems.[16] This did not mean that the church should try to imitate Christian Science, but rather that it should go it one better. Brown sharply criticized those who wanted the church to become a psychotherapeutic center, mixing medical practice into regular church work.[17]

For health, according to Brown, should not be the primary concern of Christianity. The central emphasis was and ought to be the development of moral character—qualities of self-control, goodwill, joy, peace, patience, courage, faith, perseverance, and the like. Health was a side issue. We could give attention to it, but only as part of an overall development of the individual Christian's inner life. That, he believed, was a distinctively modern need:

> It has seemed to many people that in the last half of the nineteenth century there was a widespread tendency to depend too much on the without and not enough on the within. Westward the star of empire took its way for centuries, seeking new fields for material development. Now . . . there has come a wholesome reaction from the almost idolatrous trust in material things and a quickening of interest in forces unseen. . . .
>
> And it is the belief of many thoughtful people that the main hope of our Christian world for improved health, and for the consequent larger joy and effectiveness, lies not so much in the increased efficiency of medical science in dealing with disease . . . as in so strengthening the inner life that increased immunity from the inroads of disease may be attained.[18]

Brown was suggesting, in his cautious way, that Christianity ought to turn inward, to strengthen the inner life in ways similar to the metaphysical religions.

Brown went still farther: he offered practical means to develop inner strength, by which he meant habits of right thinking and clear purpose, high expectations for oneself, firm resolve, strong will, and a constant faith in God—notice that he did not suggest anything more mystical, such as union with or likeness to God. He advised the development and use of a system employing the "healing power of suggestion," that is, "the influence exercised upon the body by the subtle power of ideas." For his proof text he quoted the biblical proverb, "As a man thinketh in his heart so is he!" Brown held, not that any single thought could transform a person, but that regular healthy states of mind could and would, over the long term, improve one's physical health; in this process the practice of certain types of thoughts could aid a great deal. "We may educate the mind by suggestion," he wrote, "to move in better channels and teach the heart to cherish more wholesome states of feeling, and in that way accomplish splendid results in securing health and developing character."[19]

Character, we recall, was in Brown's view the principal goal of Christian development; now we find him saying that suggestion can be a principal technique in achieving that goal. Brown went on to share with his readers his own system of suggestion, devised from phrases of Scripture. He instructed that one should take a comfortable position, letting the hands and lower limbs relax, and repeat a series like one of the following:

I. *To banish fear*
Fear not—only believe.
Fear not—it is your Father's good pleasure to give you the mastery.
Perfect love casteth out fear.
I will fear no evil, for Thou art with me.

II. *To bestow confidence*
In quietness and confidence shall be my strength.
Be still and know that He is God. The Lord of Hosts is with me.
The God of Jacob is my refuge.
Be strong and of a good courage. The Lord my God He it is that goeth with me. He will not fail me nor forsake me.
I know whom I have believed and I am persuaded that He is able to keep that which I have committed unto him.[20]

Brown offered eight such series, recommending one a day and two on Sunday. Then came the further instructions:

> Fix your mind upon each one in turn! Give yourself to it until it fills and possesses your entire consciousness. Seek to absorb its full significance as you dwell upon the bearing it has upon your inner life.[21]

He went on to give a lengthy exhortation elaborating on the scriptural passages. But from the instructions it is quite clear that Brown was advocating an intense meditation or focused concentration not unlike those taught in the various schools of New Thought.

In the absence of evidence, we cannot know if indeed Brown read New Thought writings. Understandably, he was not willing to credit nonorthodox sources with influencing the development of his system of suggestion. He spoke of suggestion as being a well-known phenomenon, described in all the current medical and scientific journals and elaborated by many writers. It is worth remembering, nevertheless, that he dated his own development of a better approach to health to a mere three years after his study and apparent rejection of Christian Science. It would have been surprising if he did not turn to some New Thought writers as well as to the emerging science of psychology in his search for an alternative to Christian Science; it is a safe guess that Brown was influenced by the contemporary currents of New Thought.

Brown offered, then, a Christian parallel to the practices of metaphysical religions, their meditations and affirmations. He did not respond to the deeper issues other than to condemn Mrs. Eddy's idealist metaphysics. Brown's use of suggestion was for character building, not for mystical union with God or apprehending the divine Mind. He did not consider effects of the practice of suggestion or concentration on other elements of Christianity: whether it might compete with the practice of prayer, or whether the focus on self might distract from developing a relationship to God. Brown saw suggestion as a religiously and morally neutral practice depending only on the content of the meditation. For him such neutral, pragmatic elements of the new movements could be salvaged while the philosophy itself was discarded. He introduced elements of New Thought into Christianity, yet New Thought itself gave him no reason to rethink basic doctrines about God, Christ, or human nature.

James M. Campbell, a Congregationalist of a more liberal stripe who came to Los Angeles from the Midwest shortly after 1900, was already rethinking his priorities within Christianity long before he wrote on Christian Science or New Thought. Already in 1899 he had become interested in the doctrine of the Holy Spirit and had preached a series of lectures on the subject at the University of Chicago Divinity School, published as *After Pentecost, What?* (1899). His developing interest in the inner life is indicated by the titles of some of his other books: *Paul the Mystic, The Indwelling Christ, The Presence*. The philosophical issues raised by Christian Science and New Thought were much more congenial to him than to pragmatist Brown. In two of his works, one on each of these two movements, he addressed these issues directly.

Campbell believed that Christian Science and New Thought did several positive things: they emphasized spirituality and mysticism, which had largely been lost to orthodox Protestantism; by their interest in healing they pointed to the "redemption of the body," which the church had ignored throughout most of its history; and they had found methods of suggestion and personal influence to effect physical and nervous relaxation and overall good health. Those were strong admissions amounting to a considerable claim for the truths or insights contained in the metaphysical religions. Campbell insisted that the church must take all of them seriously as criticisms pointing the way to a reconstruction of the Christian faith. He also believed, of course, that Christianity together with some psycholog-ical methods had all the resources it needed to effect such a reconstruction.

Campbell warned that people should not turn to the new move-ments simply because they offered a few advantages; they also had negative features making them unacceptable. He claimed that Chris-tian Science and New Thought were selfish and passive rather than active and loving like traditional Protestantism. Instead of fighting against wrongs, they—especially Scientists—denied that evil ex-isted. While revolting understandably against the harshness of Cal-vinism, they also suppressed sympathy, making "mothers unmoth-erly" and "drying up the springs" of true Christian grace. Since the metaphysicians never demanded self-denial or the basic Christian change from selfishness to love, their religion was incomplete. "Re-ligion has its beginnings in the soul," Campbell wrote, "but it finds its fulfillment in the social life."[22] Christian Science focused on the inner life, and New Thought emphasized the undreamed-of human potential hidden within each of us. That was good insofar as it threw the soul back on God, back to its center in mysticism and spiritual development; but neither Christian Science nor New Thought com-pleted the movement back again to the outer world, to change it and help others.

The "selfishness" of these movements was problematic for Camp-bell in another way. The metaphysicians offered relaxation, serenity, and calmness within; but they paid the price of stagnation. Physical and nervous relaxation were good, but spiritual and mental were not: "It keeps one waiting for the tide to flow in, instead of keeping him digging channels for its inflow."[23] Or, as he put it in another place, "All questioning and reasoning are given up, and the soul sim-ply floats on the stream, or an opiate is taken which puts the soul to sleep." To rest in Christ, on the contrary, was an active rest, unbro-ken even when faced with disturbances, "founded upon Him who is the world's fixed center."[24] Thus Campbell emphasized initiative and will power: the will was "a *driving* power—the dynamo of the soul." Humans, he argued, "cannot float into virtue. . . . in the outer and spiritual worlds alike, we get what we go after."[25] Campbell here was zeroing in on a tension inherent in the mind-cure movements, one that Gail Parker has observed: how could one flow with the Divine, or rest in faith in the Mind of God, and at the same time be making great efforts to overcome obstacles to that rest?[26] Or, as the paradox appears in the work of Ralph Waldo Trine, what is the difference between aimless drifting—which he criticizes—and allowing the influx of the Infinite into one's life? Campbell addressed the issue of action vs. passivity but did not resolve the paradox. Despite his courageous attempts to bring together the approaches of New Thought and Christianity, he ended up sounding, as did most of his fellow Anglo-Protestants, like a strong proponent of the work ethic.

Campbell also discussed the issue of pantheism, which, as we noted with Locke, cropped up in most discussions of the metaphysical religions. The Scientists and their kin were mistaken, Campbell said, in conceiving of man as "a bit of God"; we should rather think of him as a "child of God." Campbell insisted on a strongly personalist view of the deity, although in certain of his other works he himself spoke of God in an impersonal way. For example, in *The Presence* he described Christ as

> the abiding Presence, immanent in all things, a living redeeming reality, flooding the soul with strength, healing the body of its diseases, reducing to harmony life's discords, soothing frayed nerves, calming troubled hearts, and bringing the entire man into perfect oneness with the divine will and with the divine order. To come into touch with him is to come into touch with the Infinite; it is to tap the hidden fountains of divine energy.[27]

The language is strongly reminiscent of Christian Science and New Thought writings. Yet Campbell insisted that he was speaking not of an impersonal influx, but of an "inflow of personality into personality."[28] This illustrates the difficulty that liberal Protestants sometimes had—and Mrs. Eddy certainly had—in avoiding pantheist-sounding phraseology. Inflowing, indwelling, energy, the Presence, the Infinite are a far cry from the personal relations implied by the more traditional terms—Judge, Father, Savior, Friend—for God.

The issue of pantheism is closely connected to the issue of "active" versus "passive" religiosity. If divine-human relations are models for and of human relationships, then, on the one hand, pantheistic tendencies might manifest themselves in what a traditional Protestant would see as passivity: if there are no boundaries between self and God, the believer would look for the unity in all things and seek to merge himself with the forces of the universe. The personalist, on the other hand, would perceive diversities and be more likely to see things, forces, and wills in conflict: he would emphasize encounters between people and confrontations with the world. Campbell, by sometimes using pantheist language and speaking of rest and relaxation, while at other times emphasizing the dynamo of the will and the personality of God, was trying with great difficulty to straddle the fence. In his work, where these issues were never clearly resolved, we can see most clearly the psychological as well as the theological struggle between the two types of systems.

What Campbell advocated for the churches was, first, to make the experience of God—mystically and spiritually—more central in the religious life. In particular, he urged the churches to use personal testimonials. Second, he observed that since suggestion was known to be a powerful force, Christians could use right thoughts, along with the prayer of faith for healing, to accomplish the same practical ends as Christian Science and New Thought. Third, the churches should not give up their activist, humanitarian orientation. Christianity should not swing so far over to the spiritual side that people became passive, insensitive, or lacking in individuality; they must maintain their will to bring about changes in society. Their will, however, could be cultivated by the power of suggestion. In his book on Christian Science he observed that the power of suggestion was virtually "measureless" and quoted Emerson (also a favorite of New Thought writers) as saying that "every thought thrown into the world alters the world." Campbell himself added that "every thought thrown into the soul alters the soul; and whatever alters the soul alters the whole mind."[29] Changing thoughts and souls through renewed Christian experience and psychological methods could therefore, Campbell believed, change the world; and like most liberal Protestants of his time, he saw Christianity as aiming to do just that.

Another newcomer to California whose ideas reflected contact with the metaphysical religions was Benjamin Fay Mills (1857–1916). Mills was a nationally known evangelist, the son of a well-known Presbyterian minister, and himself a Congregationalist from his ordination in 1878 until 1898, when he became a Unitarian in Boston. In 1898 he wrote about how he became a liberal.[30] About ten years previously, around 1888, he had ceased to believe in salvation only by Christ and had begun preaching Jesus as an ethical ideal. Even earlier he had given up many orthodox doctrines. Thus, long before the turn of the century, his preaching was liberal, attracting people of many denominations.

Shortly after writing that retrospective, Mills came to minister to Oakland, having visited California once before on an evangelistic campaign in Los Angeles in 1892. After a few years in the north he moved to Los Angeles and set up an independent church, which met in a theater. By this time he was clearly straying from the fold. The Rev. Robert McIntyre, a prominent California Presbyterian, complained that "He makes much of the spirit of Christ, little of the blood of Christ." J. Wilbur Chapman, another well-known evangelist, prayed publicly for Mills's soul during his 1905 Los Angeles campaign.[31] Some liberals defended him, but he seemed to be deviating further and further from the mainstream. By 1915, however, he returned to the center as a Presbyterian in Chicago. He was even invited to speak in the evangelistic tabernacle at the Panama-Pacific Exposition in San Francisco in 1915. There his fellow ministers were glad to see him back, but bemoaned the fact that he talked very abstrusely and no longer had his former fire and vigor as a revivalist.[32]

Mills, then, displays a curious peregrination beyond the fringes of traditional Protestantism and back again. Discussions of him usually refer to his liberal period as one in which he espoused social Christianity, or the Social Gospel. That evaluation comes largely from sermons preached before the turn of the century, in which he emphasized ethical ideals and progress and occasionally spoke of himself as a (Christian) Socialist.[33] But his sermons in California, as represented in the Oakland collection *Twentieth Century Religion* (1902) and even more in *The Divine Adventure* (1907) from the Los Angeles period, developed different strands of his liberal theology. Mills became interested in Theosophy during this period,[34] and in general he was influenced more and more deeply by the currents of New Thought in California. Unlike Brown or Campbell, who approached the new metaphysical movements as a challenge, Mills absorbed them into his expansive Unitarianism. His was an interesting response, not of a committed orthodox minister, but of one deeply imbued with liberal Protestant values who allowed his views to be transformed in contact with new beliefs.

From the 1890s, and even earlier, Mills had made love the center of his Christian gospel. Loving one's neighbor, having sympathy for one's fellow, and extending the gospel of love in the unhappy or impoverished corners of society were recurring themes. His California sermons were no exceptions. Read casually they could sound much like other liberal sermons of the period; but running through them is an unmistakable undercurrent of New Thought and Theosophy. For example, when Mills preached on loving one's neighbor, he argued not from biblical commandment or social necessity but from metaphysics:

> The inner reason why a man should love his neighbor as himself, is because his neighbor is himself. In the largest sense, all that can possibly touch our lives . . . is a constituent part of our greater selves. . . . All the enemies you can recognize are a part of you. . . . You are both a part of the manifest God and neither one can be complete without the other. He is appropriate to your present state of development.[35]

In other words, the commandment signifies a deeper truth: you, your neighbor, and your enemy are part of a greater whole, and your neighbor and your enemy help reveal your deeper self to you. From this perspective, enemies were not really enemies but educational devices. Similarly, evil was not really evil: "All evil consists in an imperfect apprehension of the facts of life, a mistaken attitude of mind toward human experience, and consequent unsatisfactory conduct. . . . APPARENT EVIL IS NOT EVIL IN ITS ESSENCE." In fact, a good God is latent in it all.[36] This was, of course, one of the primary themes of New Thought as well as Christian Science: people should transform evil and negative things into positive ones by thinking differently about them.

Such ideas are quite different from those Mills preached while an evangelist trying to rescue people from evil; they are different even from his 1898 sermon in Boston on "The Problem of Evil." There he stated that "there are certain facts that we cannot call anything but evil. . . . There is unquestionable physical and mental suffering among human beings. . . . It does not explain them to say, that they are all illusions."[37] Evil, he concluded then, exists to bring out the contrast with the good, to develop strength of character, and to reveal the power of God and man to right the wrongs of the world. In the next decade he was claiming that we should not even see wrongs as wrongs; we should change our mental attitudes.

That radical shift was accompanied by others. In his Los Angeles sermons we find Mills quoting from the Buddha and Lao-Tse, as well as from New Thought writers and the American Transcendentalists Emerson and Brownson. Mills became more interested in the psychological aspect of human nature (a theme that had sometimes arisen earlier) and claimed that all people had "rare psychic powers."

He rejected the claim of some New Thought writers that our psychic or spiritual natures meant that we could claim health, wealth, or prosperity for ourselves. On the contrary, he insisted that we must learn to be unselfish and giving, not concerned for our own well-being. But Mills also held that in some sense every human being was one with God; we are "in embryo" what He is "in perfection."[38] He had stated it even more radically in an Oakland sermon on "The Divinity of Man":

> The natural God, the old idol God, the image God, the many Gods, the one God above other Gods, the only God, the Jehovah God, the human God, the Messiah God, the spiritual God, the Father, Son, and Holy Ghost—what are they all? They are simply projections out of yourself. . . .They are the photographs of our real selves. . . .
>
> Catch the real God on your sensitive plate and hold him there and you will discover a picture of your noblest self: listen to the best word that can be spoken from the deepest depths and the highest heights of your being and you will hear these words, "BE STILL AND KNOW THAT I AM GOD."[39]

We can believe in being one with God, and act on that belief; that, according to Mills, is our greater consciousness, our possibility for spiritual perfection. When praying, he said, one should keep in mind that the Lord's Prayer "is really the decision of the human soul to be divine."[40]

Such statements were especially shocking to traditional Protestants, who saw Mills as a man who had once been close to them. But his language was not accidental, not composed of occasional borrowings from the jargon of early twentieth-century California culture: it represented a coherent philosophy. Mills's new stance was perhaps best represented in the Los Angeles sermon entitled "The Life Principle of Jesus," which not only provides a succinct summary of his thought around 1905 but also shows where he stood on the interpretation of basic Christian doctrines.

Jesus's life principle, Mills said, was "Absolute Trust of Mind" and "Perfect Love" in practice: if we love and trust both God and man, we are on Jesus' path. By itself there was nothing offensive about such a principle, which was reminiscent of traditional emphases on faith and love; but the substitution of trust for faith would be slightly disturbing, for the term was more common in New Thought. Mills, however, went on to say a great deal about Jesus that would be more questionable. Jesus, he said, personified the "Universal Source, Purpose, Wisdom, Energy and End of existence" and called it "the Father." What "the Father" meant was that "all men and things were on their way from God to God." Further, "Jesus understood that all apparent knowledge derived from the senses is illusory, but that the selfless soul may know even as also he is known. To him, God was the one inescapable, knowable Reality." Jesus recognized God in nature, not only seeing natural beauty as an illustration of God's plan, but also—here Mills echoes Starr King—communing with the "inner substance" of things so as to recognize the divine within. To Jesus everything was sacred. His miracles were not violations of natural law but the fulfillment of law: "We cannot overstate the potency," Mills proclaimed, "that lies in the absolute trust of a reverent soul." Healing the sick, raising the dead, quieting storms "may be the appropriate expressions of the Infinite Energy through an entirely surrendered soul."[41]

Jesus, then, was not God any more than any very reverent or "entirely surrendered" person would be. He knew the secrets of life—the inner substances, the falsity of sense knowledge, and the sacrality of everything and everyone on their way "from God to God." He exemplified all that we can achieve. Clearly for Mills the traditional doctrines about Jesus's divinity or his humanity were irrelevant, since all humans are the same sort of beings. And difficult theological questions were resolved by making Jesus virtually immaterial—as indeed most New Thought writers did. He was the embodiment of divine love, but in a more abstract way than in traditional portrayals. He was also the embodiment of divine power, meaning an inner spiritual power accessible to all.

In Mills's development we see an evangelist moving first to an ethical, humanitarian view of Jesus and religion, then to a universal religious perspective in which specific ethical issues nearly disappear. Mills still preached a gospel of love, but whereas earlier he had spoken of applying love to poverty or governmental relations, by the time of the Los Angeles sermons he spoke only of inward loving attitudes. That is precisely what James Campbell had feared would happen if Christians turned too much toward New Thought spirituality: the emphasis on inwardness might lead to a neglect of humanitarian Christianity. Mills, as it turned out, eventually returned to the fold. No published sermons survive from that later period, and virtually nothing is known about his later beliefs. But while in Cal-

ifornia, he had continued to move from doctrine to ethics to elevation of inner consciousness. He gave up personalistic theology with
its dramas of man's Fall, of Christ's passion and death with its mysterious atonement for sin, and of the future life in heaven or hell. Instead he preached an exemplary Jesus, a humanitarian and symbol
of inner power. Simultaneously, he deemphasized the dramatic conversion experience in favor of a confidence in personal growth and
suprarational mysticism. So long as he was strongly influenced by the
socialist tendencies growing on the East Coast, he had held to humanitarian forms of rational religion. But as a result of his reading
and his work in California, he adopted a spiritual concept of existence and a mystical approach to the divine that was, nevertheless,
still rational, with a general concept of God as the Infinite. Like
Campbell, Mills saw the Christian as developing the inner life, aiming to be in the presence of God and to be touched by the Infinite.
Unlike Campbell, he did not see the difficulties in accepting this new
view. Nevertheless his thought clearly shows a movement with its
own inner logic. Notable for our purposes, of course, is that his
movement from social Christianity to a more eclectic mysticism coincided with his move to the West Coast. In California, tolerance was
the watchword; the sense of community was weak, especially in the
south; and there was already a strong cultural movement in the direction of the metaphysical religions. These factors could support, if
not actually give rise to, Mills's turn to mysticism.

Joseph Pomeroy Widney, our last illustration, was perhaps the
best known and most influential, over a long term, of these ministers.
His connections to the East were weakest and to California the
strongest. Born in 1841 near Piqua, Ohio, he grew up in that region
and attended Miami University. After a brief enlistment in the Civil
War, he came to California for his health while still quite a young
man. He completed with honors a ten-month course in medicine at
Tolad Medical College (San Francisco), spent two years with the
army as a surgeon in the Arizona Indian wars, and then settled in
California before the big booms. (We have already met his brother
Robert Maclay Widney as one of the planners of the University of
Southern California.) Joseph Widney never left until he died in 1936
at the age of ninety-five. One of the first southern Californians, he
was a cultural leader there for nearly seventy years.[42]
Widney's profession was medicine: he founded and served as dean

of the University of Southern California College of Medicine in
1885. But his real love was the study of mankind, especially religion
and history. As trustee of the University from 1880 to 1895 and as
its president for the last three of those years, he expressed broad
aims. In an 1892 address to graduating students of the Maclay College of Theology, for example, he urged all to fulfill mankind's basic
aim: "to become seers."[43] And in the years that followed he devoted
less time to medicine than to developing his deeper interests through
historical research and the ministry.

A Methodist, Widney was briefly a part of the holiness movement
in Los Angeles and co-founded, with Phineas F. Bresee, the Church
of the Nazarene in 1895. He left the church late in 1898 because he
believed in gradual spiritual growth rather than an identifiable experience of sanctification. Shortly afterward he returned to the
Methodist ministry and was appointed to the church's City Mission
of Los Angeles (formally organized in 1908), where he ministered to
thousands over the next several years.[44] He also built his own mission church, essentially a chapel, seating 100 persons—for a "wider
faith." He called it Beth-El, dedicated it to the "All-Father," and conducted Sunday services there for thirty-six years.[45]

In 1876 Widney had written, together with J. J. Warner and Benjamin Hayes, the first history of Los Angeles County; he had also
penned some brief essays on holiness in 1900, and another on the
"Faith Cure Fallacy" denying that healing was a sign of true Christianity.[46] But his most substantial writing on religious subjects appeared in 1907, when, at the age of sixty-six, he published the two-
volume *Race Life of the Aryan Peoples*. He published little again until his old age in the 1930s; then, with the aid of his daughters (for
he was going blind), he assembled several books, including *The Genesis and Evolution of Islam and Judeo-Christianity* (1932), *The Faith
That Has Come to Me* (1932), *Whither Away?* (1934), *The Three
Americas* (1935), and *Race Life and Race Religions* (1936). Although none of these books could have influenced southern California until after his death, it is clear that the basic elements of his ideas
were already formed when he wrote *Race Life of the Aryan Peoples*.
Some passages from this work are repeated verbatim in later books,
and he indicates that he had been writing for some time before
he finally gathered his ideas into publishable form. Probably he
preached and taught, between 1907 and 1930, many of the ideas that
appeared later. Thus, while relying primarily on his 1907 work, we

can draw occasionally on elaborations made later to explicate Widney's thought.

Widney was a dramatic example of a midwestern Protestant who turned away from church and creed toward an independent religious system that had some affinities with New Thought. His great passion was to understand and explain the direction of history from the remote past into the future. His explorations in the history of the Aryan race and the American continents were all part of an effort to map the human cosmos with its amazing diversity of present and past peoples. On his map the Aryans had the central place, while the other races—black, yellow, red—were passing from the scene. Among the Aryans he selected the Scots-Irish and English for special attention as representing the ultimate in the Aryan conquest of the planet. Widney was not original in these beliefs, of course, though he comprehended more territory than most. In large part, his 1907 volumes can be understood as a defense of the imperialistic attitudes held by many Americans, and attacked by some, at the turn of the century. Imperialism, he declared, was a "bogy" [*sic*] that Americans used to frighten themselves away from fulfilling their destiny. In fact, the "resistless working of the higher law of race expansion" overrides any protests and any treaties or agreements between countries; it is best simply to recognize the facts. The strong and highly civilized must and will replace the weak and barbarous peoples.[47]

At the same time as he stood strong for Aryan particularism, however, Widney also wished to transcend it. He recognized that any race life also has its death, though he expected the Aryans to be around a long while yet. More importantly for the immediate future, he believed that enlightened members of the race were turning to a less provincial view of things. Especially in religion, he believed that all could be united. Widney argued that the exclusivism of Christianity had blinded us to other forms of revelation, such as had come to Socrates, Confucius, or Gautama the Buddha. He suspected that Jesus and Paul had been influenced by non-western wisdom themselves. For Widney the event of Calvary was not the central fact in the divine plan of the universe, but merely a passing episode, however dramatic, affecting one portion of human history.[48] Now the traditional Christian creeds and the older churches were dying away. The "Teuto-Aryan," he said, was letting doctrinal controversies pass by, "while he turns more and more to the kindly life of the Christ who walked the troubled earth as the helpful Brother of Man."[49] Jesus, in short, was not the ultimate Savior, but our "Mystical Elder Brother."[50] He was one of those "men with a Message" who appear in various places and epochs with news from the beyond. We cannot say definitely who Jesus was, nor can we say any more about God than that he is "the One Great Central Life-Force of all," the one who has said "I AM."[51] We would do better to drop our creeds and theologies and turn to a different kind of religion.

Widney's new religion would recognize that all religions are essentially one. Its basic principles included a positive view of human nature: "more of the self-respecting manhood of one made in the divine image; less of that old monkish idea of an utter and unworthy self-abasement which dishonors God in dishonoring His handiwork." It recognized that heaven and hell are "essentially conditions," that "man makes his own heaven and hell." This view provided a foundation for basic ethical principles such as justice and love, and a few basic beliefs that Widney assumed all religions already had: belief in God; in sin, repentance, and forgiveness; in a life beyond the grave with just rewards for all; and in the common brotherhood of man. All existing religions should strive to peer beyond their myths and images "to the calm, clear face of the All-Father himself."[52]

In advocating the unity of all religions, in viewing Jesus as human yet mystically in tune with higher forces, in understanding God as the great Life-Force, and in relativizing the concepts of heaven and hell, Widney sounded much like a New Thought philosopher. Yet he held onto the "All-Fatherhood" of God and traditional Protestant concepts of sin, repentance, and forgiveness. He did not mean something entirely traditional by these, but neither did he hold that humans are already essentially divine.

Widney was widely read in the thought of his day, and there are any number of sources from which he could have developed his ideas. In fact, however, his interest in liberal religion went back to his student days at Miami University, where he heard the teaching and preaching of David Swing (later a popular liberal preacher in Chicago, tried for heresy there). Widney called Swing a "poet-preacher" and compared him favorably with Thomas Starr King. "His life work, like that of Star [*sic*] King in San Francisco, was the preaching and the teaching of a faith broader, kindlier, sweeter than that written in our creeds." According to Widney, these two felt "called upon to step over the ecclesiastical lines which we have drawn about the simple, kindly, trusting life and teachings of Him we call Jesus of Nazareth."[53] From his reference to Starr King we can see that Widney was connected to the earlier branch of liberal thought in northern California and drew from it at least part of his inspiration. He seems not to have been attracted to the mind-cure traditions; as a physician, he upheld the value of physical care and natural cures. With his interest in many religions, he may have been attracted to Theosophy; but with his firm grounding in Christianity, he wanted to remain true to Western traditions. He was striving to be an independent thinker in religion.

Appropriately enough for a man of midwestern Protestant background, Widney had once had an experience that he described retrospectively as focal for his religious life. Neither a conversion nor a sanctification, neither a healing by the Divine Mind nor a floating on the Infinite, it was nevertheless peculiarly Californian in the independent style that Widney had adopted. Afterward Widney claimed it was his revelation of God. While an army surgeon during the Arizona Indian wars, he rode out one day into the northern desert and stayed alone much of the day. In the "utter hush" of the desert noon, he recalled,

> as I sat looking out over the brown, dry plain to the simple outline of the far-off mountains, a strange sense of a new life seemed to come to me. I somehow seemed, as with a new-born perception, to awake to a sense of life about me: intangible, unseen, but Life. . . . I seemed somehow to have stepped out of the old, narrow bounds and bonds of the flesh, and to stand within the portals of a new and broader existence. . . . I had found the desert—and God.

Afterward Widney was never the same. He saw modern urban civilization as the true desert, while knowing that the desert itself—to which he never returned—was life.[54] Often in his later works he referred to the God of the desert and of "the Open," identifying his experience and his faith with that of the ancient Semites from which Judaism later sprang, and with the religion of primitive man generally.[55] He called his own independent church Beth-El, "House of God," from the Old Testament name. In a certain sense, then, his attempt to unite all religions around faith in the "All-Father" was also a return to what he saw as his own root in the American West, via the desert; to the roots of Western culture; and to the roots of humanity in a primitive sense of nature and life.

That an uprooted Midwesterner would search for roots in this intense way and end up sounding like a Theosophist or at least a Transcendentalist is not surprising. As we have seen, discarding or loos-
ening traditional church loyalties in favor of an abstract unity of
faiths was a typical direction for white Protestant Californians. In
southern California particularly, people tried to attach themselves to
the culture before them and to other roots they could identify. At the
same time they sought, by the use of religious images or philosophies,
to enrich their sense of themselves in relation to God. Widney was
unusual in the independence of his search, in his intellectual thor-
oughness (for his time and situation), and in moving toward the Old
Testament rather than the New. But the results were congruent with
what other southern Californians were doing. As Theosophists attempted to find the perennial philosophy by accepting all gods, so
Widney too looked to the mystical beyond and its many messengers
for his inspiration. From the time of his transformative experience in
the desert, he increasingly rejected dogmatism in anything. Unlike
some of his fellows, he was not a likely candidate for any single system of thought; but like the other metaphysicians of southern California, Widney forged a California theology of his own.

Brown, Campbell, Mills, and Widney represented a new stream in
California liberal Protestantism that attempted to address the vocal
metaphysical religions. Their range was wide, from Brown's Pragmatism and emphasis on character building to Widney's Aryan philosophy and desert mysticism. They had in common an appreciation
of the needs of Anglo-Protestant Californians to develop inner
strength while at the same time maintaining the essentials of their
faith.

The common thread that still tied them to tradition was their
commitment to humanitarian activism. These four men were not
necessarily committed to the Social Gospel, but each was concerned
about Christianity's mission to transform the world. Even Benjamin
Fay Mills, who had abandoned most traditional doctrines, continued to preach unselfish action as crucial to Christianity, in contrast
to New Thought people, who, he believed, were seeking blessings for
themselves. Widney translated activism into a sense of Aryan destiny, as many Protestants before him had done. All felt the necessity
of maintaining some outward orientation to avoid the pitfalls of pas-

sivity, quietism, and selfishness that many critics saw as characteristic of the metaphysical religions. Besides the (related) accusation of pantheism, nothing worried them more.

At the same time, as Brown recognized, many Protestants felt that the outward orientation of religion had been too strong, and that some problems might best be solved by turning to the inward resources of Christian life. The metaphysical religions seemed to offer restoration of a lost balance. Campbell, Mills, and Brown all tried to resurrect the appropriate resources within their own tradition: thus Brown and Campbell used Scripture or other religious passages as affirmations. It was difficult, however, to find orthodox resources. Campbell had to turn to Emerson, while Mills strayed farther afield into other religions. Widney, with his grand aspirations to be a universalistic thinker, embraced the general truths of all faiths; yet he validated his stance in a way closer to his Methodist and holiness predilections, through personal mystical experience. Consistent with that position, he urged all to become "seers."

Putting such prescriptions into action must have been another problem. Most churches did not support the kind of inner work these men were suggesting, and it is uncertain that they even tried to develop such support in their own churches. Nevertheless their ideas reached a large audience and may have been put into practice by individuals, as a kind of private devotionalism. Campbell's works were known in clerical circles and may have influenced other liberal ministers. Mills and Widney were popular and well known; Brown influenced the upper echelons of Oakland society and was one of the most prestigious ministers in northern California. Through these leaders and others they influenced, a significant proportion of the Anglo-Protestant population was introduced to new religious methods and insights.

Of course, the men considered here were on the liberal fringe—Congregationalist or Methodist in background, independent in thinking. Mills was temporarily out of the mainstream, as usually defined. There were other, equally well respected ministers in the urban areas who paid little attention, at least publicly, to the issues raised by the metaphysical religions, concentrating instead on strengthening traditional beliefs, building churches, and working for the betterment of their communities. We need only think of Robert Burdette and William Stewart Young, famous for the churches they built in Los Angeles; or Dana Bartlett, proponent of the Social Gospel and author of *The Better City* and *The Better Country*, who once received the Los Angeles Citizen of the Year award. Such men represented the strong center of Anglo-Protestantism in southern California. Their prominence might lead us to think that the influence of the new religions reached only a few, perhaps the educated elite or the more wealthy, or certain people in the churches who had special personal, psychological concerns. But in fact the divisions are not so clear. There was another dissident movement centered in southern California that touched a different range of church members. This was the holiness movement, which appealed to the less wealthy and, at least on the surface, seemed to be far more conservative. In the next chapter we will find that it too was influenced by the metaphysical and mystical traditions.

7. Holiness in California

The holiness movement, especially as it culminated in the founding of the Church of the Nazarene in 1895, was another Protestant response to conditions in California. Like Christian Science and New Thought, the holiness movement originated elsewhere. But under the leadership of Phineas F. Bresee in Los Angeles it gained new momentum, developed a strong organization, and offered, for some years, a gospel that rang of California at least as much as of other regions. Especially important is that Bresee reached a sector of the population other than the upper-middle-class, educated populace who were the primary supporters of Protestant liberalism. Bresee helped the less wealthy and less articulate express their religious experience in a California context, just as Campbell and Widney did for other parts of the population. We will see how he did that, after reviewing the development of the holiness movement.[1]

Holiness originated in the period immediately following the Second Great Awakening. Besides the movements for social reform, utopian experiments, and new sects that followed the revivals, some evangelicals of that era were inspired to seek a greater sense of Christian grace, purity, and devotion within themselves. Presbyterian leaders like Charles Grandison Finney and Asa Mahan, both at Oberlin College, began around 1839 to preach that it was possible to attain Christian perfection or, as it was also called, "entire sanctification" or "holiness." The Methodists found antecedents to this idea in the thought of John Wesley himself, and among them the idea spread widely. One of its chief proponents was Phoebe Palmer, who became famous for her "Tuesday Meetings for the Promotion of Holiness," beginning in 1837 in New York City and continuing for over twenty years. The Plymouth Brethren promoted another version of the idea. By the late 1850s ministers of other denominations were also preaching holiness: A. B. Earle, for example, a Baptist evangelist who held interdenominational revivals all over the country, professed sanctification in 1858. Earle, as we have seen, brought his message to northern California shortly after the Civil War, preaching in many towns and cities at the invitation of the San Francisco Ministerial Union. National holiness leader John S. Inskip evangelized in California in 1871; and from the 1860s on, the Methodist *California Christian Advocate* regularly discussed issues pertaining to the "higher life."

There were various definitions of what "holiness" or "entire sanctification" meant, but generally it was understood as a dramatic experience comparable to, but higher than, conversion itself. Phoebe Palmer called it "laying all on the altar," meaning giving one's life entirely to God. In return the Christian received a gift of grace that purified his or her soul from sin. Whereas conversion had brought forgiveness and cleansing from the guilt of past sin, sanctification brought a cleansing from the tendency to sin. Some would understand it as the indwelling of the Holy Spirit, filling the soul with goodness so that it excluded sinfulness. The sanctified believer would not yield to temptation or have any sympathy with sinful passions, thoughts, or deeds; he would enjoy peace and rest in his soul and would be granted the graces of humility, charity, and love. One could progress in the awareness and manifestation of holiness throughout one's life. One could also fall from it; but while in the state of holiness, even though one might make mistakes or misjudgments, one could not truly be said to sin. As Jesse Peck wrote in his classic on holiness, *The Central Idea of Christianity*, one could sin after conversion, but not after being sanctified in the Spirit:

> We have inward convictions of remaining corruptions. . . . The conscience recognizes the stain. We feel the struggle arising again from unholy elements, "roots of bitterness springing up trouble us." Hence our weakness in Christian effort, our inefficiency as laborers in God's vineyard; our oft-repeated failures in representing the true spirit of Christianity, and those outward vacillations and sins into which we are suddenly betrayed. But, in the work of entire sanctification, these impurities are all washed away, so that we are wholly saved from sin, from its inward pollution.[2]

Gradually the idea developed that holiness could make one Christlike or godlike in one's inner heart—although of course that did not make one perfect in all actions.[3]

In the 1870s the movement attracted greater numbers, both

within and beyond Methodism. Each summer, from 1867 on, the National Camp Meeting Association for the Promotion of Holiness gathered hundreds or thousands at its retreats. Some significant divergences developed, however. In the late 1870s some leaders, influenced by the parallel Keswick Conferences held in England from 1874, began to question the idea of eradication of a person's sinful nature and to see growth in perfection as more gradual. In general, the Keswickians viewed holiness not as a cleansing from sin but as an "enduement of power" counteracting one's tendency to sin and turning outward to service more than inward. People influenced by this branch of the movement tended to emphasize mission work, conversion of others, and alleviation of social problems, especially in urban areas. A number of well-known evangelists and holiness leaders—Dwight L. Moody, Reuben Torrey, J. Wilbur Chapman, A. J. Gordon, A. B. Simpson—were influenced by the Keswickians, as was the Salvation Army, which had been founded in England by William Booth.[4]

While the leaders were developing a language and theology of holiness, there were other sources of division at the grass roots. Especially in the Midwest and the South, many groups wished to define holiness in terms of specific standards of behavior and practice; they tended to emphasize stricter codes of dress and morality than those in the urban Northeast, where the movement had originated. All holiness people insisted, of course, on basics of evangelical morality such as chastity and abstinence from liquor. The stricter groups also forbade ostentatious clothes or jewelry, with the aim of preserving simplicity in the church. In this way they distinguished themselves from the wealthier urban churches that had gained power in the denominations in recent years and which, the rural groups believed, were lax in discipline and membership standards and expended too much energy on grand church buildings and imposing ecclesiastical bureaucracies. In this respect, one branch of the holiness movement was very populistic.[5]

The same branch was also the most radical in its separatist tendencies. By the late 1870s some rural holiness preachers were organizing their converts into holiness "bands" independent of the regular denominations, and more local and regional "associations" were sprouting. By the 1880s the first independent holiness churches had begun to form. In California a radical Methodist named Hardin Wallace, who had already evangelized throughout Texas, began to preach in Los Angeles and elsewhere, often together with evangelist Harry Ashcraft and gospel singer James Jayns. Out of their work the Southern California and Arizona Holiness Association was formed, led by James and Josephine Washburn. This organization was very strict: all members had to experience sanctification; all had to dress plainly, abstain from tobacco and the use of gold ornaments, and abjure membership in any secret society. They erected plain buildings and forbade musical instruments in church; ordination was by the "baptism of fire," with no preacher designated before the service. The Southern California and Arizona Holiness Association remained quite small, establishing churches in only a handful of southern California towns; a more moderate organization, the Pacific Coast Holiness Association, appeared in 1885. Nevertheless the radicals caused concern in the Methodist church when in 1885 one of their leaders, B. A. Washburn, proposed that all holiness groups separate from the mainstream churches. The California Methodist establishment was not at that time antagonistic to the holiness movement—quite the contrary. The radicals, however, felt alienated from the regular Methodists. Eventually (1896) they organized into the Holiness Church, which continued to be very small.

The urban sector of the movement, more intellectual and interdenominational, less concerned about regulating details of outer behavior, had so far stayed within the Methodist church. Nevertheless tensions were building. Holiness Christians were inclined to ally with those in other denominations, at least for revivals and general meetings. They wanted more evangelism focusing specifically on sanctification, whereas the Methodist bishops believed all church activities were already designed to promote holiness, and no special means should be instituted. Meanwhile many churches supported activities such as fairs, plays, and concerts—not to mention higher biblical criticism—which, to holiness people, were tangential to the Christian life. Those seeking to help the poor through missions to urban families and neighborhoods were not getting much support for their efforts. The stage was set for a split in the Methodist church.

Southern California was rapidly being urbanized as Los Angeles grew, and developments there were similar to those in other large cities. The city mission approach was vigorously represented by the work of T. P. and Manie Ferguson. T. P. Ferguson, born in Ohio in 1853 and converted at Oberlin in 1875, came to Santa Barbara in 1879 and soon thereafter was sanctified at a holiness revival. He be-

came an itinerant preacher and settled in Los Angeles during the
boom of 1885–86. Late in 1886 he set up the Los Angeles Mission,
the first in what would become a chain of Peniel ("Face of God")
Missions dotting the Pacific Coast and mountain states. Together
with his wife Manie, he offered street-corner meetings in the after-
noons and evangelistic services nightly, with a meal afterwards.
Their entire work, like that of most of the city holiness missions, was
oriented toward soul saving and the promotion of holiness. The mission was not a church, however; converts were supposed to join one
of the regular denominations. It was, rather, a holiness revival station spreading the message of Christian perfection.

The crucial development in Southern California came when Phineas F. Bresee arrived on the scene. Born in 1838 in Delaware County, New York, he had gone to Iowa in 1855 as a circuit pastor, and
was highly successful for a time. In the early 1880s, however, he went
bankrupt due to the failure of some Mexican iron mines in which he
had invested, and he left Iowa for California, arriving in 1883. Soon
he won fine appointments in the Methodist church, notably as pastor
of First Church in Los Angeles and as one of the editorial committee
of the *Southern California Christian Advocate.*

Bresee identified himself with the holiness movement and experienced sanctification himself in 1884 or 1885. In his church he emphasized revivals, gospel singing, and spontaneous congregational
responses. Some ministers opposed his outright holiness stance, but
he was supported by his general popularity and the approval—or at
least the neutrality—of the bishops until 1892. In that year an anti-
holiness clergyman, John Vincent, became Bishop, and he assigned
Bresee to churches that could not offer adequate financial support.
In 1894 Bresee sought a supernumerary relation so that he could do
mission work instead of a regular pastorate, but Vincent refused permission. At that point Bresee withdrew from the Methodist ministry.

At first Bresee joined with the Fergusons at the Peniel Mission in
Los Angeles, where he tried to persuade them to open a school and
organize to receive members like a church. They refused, however,
and other difficulties led to his parting with them after one year. In
the fall of 1895 he, together with Joseph P. Widney, began holding
independent services in a rented hall. Their ministry was so popular
that three and a half weeks later they organized as a church, the
Church of the Nazarene. Bresee and Widney were appointed to life
tenure as pastors and superintendents.

The accession of Vincent to the bishopric in southern California represented a turning of the tide. About the same time, all across the nation, the church establishment was beginning to come down hard on holiness people and their associations. As a result, independent churches were being formed even among many who had loyally remained with the regular church. Phineas Bresee was one of these. When he left the ministry, it is clear that he wanted to gather holiness people into an independent church, hopefully by using the Fergusons' organization, but when that did not work out, by organizing on his own. This was no small step for a man of fifty-seven years (Widney was fifty-four), but his popularity and organizational ability held the group together and it grew rapidly into a large church. Ultimately, after merging in 1908 with other regional holiness churches, the Church of the Nazarene would become the largest holiness denomination in the nation.

In Los Angeles Bresee was soon on his own, for Widney, as we have seen, returned to Methodism in 1898 because he held the view that sanctification could be progressive rather than a single dramatic experience. Bresee held to plain services and plain buildings—his tabernacle was soon nicknamed the Glory Barn—and regarded his evangelical work as directed to the poor. Nevertheless some prominent citizens joined his church and gave financial support. He attracted well-known evangelists and singers, and began to publish the *Nazarene Messenger* in 1898. After the turn of the century and even more after 1905, the Nazarene work expanded into the Northwest and Midwest, especially in urban centers.

The church was attractive to those who sought a more revivalistic religion than the regular churches offered. Compared to the early radicals, the Nazarenes were moderate. Yet their emphasis on conversion and sanctification contrasted with the increasingly lax membership standards of mainstream denominations. The rules against drinking and dancing were probably reminiscent, for many former Midwesterners, of the moral codes of their home towns. The Church of the Nazarene thus offered a familiar environment to the middle-class and less wealthy Angelenos who had recently moved from farms and small towns.[6] Yet we should not emphasize the structure and format of the church to the point of overlooking the importance of Bresee's popularity and the central ideas of the holiness movement itself. A familiar environment with similar customs would certainly be attractive, but the church's growth suggests that Bresee's teaching must have struck responsive chords in his listeners. In general, Bresee's was an evangelistic teaching that emphasized experience, similar to that of revivalists who had dominated American Protestantism in earlier generations. But beyond conversion, Bresee preached a spirit-filled life available to believers.

For Bresee the center of Christianity was "the coming of the Holy Ghost," the disciples' experience of Pentecost. This event superseded the incarnation, suffering, atonement, and resurrection of Jesus. "But for the coming of the Holy Ghost all else were lost," he said in a 1903 sermon, "all that went before would have disappeared. The coming of the Spirit established Christianity, and continues to give it power and efficiency." Likewise, the experience of the Holy Spirit in the believer's individual life was the center of Christian faith for each person today. Bresee believed in the experience called sanctification, but he insisted that this was the beginning of spiritual growth, not its end; the Christian's spirit, edified by the Holy Ghost, would learn more about Jesus and his meekness and lowliness, and receive the graces of courage, love, kindness, and knowledge of God. "It is not for the thrill of a moment," he warned, "but for the heart-to-heart fellowship with the Holy Ghost as he pours His own life and transforming glory through and through us for all ages."[7]

Much of Bresee's preaching, as it has been preserved in the church, was devoted to reemphasizing and elaborating the meaning of that pivotal experience, the reception of the Holy Ghost. He assumed that right action would follow on the experience, but he did not accentuate the social aspect of Christian life or even the importance of mission work or evangelism. In this respect he was in line with traditional Methodist holiness doctrine, not the Keswickian branch that had become popular among many who worked among the urban poor.[8] Even though he saw his preaching as aimed at the poor, he urged his listeners to seek deeper inward experience that would continuously transform their lives.

In this process, people were to become more and more like Jesus himself. At the outset, the Holy Spirit would reveal to them their present imperfections while at the same time making it possible for them to come nearer and nearer to union with the Divine. Bresee called this gaining a "deeper knowledge of self," which meant first learning about one's lack of conformity to Christ. Then, as one put away earthly attachments, one could gradually gain in knowledge and become increasingly "in soul united with Him in His passion for dying men." Ultimately the believer would learn that "*they whom Je-sus sends are absorbed in Him. . . .* They are one with Him, united in mystic unity," as he was with the Father.⁹ Lived in the presence of the Holy Ghost, the life of holiness was a divine life.

Bresee envisioned that every Christian could achieve a high spir-itual level, experiencing the "all-pervading presence of God" and recognizing that "human life is in this Divine Presence. Not in the presence of God, but in God. . . . God is the element in which we live, and . . . all things must be adjusted to Him."¹⁰ This image of God as the ambient of all human life is surprising, because it sounds remarkably impersonal. Whereas "in the presence of God" might suggest being in front of a certain being, Bresee replaces that familiar phrase with "in God." Here, he is taking a new and mystical turn.

Like most holiness leaders, however, Bresee focused on the per-sonal when it came to the individual soul. He insisted that each per-son must come to experience the presence of God in his own way, unmediated by any particular ritual or religious leader. The sole pur-pose of all religious institutions—the teachings of the church, its meetings, its worship—was to aid the individual to achieve "an open vision discerning the divine presence," and finally to be "transformed into the likeness of His Son." In this respect Bresee, though a for-midable organizer, was anti-ecclesiastical. If institutions impaired or impeded an individual's way to God, they were not being truly Chris-tian. God's work in the world was not the establishment of institu-tions but personal transformation: "God's great work is the mani-festation of Himself in Human [*sic*] consciousness."¹¹

From Bresee's language in the passages quoted, it appears that he was moving beyond a traditional Protestant vocabulary. Nineteenth-century Anglo-Protestants describing the divine-human relationship had generally relied on either the legal models of guilt and forgive-ness or on the personalistic models of Jesus as a friend or God as the loving Father. Bresee, in contrast, spoke of being "in" God and "united with" Jesus. Moreover, one would expect a gospel preacher to speak about emotions a great deal, or at least to appeal to emo-tions in an explicit way. Bresee did very little of either. The heart or affections must be touched by the message of Jesus, he said, but then the person develops a kind of intensity that is not simply emotional. He wrote that the heart is the opening of vision: "*The eye of the soul is the heart.* All the light that ever comes into a man's real being comes in through the heart." Further, the heart must be "melted down by the love and tears of the Son of God, mingled with the love and tears of his servants."[12] Yet more often he spoke in another vein: the "passion of the soul" for Christ meant intensity and thoughtfulness:

> Thoughtful passion is the warp of the Christian life. An intensity which makes it impossible for anything else to get the attention. A clear thoughtfulness which has considered the matter, and has the mind fully made up.[13]

In another place, describing the correct attitude of the spirit ("Blessed are the poor in spirit"), Bresee emphasized that "a necessity to poverty of spirit is clear thought. Thought is the spirit's eyes. Clear thought is one of the necessities of men. . . . To think is the concentration of the soul's forces."[14]

If the heart is the opening of vision, Bresee was saying, then clear thought is what brings everything into focus, in full light. This is the fullness of devotion to God, the fullness of holiness. "The emphasis of loving God with all the mind," he wrote, "is a Christly emphasis. The Old Testament has heart and soul and might, but the New Testament . . . emphasizes mind. The Holy Spirit having come to abide in us, peculiarly clarifies, fills and thrills the thought-life. As a man thinketh in his heart so is he."[15]

Further, the transforming power of Christ and the Holy Spirit comes from Jesus' own pure thoughts. Following on his comments on the heart as the eye of the soul, quoted above, Bresee described the spiritual experience of the love of Jesus in terms of Jesus' thought entering the believer like light:

> He fills the spirit with the light of his thought. . . . His presence . . . brings us into highest relationship to eternal verities, and into fellowship with immortal personalities. . . . When [He] pours his infinite exhaustless thought, in perennial and increasing streams through the soul; when the virtue of His own soul-life flows in infinite purity through all the avenues of our being; when His love, all aflame and aglow, fills the fountains of our being; we are almost touching the mount of transfiguration. . . . There is such a thing as overcoming gravitation. You fill a body with a substance so much lighter than air that you overcome the weight of the body and it will rise. A soul in which Jesus Christ lives is so filled with heavenly atmosphere that it mounts heavenward.[16]

The emphasis on "infinite exhaustless thought," on "eternal verities" and virtue, and the allusion to rising higher all suggest a sort of piety different from that of earlier Protestantism.

We do not find such language in other contemporary holiness writers. Most of them employ a variety of metaphors and descriptions of the work of the Holy Spirit and the Christian's experience of it. Purity and cleansing, light, love, power, filling of an emptiness— all these are common ways of speaking of the Pentecost experience. Occasionally one sees the older, strikingly personalist metaphors, as when A. B. Simpson wrote that the Holy Ghost corresponds to motherhood, while the other parts of the Trinity correspond respectively to fatherhood (God) and brotherhood (Christ).[17] More often we find general concepts such as power, the "enduement with power" being a distinctive emphasis of the Keswickians. As George Marsden has observed, the emphasis on power, action, and preparation for service was predominant in the tradition dominated by Reformed holiness people. "Unlike the holiness movement of the Civil War era," he writes, "this newer Reformed holiness movement was male-dominated and masculinity was equated with power and action."[18]

A few writings express some of the same ideas—mind, thought, wisdom, knowledge, truth—as Bresee's sermons. Simpson spoke of the Holy Ghost as the Spirit of wisdom and of a sound mind, but he did so in the much broader context of how the Spirit guides all the work a person has to do. A. J. Gordon made wisdom somewhat more prominent. He wrote of the three dimensions of the enduement of spirit as sealing, filling, and anointing: "Each of these terms," he explained, "is connected with some special Divine endowment—the seal with assurance and consecration; the filling with power; and the anointing with knowledge."[19] For Gordon, knowledge, in a spiritual sense similar to Bresee's, was one of the features of life in the Holy Ghost.

Nevertheless, unlike Bresee, none of these writers devoted such attention to the influence of the Holy Spirit on the human mind. Bresee, of course, was not speaking of mind in the sense of an operative mentality; he was not advising logical argument or analysis, but urging people to an experience of intensity, focus, and clarity. Thought was the "concentration of the soul's forces," a grasping of something with all the faculties. When he spoke of "knowledge" of God or "learning" more of Jesus, he was pointing to spiritual transformation. "This is not growth, nor culture, nor morality," he emphasized, "but

Jesus' own personal presence and life."[20] As the clarity and intensity of awareness that accompanied the experience of the divine presence, thought was the experience of unity or absorption in God. With these ideas, Bresee was communicating in a style different from that of those holiness writers who wrote of being filled with power, being purified or cleansed, or finding peace and rest.

Beyond the imitation of Christ and the clarity of thought that was the experience of the Holy Ghost, Bresee also described the experience of holiness as involving a kind of disembodiment, a becoming more nearly pure spirit. He wrote:

> Now spirit-life is the enlarged life, the full circle of our being. . . . There are worlds about us which we scarcely touch [with our bodies]. There are no doors through the senses to them. We close our eyes to see some things. There are some voices to hear which we close our ears. There are some [paths] we can traverse only as we disembody ourselves. Some ways which we call abstract thought. What is that? To simply close all the highways of the senses and go out along spiritual lines. . . . If you seek to know pure mathematics you cannot see with your eyes but must see with your thought. The fountain of moral obligation, the great fact of holiness, the vast verities of destiny are so.[21]

Spirit life was truly beyond the life of the body; the analogy with mathematics and abstract thought indicates that it was not rooted in anything earthly. Indeed, one who became fully spiritual would not even seem to be in his ordinary personality:

> While [a holy person] is personally enlarged and strengthened, yet he is more of an avenue, more of a transmitter, more a viaduct, than a personality, i.e., he is filled with and clothed upon with power so much greater than himself that he is comparatively lost sight of.[22]

To become lighter than air, to have one's personality replaced by the Spirit's presence, to "gaze into the heavens," as Bresee liked to say, in order to see things beyond the senses—these were the ultimate in the life of holiness. These could only come, of course, from outside humanity, from the coming of the Holy Ghost.

While Bresee's peculiar emphases depart from earlier Anglo-Protestantism and contemporary holiness writers, they bear a similarity to certain New Thought concepts in the quest for a state beyond the physical human embodiment, in the unabashed use of mystical language in speaking of likeness to or unity with Christ, and in the centrality of the concepts of thought, knowledge, and mind. His approach is more concrete than New Thought, much more personalist in its theology, and more traditional in its emphasis on the Christian's dependence on God's grace; yet it sounds similar in its aims and its general sense of the nature of spiritual goals. Of course, he would not have borrowed knowingly from New Thought or related movements, for most were too far from Christian tradition. Yet Bresee shared with other southern California religious thinkers a cultural ambience that influenced him, and to which he contributed. His association with Joseph P. Widney is probably the most significant; until 1898 they worked closely together, and the relationship remained amicable even when they went their separate ways. Considering that the period of Bresee's work with the Church of the Nazarene coincided with the most intensive period of growth of the metaphysical religions (1895–1915), it is not unlikely that their approach to spirituality influenced his attempts to describe the experience of holiness.

Here the historian is on shaky ground, for it is difficult to trace the threads of popular tradition. The accounts of Bresee's life do not show his intellectual indebtedness to anyone else; indeed, his synthesis of traditional doctrine with mystical concepts is highly original. Most of his associates left few traces of their thoughts in writing, and the men who later led the church, even in California, were mostly from the Midwest or East. However, we can identify one significant relationship, with the man who later became the systematizer of theology for the Nazarenes, H. Orton Wiley. Though born in Nebraska, Wiley spent most of his life in the West (though he was born in Nebraska). He experienced sanctification while a college student in Berkeley in 1902, and became close to the Nazarene pastor E. A. Girvin, who was a friend of Bresee. Wiley was invited in 1910 to become dean of Deets Pacific Bible College in Los Angeles, of which Bresee was president. This school later became Pasadena University, and Wiley was advanced to its presidency in 1913.

Wiley's theological work was not published until the 1930s and later, and his major systematic work is largely a synthesis of earlier thought.[23] Of most interest to us is that during and immediately after the years he worked most closely with Bresee, he was completing the M.S.T. degree at Pacific School of Religion; his 1917 thesis was entitled "The Logos Doctrine of the Prologue of the Fourth Gospel." While the Logos was a natural subject for a holiness theorist concerned with the works of the Holy Spirit, Wiley's interpretation, while drawing on insights from other commentators, had some special emphases. Wiley argued in general that the Logos prologue represents three levels of God's power: in nature, in humanity as a race of historical and ethical beings, and on the level of spirit. Nature, as God's creation, is connected to spiritual experience because our knowledge of God is mediated through our experience of nature; Christian mysticism is rich in nature symbolism. The historical-ethical level is the Logos leading humankind to advance in civilization and general understanding. The spiritual level appears in the Logos bringing the revelation of God in fullness—first in Christ as Logos, and ultimately in the lives of all. Interestingly, Wiley argued that the coming of Christ was necessary not only because humans had sinned—Christ would have come with or without sin—but also because the revelation of God had to grow in fullness.[24]

We find here an organic conception of the Logos, connected with growth and progress, and somewhat disconnected from the idea of sin and the need for atonement. Wiley amplified on his conception by using analogies from psychology: just as in psychology "progress is from the lower centers to the higher," he said, so it is in the realm of spirit. After rising, the higher center then controls the lower: the Logos comes, expressed in the humanity of Christ, then he "dominates in love the race which has given him birth." The human race in turn then becomes a "higher, more perfect revelation" of the eternal Logos. This growth is possible, Wiley asserted, because the Logos is not only a revelation from the outside, a transcendent being felt in our conscience as moral director, but also comes from the inside, within the personality. Psychology shows that human beings possess a personal religious impulse, a tendency toward religious experience, that Wiley called "God-consciousness." From this impulse even the minds of primitives produce rudiments of the "Logos truth"; the Logos within exists universally. Thus from the inward being that turns to God, and from the outward progress in morality directed by conscience, the Logos is manifested more and more fully.[25]

Wiley's conclusion was that both in the transcendent and in the immanent sense, the Logos should be understood as guiding history to its fulfillment and each person to his completion. This was the truth that he saw in mysticism of all kinds, which recognized and developed the inner God-consciousness. Mysticism was a positive reaction against rationalism; its danger was its tendency to "Quietism" or emotion alone. Mysticism had to be grounded in the "entire, personal constitution of man," by which Wiley meant that it must be connected to the growth of the whole personality.[26]

The thesis is by no means fully argued, nor is it highly original. But as the work of a holiness leader it is striking. Like liberal Protestants, Wiley valued mysticism positively (while warning against "quietism"). He emphasized the organic and developmental nature of spirit manifest in the world and recognized in a positive way the spiritual yearnings of all humankind. Spirit was not a correctional officer keeping people from falling back into sin, nor was it an empowering impulse; it was, rather, the inner guiding force for human perfection. Another similarity to liberal Protestantism is the fact that he called on "modern" psychology (without citing secular sources) as support for his interpretation; psychology was still a new science, more often used by liberal than by conservative Protestants.

These ideas were congruent with, but not derivative from, Bresee's thought. Unlike Bresee, Wiley did not use concepts like thought and knowledge to interpret the Logos; whether he consciously avoided them or simply preferred a more traditional approach we cannot know. But his organic conception reminds us of Bresee's insistence that "spirit-life is the enlarged life, the full circle of our being." Like Bresee, Wiley had an open, expansive attitude that understood the Holy Spirit both broadly, in reference to all people and all aspects of life, and deeply, in that it made possible the completion of each individual. Thus, while not directly indebted to any particular religious tradition outside the regular churches, Wiley's interpretation rings of the open spirituality and even of the liberalism in thought that we find in so many California thinkers influenced by alternative traditions.

Thus even the holiness movement, though directly derived from traditional evangelicalism and usually regarded by historians as very conservative, was susceptible to influence and modification in the ambience of California Protestantism. In certain respects Bresee's approach made the Nazarene church similar to liberal popular movements that were also focused on the inner search, and this similarity helps to account for the church's popularity. For not all holiness groups succeeded like the Nazarenes; most remained small and relatively insignificant. Nor did the Nazarenes in California grow so rapidly after Bresee's death in 1915. When the California body was the only Church of the Nazarene, before the 1908 merger, it had nearly 2,500 members, having grown from a small group in 1895. In 1916 California membership totaled nearly 3,500. While the church continued to add members after Bresee's death, at the rate of about three thousand in each of the next two decades, this rate of growth was small compared to the mushrooming of the national Nazarene church, which grew from a little over thirty-two thousand in 1916 to over one hundred thirty-six thousand in 1936, a 415 percent increase compared to California's 280 percent in the same twenty years. It was also small compared to the total growth in California population, and only slightly larger than the general growth in non-Catholic groups in California.[27] While there are various reasons for the relatively weaker growth of the California Nazarenes, one was certainly the loss of Bresee's leadership. After his death a struggle ensued between "spiritual" and "ecclesiastical" factions,[28] and the holiness message brought by new leaders from other regions did not fit with the approach that members had appreciated in Bresee.

This hypothesis is substantiated by the history of pentecostalism, which preached a message similar to that of the holiness leaders of other regions, but did not succeed in California. Pentecostals looked for an enduement of spiritual power in the form of specific gifts, usually speaking in tongues. Partly an outgrowth of the holiness movement, they were generally strongest in the same regions as the radical holiness groups, namely the rural Midwest and the South. They tended to be poorer than holiness church members. Most important from our point of view, they were not particularly successful in California before 1920.

This last statement may seem strange, for it is widely known that one of the great early pentecostal revivals was the one led by black minister William Seymour at Azusa Street in Los Angeles, beginning in 1906. Yet all accounts of that revival show that it was a cosmopolitan pentecostal station that had little long-term effect on its region. After the first outbreaks of glossolalia, Azusa Street became well known, and church people from many parts of the country visited it to see the great events and participate in the spiritual blessings. Most of the visitors soon left, returning to their home states or mission areas to evangelize and spread the news. California was left with a few small pentecostal churches, but nothing like what one would expect from the impact of Azusa Street on the rest of the nation.[29] Not until after World War I, when Aimee Semple McPherson established her International Church of the Foursquare Gospel, did a large pentecostal church take root and make a significant impact on southern California Protestantism.[30]

Bresee's Church of the Nazarene from 1895 to 1915 was a unique movement. Thoroughly evangelistic in format and doctrine, it nevertheless had a distinctly mystical slant. Bresee's Wesleyan background made that an easy development; the early holiness movement sought a dramatic purifying experience that would bring one inwardly closer to God, making one become like God. Bresee took the holiness theology a step farther, defining it more precisely as a mystical experience centered in the mind—the transrational mind, not the mind of ordinary logic. As a result his descriptions sound like a combination of Transcendentalism and Holiness. Similarly, his young colleague Wiley integrated an organic and expansive view of the Spirit into his theology, while also acknowledging the mystical tendencies in every soul. Neither man went the way of New Thought with its "floating on the Infinite": Wiley warned against "quietism," while Bresee found a different language of religious experience that seems to have avoided the paradox of activity and passivity that plagued liberals like James Campbell. Bresee thus communicated a mysticism that was truly inward and empowering, yet neither totally passive-receptive nor urgently active, willful, and outgoing.

Bresee's originality, command of language, and obvious expertise in holiness experience account for much of his power and popularity during the first twenty years of the Nazarene church. As a preacher he encouraged congregational participation and held a lively service without relying on special spiritual events such as speaking in tongues. His relationship with his congregation and the message he preached were apparently successful in guiding southern California Protestants along the holiness path. Bresee's idiosyncratic language could capture their hearts and minds because they were open to his style of religiosity: like their upper-middle-class counterparts in the liberal churches, his followers sought a mystical experience that was more than emotional, one that would grow over time and help them gain in clarity and strength. Bresee seldom reminded his audiences of their fears and anxieties, let alone their nervous or other ailments, nor did he use psychological language in speaking of the results he hoped people would achieve. Yet he helped his followers, as did the New Thoughters and liberals we have considered, to find stability, direction, and strength within themselves.

The urban holiness movement in southern California, under Bresee's leadership for two decades, thus provided a highly integrative religious experience for those Protestants attracted to it. For middle-class midwesterners it provided a familiar revivalistic context, while Bresee's message in particular was relevant to their life in California, both outwardly and inwardly so new and disturbing. Bresee's synthesis shows that the influence of alternative, metaphysical-mystical thought was not limited to a single Protestant tradition or socioeconomic stratum. Furthermore, where our records tend to show traditional Protestantism in conflict with the new ways of thinking, Bresee went beyond debate to create a satisfying and inspiring understanding of Christian experience that was congruent with the new waves of thought as well. Whether his synthesis, or those of men like James Campbell and Joseph Widney, would affect Protestantism in California in the long run remained to be seen.

8. Into the Sierras

By 1910 the Anglo-Protestant tradition in California found itself sharing its territory, already small, with a vocal alternative tradition that was more mystical, individualistic, and inward-directed. The major institutions of this tradition were the metaphysical religions: Theosophy, New Thought, and Christian Science. According to the 1906 census, the metaphysical groups constituted nearly 5 percent of the Protestant population; if we add the Unitarians, the major liberal denomination, the total is 6 percent. While that may seem a very small minority, it was larger than in any other state except Massachusetts, where these groups amounted to over 10 percent, due in part to an unusually high Unitarian membership and a disproportionate number of Christian Scientists registered as members of the Mother Church in Boston (though they did not necessarily reside there). Even in New York and Illinois, the next closest contenders, only 2.4 and 2.5 percent, respectively, of the Protestant population belonged to these groups. These figures do not include the many people influenced by the literature of these groups or by churchmen who adopted language or concepts from the metaphysical, mystical traditions.

In California, the metaphysical religions and a handful of liberal leaders were not the only ones tending toward a broader concept of spirituality. The metaphysical traditions were weak in one area where our first liberal, Starr King, had excelled: appreciating nature and understanding the natural world in a spiritual framework. Some Californians took up the path of nature and, with a devout attachment to the Emersonian Transcendentalism that had inspired many dissenters, created yet another form of spirituality. They sought their religious experience and their source of personal stability outside all organizations, in nature itself. Like Starr King, they found messages from the divine in nature, and looked for virtually nothing from books or organizations. We cannot analyze this group sociologically; except for a few conservationist groups, they were unorganized. But by the turn of the century they too had a leader, whose name became almost synonymous with the cause of nature in California: John Muir.

Born in Scotland in 1838, John Muir came with his family to Wisconsin while still a boy. Raised in a strict Protestant home—his father did not hesitate to use violence to "help" his children learn—John took every chance he had to follow his own inclinations. He loved to invent machines and discover how things worked; this trait would later blossom into a great scientific mind. When he could steal a moment out of his father's sight, he loved to read literature and poetry instead of Calvinist teachings. He survived the rigors of his upbringing, left home at age twenty-two, and went to the University of Wisconsin at Madison in 1861. He intended to go on to study medicine at the University of Michigan, but traveled in Canada instead. He worked for a brief period in Indiana to earn money. Then an eye injury that resulted in temporary loss of sight led to his decision to take another journey. He wrote:

> As soon as I got out into Heaven's light I started on another long excursion, making haste with all my heart to store my mind with the Lord's beauty and thus be ready for any fate, light or dark. And it was from this time that my long continuous wanderings may be said to have fairly commenced. I bade adieu to all my mechanical inventions, determined to devote the rest of my life to the study of the inventions of God.[1]

"The inventions of God" was no mere metaphor. John Muir's writings reveal an intensely religious man who believed that religion in his time had become so constricted that people did not know what their lives were about. His conviction grew that only a return to contact with nature could restore one's true soul. He felt himself driven to wander, "carried of the spirit into the wilderness," he wrote. He walked a thousand miles from Indiana to Florida. Hoping to go on to the Caribbean and South America, he changed his mind after an attack of malaria and headed for California. The wilds of the golden state, and especially the Sierra Nevada, became his home. Though he dearly loved family and friends, though he married and spent some periods of time in the lowlands to work, farm, write, and talk about his concern for preserving natural sites, he always returned to the mountains, spending long stretches alone in the forests, meadows, and valleys of the Sierra. By 1872 he had begun writing articles for

Overland and other periodicals, describing the wonders of Yosemite and arguing for the theory of glaciation (rather than the accepted catastrophic theory) in the formation of the great Yosemite Valley. By 1875 he began to be active in what would be his great public mission, the preservation of the wilderness for future generations. An article in the *Sacramento Record-Union* on February 5, 1875, was his first public argument. Headlined "GOD'S FIRST TEMPLES," it began, "How Shall We Preserve Our Forests?"

As this first headline indicates, however, Muir was not making merely aesthetic or even scientific arguments for conservation. In his writings, public speeches, and private communications he liberally spoke of God behind all the beauty that humans experience. Like Emerson, whom he deeply admired, he had an expansive concept of God that went beyond all organized religion. Already in 1865, writing in the journal of his thousand-mile walk, he criticized traditional concepts of death:

> [On] no subject are our ideas more warped and pitiable than on death. Instead of the friendly sympathy, the union of life and death so apparent in Nature, we are taught that death is an accident, a deplorable punishment for the oldest sin. . . . And upon these primary, never-to-be-questioned dogmas, our experiences are founded, tissue after tissue in hideous development, until they form the grimmest body to be found in the whole catalogue of civilized Christian manufactures. . . . But let a child walk with Nature, let him behold the beautiful blendings and communions of death and life, . . . and they will learn that death is stingless indeed, and has no victory, for it never fights. All is divine harmony.[2]

At a time when many liberals were questioning received doctrines about death and the afterlife, Muir was developing a way of thinking that understood humans as only "a small part of the one great unit of creation."[3]

On coming to California, Muir developed and enriched his sense of harmonious being in the natural world. After walking with a companion in the Santa Clara valley (the San Jose area) shortly after his arrival in 1868, Muir exclaimed about the pure air, the bright skies, and even the variety of tastes in the air itself. "We were new creatures," he wrote, "born again; and truly not until this time were we fairly conscious that we were born at all. Never more . . . shall I sentimentalize about getting free from the flesh, for it is steeped like a sponge in immortal pleasure."[4] Yet Muir was not about to become a

materialist; he did not give up traditional beliefs, only narrow interpretations of them. He fully believed in the spiritual aspect of human
beings, and he experienced in nature continual confirmation of it:

> No sane man in the hands of Nature can doubt the doubleness of his life.
> Soul and body receive separate nourishment and separate exercise, and
> speedily reach a stage of development wherein each is easily known apart
> from the other. Living artificially, we seldom see much of our real selves.
> Our torpid souls are hopelessly entangled with our torpid bodies, and
> . . . we hardly possess a separate existence from our neighbors.[5]

He believed in the immortality of the soul; he wrote to a friend in
1900 that death does not merely separate two loved ones, it also
unites them: "The sense of loneliness grows less and less as we become accustomed to the new light, communing with those who have
gone on ahead in spirit, and feeling their influence as if again present
in the flesh."[6] His understanding of traditional rites and ceremonies
was also highly spiritualized; he saw them as beautiful and impressive, communicating good to everyone involved when done rightly.
The mistake of traditional religion, he believed, was in letting the
beauties of spiritual things become points of dispute and arguing
over who should be allowed to take communion or how baptism
should be performed. All beliefs and rituals were figures through
which God communicated with us, and which were understood
most fully in our own experience. For Muir that always meant
experience of nature. Thus, after expounding angrily against the
narrow-mindedness of the church in an 1870 letter to his brother
David, he wrote in a more jocular vein:

> I was baptized three times this morning, 1st (according to the old way of
> dividing the sermon), in balmy sunshine that penetrated to my very soul,
> warming all the faculties of spirit, as well as the joints and marrows of
> the body; 2d, in the mysterious rays of beauty that emanate from plant
> corollas; and 3d, in the spray of the lower Yosemite Falls. My first bap-
> tism was by immersion, the 2d by pouring, and the 3d by sprinkling. Con-
> sequently all Baptists are my brethering [*sic*], and all will allow that I've
> "got religion."[7]

Within his lighthearted parody is an allegory of nature and spirit that
was becoming familiar to many Californians.

In the writings that reached the California public from the early
1870s to his death in 1914, Muir continued to put forth a view not

unlike that of Thomas Starr King in the 1860s: nature is God's book; through sensitivity to nature we can appreciate God directly. Yet, as Starr King was remembered mostly as a patriot, so Muir was viewed mostly as a conservationist. As president of the newly formed Sierra Club in 1892, and as a hiking companion of Theodore Roosevelt, Muir became guardian of the wilderness. But Muir, like King, was also a prophetic voice in that wilderness, calling on Californians to restore their spiritual as well as their physical health by rediscovering the world beyond civilization. Human beings had to be understood anew in the light of nature itself:

> How little do we know of ourselves, of our profoundest attractions and repulsions, of our spiritual affinities! How interesting does man become considered in his relations to the spirit of this rock and water! How significant does every atom of our world become amid the influences of those beings unseen, spiritual, angelic mountaineers that so throng these pure mansions of crystal foam and purple granite.[8]

Like Starr King, Muir never urged anyone to leave a church or give up any religious customs, but only to discover deeper levels of themselves and reach out for broader understanding.

Muir needed none of the metaphysical religions, with their belief that thought could heal; he received healing and strength from the wilderness. Yet the metaphysicians and Muir are related in their rejection of the Anglo-Protestant tradition in favor of other models of spirituality. The New Thoughters had a non-doctrinal attitude toward religion, just as Muir tried to wipe away the constriction and negativity of dogmas and debates. Many of them emphasized the unity of creation, seeing the glory of God in all of it: for example, Joseph Widney, with his God of "the open." Muir knew the power of being alone with oneself in the wilderness; the mystics also spoke of the strength one could gain from an inward journey.

Muir experienced in the mountains what thinkers of the alternative tradition would call the "divine influx" or "indwelling of the presence." Unity with the divine came to him mediated through nature and the experience of his own physicality. In *My First Summer in the Sierras* he wrote:

> We are now in the mountains, and they are in us, kindling enthusiasm, making every nerve quiver, filling every pore and cell of us. Our flesh-and-bone tabernacle seems transparent as glass to the beauty about us,

as if truly an inseparable part of it, thrilling with the air and trees, streams and rocks, in the waves of the sun, —a part of all nature, neither old nor young, sick nor well, but immortal.

Kevin Starr has pointed out that at times of this sort of mystical union, and at times of crisis, Muir "felt himself in contact with an Other Self, a spiritual projection of his ego in mystical harmony with the mountains."⁹ This other self was his source of deliverance from danger, a source of spiritual sight and wisdom that at times was literally his salvation. The means were different, but the end was in some respects similar: the metaphysicians' effort to transcend the ordinary mind and Muir's work of climbing mountains could both bring a spiritual apprehension or sense of divine unity that was beyond ordinary experience.

Those who followed Muir's paths into the wilderness and those who joined his efforts to save California's beauty for future generations also were heirs of the Transcendental tradition. They sensed the mystery of God as creator more than as judge or redeemer from sin. Like their metaphysical relatives they longed for inner peace and closeness to God, and they found it in opening themselves to the wonders of nature. They could leave the building of cities and railroads to others. Yet, if we can judge from the founders of the Sierra Club, these Californians were not withdrawing from society; as Kevin Starr points out, they were upper-middle-class professionals (not necessarily the very wealthy), many of them educators. Like David Starr Jordan, president of Stanford University, they would pass on to succeeding generations their feeling for the beauties of nature and their broad-minded consciousness of God. The Anglo-Protestant tradition many of them had inherited had been transformed into a transcendental faith; for they, like John Muir, were Californians rebaptized in the wilderness.

Epilogue

The forms of religious expression and experience that the Anglo-Protestant churches mediated dealt in one way with the inner conflicts, social upheavals, and new environment that Protestant Californians experienced, but for many they were insufficient. As a result, certain alternatives developed in California to a greater degree than elsewhere. Among these alternatives were the metaphysical religions, already begun in the East but far more popular on the West Coast. A number of church leaders—ministers such as James Campbell, Charles Reynolds Brown, and even in a denomination usually regarded as conservative, Phineas Bresee—adopted some of their ideas. Others, such as Benjamin Fay Mills, immersed themselves fully in one of the new traditions; while an occasional individual like Joseph P. Widney preferred to carve his own path. Although these Protestants do not fit into a single category or well-defined movement, they resemble the popular liberals of an earlier generation, Thomas Starr King and Laurentine Hamilton. So do the lovers of nature like John Muir. With Emerson's writings his constant companion, he made transcendentalism an active religion and eventually put it to work behind the cause of conservation. For many, Muir's writings became the impetus for their own spiritual development, which was, like the metaphysical religions, away from the confines of tradition.

We began this study by asking what happened, in California, to the great evangelical tradition that had conquered earlier frontiers. The many complaints of ministers about secularism and materialism certainly indicate one side of the truth: many Californians made wealth and pleasure their primary pursuits. Also, the cosmopolitanism of the region from the beginning restricted Protestant success: large numbers of Roman Catholics and Orientals and significant minorities of blacks and Jews started off on a more or less equal footing in California, while the secular democratic tradition limited outright persecution and discrimination.

Given these constraints, however, a strongly unified Anglo-Protestant population might yet have made a deep imprint on California society. The leaders certainly tried. With schools and universities as well as churches, they made great efforts to shape California in the mold of the upright Protestant societies they had known. But they found their potential supporters reluctant to put their energies fully behind the traditional enterprises. Some Protestants had undoubtedly given up religion for the pursuit of wealth. Others, however, saw institutional religion as barren, while yet retaining some of their faith. Like John Muir, they could not accept certain traditional doctrines, and certainly could not see the point of engaging in disputes over them. These, we may expect, were the people most open to new spiritual explorations.

To traditional ministers these Protestants may have seemed very secular, taking their pleasures in mountain vacations or focusing on their physical health. Some, with their interest in esoteric doctrines or meditations, may have seemed on the verge of idolatry. Behind the appearances was a search for a different kind of spiritual satisfaction and a different orientation toward the world. The practitioners of the alternative traditions believed they had found a religiosity less severe and more rational—but also beyond the rational, promising inner growth and an increasing sense of closeness with God.

We have suggested that the relative isolation of many Anglo-Protestant Californians contributed to the search for another religious alternative: without strong family connections or traditional communities, they sought forms of spirituality that could be practiced alone. Adventurers in many ways, they were drawn to the spiritual frontiers beyond traditional doctrine and practice. At the same time, while their journeys into the mind or the wilderness could be undertaken alone, the groups that formed around this common search could be sources of support making the break with family and tradition easier while not restricting individual freedom. The independence that early Californians so valued could continue in many of the metaphysical traditions and in the religion of nature.

The fact that significant numbers of Anglo-Protestants took up such alternatives does not mean, as we have emphasized before, that the very existence of the churches was threatened. Many people continued to cherish the old communities and traditions and use the forms of spirituality that had been handed down. Many, for example, experienced themselves as sinners needing to be relieved of their guilt; they saw the imperfections of human nature and rejected the perfectionist impulses of New Thought. Most of all, they expressed over and over again a concern for social order, and they brought together the resources, financial and organizational, to help build a new society. The churches they built thus remained important features of Anglo-Protestant social systems and a highly positive moral force. The weakness of the churches appears only when compared to other sections of the nation, and is seen in somewhat smaller membership figures and a noticeable lack of "enthusiasm," as Josiah Royce observed. It was as if Anglo-Protestant churchpeople, for much of the period between 1850 and 1915, had to live with a continual question mark, a recurring suspicion expressed by advocates of the alternative tradition: Do our religious differences really matter? Is God really the kind of being we have learned he is? Is this the most effective way to relate to God? Is this, ultimately, real religion? The reservations such questions created subtly diminished the power of the Anglo-Protestant tradition in California, even among its own people.

Thus, while Anglo-Protestantism lost its cultural power for many reasons, one highly significant factor was the presence of the alternative traditions with their metaphysical and mystical emphases. They offered an attractive picture of the "substance" behind the "show," to use Starr King's terms, and showed how a person could apprehend that true spiritual substance. Mary Baker Eddy's Divine Mind, Benjamin Fay Mills's "divinity of man," Phineas Bresee's divine Presence, all suggested the broader, deeper spiritual world. Even though their numbers were small, the people who voiced these alternatives weakened tradition and in some ways strengthened secularism, as the Seventh-day Adventists had unwittingly done in the 1870s and 1880s. For by offering a version of religion that claimed to be spiritual rather than traditional, they broadened the concept of religion and made it impossible for any one group to speak for God's truth.

The Protestant landscape in 1915, the result of three or more generations of adjustment to California, contained a well-established network of denominations, each strong in its own right while cooperating on occasional joint ventures, plus a strong undercurrent of unrest related to the explorations in mind, nature, and holiness that had attracted many. That landscape would change in the period following World War I. Another important wave of immigrants, especially from the South, would bring a strong conservative Protestant population that would support, in Los Angeles, revivalists like Aimee Semple McPherson and Robert Schuller. Nevertheless the soil that welcomed unorthodox religious movements had been well fertilized, and there would be a congenial atmosphere for Hindu and Buddhist leaders organizing to bring their versions of religious truth to America. These and other alternative groups would, however, remain very small until after World War II.

But these developments were in the future. Looking back to 1910, we can see that the culture of Anglo-Protestants in California over the generations since the American conquest had developed certain tendencies and nourished certain potentials that made it distinct from the rest of the nation. From the visionary oratory of Starr King to the wilderness mysticism of John Muir, from the liberal rationalism of Laurentine Hamilton to the positive thinking of New Thoughters, from the embattled orthodoxy of Sabbath campaigners to the careful constructions of Charles Reynolds Brown and James Campbell, from the street preaching of William Taylor to the expansive holiness of Phineas Bresee, California Protestants wove a rich tapestry of religious culture, of many different yet complementary threads. The early missionaries had failed to construct a replica of the society of Iowa or Massachusetts; but the interaction among Protestants of many different tendencies created a history and a culture with its own character, a part of California whose traces are still with us. In the battles they fought, the issues with which they struggled, and the adjustments they made in lifestyle and attitude, we can see issues of social, moral and religious significance for modern America as a whole.

Notes

Preface

1. Very recently, there has been additional interest in western regional studies in religion. See Carl Guarneri and David Alvarez, editors, *Religion and Society in the American West* (forthcoming: University Press of America) and, for bibliographical assistance, essays on religious archives in Doyce B. Nunis, Jr., and Gloria R. Lothrop, editors, *A Guide to the History of California* (forthcoming: Greenwood Press). Regional American religious history has also received some general attention; see, for example, Samuel Hill, "Religion and Region in America," *The Annals of the American Academy of Political and Social Science* (July 1985).

Chapter 1: California Dreams

1. Joseph A. Benton, *California As She Was: As She Is: As She Is to Be* (San Francisco, 1850), 5, 12. Kenneth L. Janzen, in "The Transformation of the New England Tradition in California, 1849–1860" (Ph.D. thesis, Claremont Graduate School, 1964), uses Benton as the prime example of the New England mind. For an Episcopal bishop's version of the transformation hoped for from civilized cultivation of the land, see William Ingraham Kip, *A California Pilgrimage* (Fresno, Calif., 1921), 26.

2. William C. Pond, *Gospel Pioneering: Reminiscences of Early Congregationalism in California 1833–1920* (Oberlin, Ohio, 1921).

3. James A. Woods, *A Sermon at the Dedication of the Presbyterian Church of Stockton, California, May 5, 1850* (Barre: Patriot Press, 1851), 14. Woods added the hope that now, through California, Christianity could shed its light on China and "Hindostan." The Pacific orientation recurs throughout California literature, but its effects on religion are small in the early period. As we will see, a few Protestant ministers, notably the Reverends A. W. Loomis and Wil-

liam Speer, tried to pass on to their fellow Protestants an appreciation of Chinese culture while at the same time trying to convert the
Chinese to Christianity.

4. *California Christian Advocate*, October 10, 1851.

5. Darius Stokes, *A Lecture Upon the Moral and Religious Elevation of the People of California* (San Francisco, 1853), delivered
June, 1853, at the AME Church, Sacramento. Compare Mifflin Wister Gibbs, another black minister, who claimed to see in the American expansion into California the exemplary fulfillment of moral law
(*Shadow and Light: An Autobiography* [Washington, D.C., 1902]).
In this kind of imperial consciousness, black Protestants were in ac-
cord with their white counterparts. They also had to struggle, however, for their own rights in a California that was as discriminatory
as most northern states at this time. See Douglas Henry Daniels, *Pioneer Urbanites* (Philadelphia: Temple University Press, 1980).

6. Lorenzo Waugh, *Autobiography*, 3rd edition (San Francisco:
S. P. Taylor & Co., 1885), 194–95, 217–19. Waugh came to California in part because of a vision in 1851 of a beautiful valley, which
he claimed to recognize when he arrived in Petaluma. This is the
same Waugh who was a famous midwestern circuit rider and Indian
missionary. For similar glorification of California, see J. C. Simmons,
My Trip to the Orient (San Francisco: Whitaker and Ray, 1902),
182: "Of all the lands I have seen, there is none to compare with
America, and in America, none to compare with California."

7. William Taylor, a Methodist street preacher and later a famous
bishop, saw San Francisco as "the Sebastopol of his Satanic majesty"
(referring not to California's town of that name, but to the seige of
the Russian city Sebastopol). See Taylor's *Seven Years Street Preaching in San Francisco* (New York, 1856), 342; and Douglas Anderson,
"Give Up Strong Drink, Go to Work, and Become a Man: William
Taylor in Gold Rush San Francisco," paper presented at the American Academy of Religion, Western Region, March 1982. For other
concerns about the temptations of California, see the *Pacific* and the
California Christian Advocate in their early years. As late as 1868
the *Occident* was complaining about the lack of home influence, of
respect for reputation, and of watchful neighbors to keep society's
morals in order. On the lack of unity, see Albert Williams, *A Pioneer
Pastorate and Times* (San Francisco: Wallace & Hassett, 1879), 193.
For an excellent description of the subtle differences in ministers' attitudes and aims, see Kevin Starr, *Americans and the California*

Dream, 1850–1915 (New York: Oxford University Press, 1973), especially 87–97; see also Richard Lyle Power, "A Crusade to Extend Yankee Culture," *New England Quarterly* 13 (1940): 638–53; and the comments on manifest destiny by Colin B. Goodykoontz, "Protestant Home Missions and Education in the Trans-Mississippi West, 1835–1860," in *The Trans-Mississippi West*, edited by James F. Willard and Colin B. Goodykoontz (Boulder: University of Colorado, 1930).

8. Quoted in Power, "Crusade," 645.

9. Ibid., 647.

10. S. D. Simonds, in the *California Christian Advocate* of July 1, 1852, was proud that the first ceremonial cornerstone laying he had seen was at a church in Sacramento, suggesting that churches were indeed the pillars of society.

11. *Pacific*, August 1, 1851, 1.

12. *Occident*, January 4, 1868, 2.

13. *California Christian Advocate*, October 10, 1851, 1.

14. Ibid., August 22, 1867, 2.

15. Ibid., November 7, 1867, 1.

16. *Occident*, January 4, 1868, 1.

17. *Evangel*, January 29 and February 6, 1874.

18. *California Christian Advocate*, November 7, 1867, 1.

19. For accounts of various aspects of California religious enterprises, see Starr, *California Dream*, chapter 3; William Hanchett, "The Question of Religion and the Taming of California, 1849–1854," *California Historical Society Quarterly* 32 (1953): 49–56, 119–44; William Warren Ferrier, "The Origins and Growth of the Protestant Church on the Pacific Coast," in *Religious Progress on the Pacific Slope*, edited by Charles Sumner Nash and John Wright Buckham (Boston: Pilgrim Press, 1917); Norton Wesley, "'Like a Thousand Preachers Flying': Religious Newspapers on the Pacific Coast to 1865," *California Historical Society Quarterly* 56 (1977): 194–209; Charles S. Greene, *Magazine Publishing in California* (San Francisco: Library Association of California, 1898). Denominational histories include Sandford Fleming, *God's Gold: The Story of Baptist Beginnings in California, 1849–60* (Philadelphia: Judson Press, 1949); C. V. Anthony, *Fifty Years of Methodism* (San Francisco: Methodist Book Concern, 1901); Arnold Crompton, *Unitarianism on the Pacific Coast: The First Sixty Years* (Boston: Beacon Press, 1957); Clifford M. Drury, "The Beginnings of the Presbyte-

rian Church on the Pacific Coast," *Pacific Historical Review* 9 (June 1940): 195–204, and *The Centennial of the Synod of California* (Presbyterian Synod, 1951); Janzen, "Transformation"; Floyd Looney, *History of California Southern Baptists* (Fresno, Calif., 1954); E. B. Ware, *History of the Disciples of Christ in California* (Healdsburg, Calif., 1916); W. B. West, Jr., "Origin and Growth of the Churches of Christ in California" (M.A. thesis, University of Southern California, 1936). See also Kenneth Wilson Moore, "Areas of Impact of Protestantism upon the Cultural Development of Northern California, 1850–1870" (M.A. thesis, Pacific School of Religion, 1970). It is no accident that most of these studies deal with the first ten to twenty years of California Protestantism; for, as I will show below, after that time much of the energy of church leaders goes into maintaining what they have built and dealing with the challenges of other groups.

20. On schools, see Clifford M. Drury, "Church-Sponsored Schools in Early California," *Pacific Historian* 20 (1976): 158–66; on Sabbatarian agitation, William Hanchett, "The Blue Law Gospel in Gold Rush California," *Pacific Historical Review* 24 (1955): 361–68, and below, Chapter 4.

21. The Vigilantes appear in any basic California history; for their connection with evangelical Protestantism, see Starr, *California Dream*, 106. Starr argues that the mercantile establishment controlled the whole enterprise and that the ministers simply allowed themselves and their pulpits to be used because the Vigilantes represented their fantasies of cleansing regeneration. Such an extreme interpretation is unnecessary; it is likely that the Protestant leadership for the most part shared the same social and moral values as the merchants. Most preferred not to see that the Vigilantes were sometimes perpetrating evils as great as their opponents were.

22. Josiah Royce, *California: From the Conquest in 1846 to the Second Vigilance Committee in San Francisco: A Study of American Character* (New York: Alfred A. Knopf, 1948), 316–17. There is considerable evidence supporting Royce's contention that people wanted churches to prosper, in the first ten or fifteen years of the American period in California. Despite clerical complaints about an unsympathetic press, the early papers, especially those outside San Francisco, urged the importance of religion without favoring denominations as such. See, for example, the *Petaluma Journal* and the *Sonoma County Journal* (Santa Rosa), both of which extolled the

spiritual influences of home and mother and carried occasional reports of camp meetings or revivals in the churches. In the mining country, when the *Placerville Herald* in 1853 published "The Miner's Ten Commandments," reminding the men especially of the duty of Sabbath observance, the paper sold triple editions. See also Rodman Paul, *Mining Frontiers of the Far West 1848–1880* (New York: Holt, Rinehart & Winston, 1963), 46, 164–65. Even in San Francisco, the *Herald* was kind enough to report in 1856 that religion there would compare well with that in any northern city (cited in Fleming, *God's Gold*, 118). It is true, however, that the secular papers declined over the years in their promotion of, or kind words for, specific religious activities.

23. Denominational and general secular histories of California usually do not mention the 1858 revival; an exception is Fleming in *God's Gold*. Starr, *California Dream*, reports simply that "a religious revival followed the upheavals" of 1856 (p. 95), thus linking it to the Vigilantes. Revivals in general were far less popular than on earlier frontiers. Anthony's *Methodism* mentions a few traveling evangelists, notably Maggie Van Cott and A. B. Earle (Earle's were holiness revivals); Pond, in *Gospel Pioneering*, also refers to an Earle revival in Petaluma in 1866. Anthony mentions that the Methodists did not do well at union (that is, interdenominational) meetings. For a treatment of later mass revivals held by D. L. Moody, see Douglas F. Anderson, "'You Californians': San Francisco Evangelicalism, Regional Religious Identity, and the Revivalism of D. L. Moody," *Fides et Historia* 15 (Spring/Summer 1983): 44–66.

24. Williams, *Pioneer Pastorate*, 158.

25. Philo F. Phelps, *The Relief Signal in the Hour of Need*, sermon at First Presbyterian Church (San Francisco, 1880).

26. *Pacific Methodist*, December 21, 1871.

27. *Petaluma Daily Crescent*, December 11, 1870, 2.

28. "Selected Letters of Osgood Church Wheeler," edited by Sandford Fleming, *California Historical Society Quarterly* 27 (1948): 9–18, 123–31, 229–36, 301–9; letter of August 1, 1849. A similar observation was made in later years by Presbyterian minister Robert Mackenzie, reviewing the history of his denomination in California: the pressure of material things was always so great that it took a great effort to make people pay attention to the cause of the kingdom of God (in *Californian Illustrated* [April 1892]: 441). Charles A. Farley, a Unitarian minister, wrote that in California "a

nation has literally been born in a day; a nation the strangest and most miscellaneous ever brought together . . . animated primarily, it must be confessed, by . . . a passion for money." See "The Moral Aspect of California: A Thanksgiving Sermon of 1850," introduction by Clifford M. Drury, *California Historical Society Quarterly* 19 (1940): 302.

29. William Taylor, *Seven Years*, 342.

30. For some description see Paul, *Mining Frontiers*, and Earl Pomeroy, *The Pacific Slope: A History of California, Oregon, Washington, Idaho, Utah, and Nevada* (New York: Alfred A. Knopf, 1966). Dorothy O. Johansen has argued persuasively that California immigrants were self-selected to be of a different temperament than other westward migrants who went, at roughly the same time, to Oregon. Because of different kinds of promotion and publicity, the Oregon fever of 1842 had attracted more sober, conservative, and "respectable" people; California attracted the risk-takers. See "A Working Hypothesis for the Study of Migrations," *Pacific Historical Review* 36 (1967): 1–12.

31. The cosmopolitan character of early California is treated in Pomeroy, *Pacific Slope*, 160–62; Moses Rischin, "Immigration, Migration, and Minorities in California," in *Essays and Assays: California History Reappraised*, edited by George H. Knoles (California Historical Society, Ward Ritchie Press, 1973); and Doris Marion Wright, "The Making of Cosmopolitan California, 1840–1870: An Analysis of Immigration," *California Historical Society Quarterly* 19 (1940), 20 (1941).

32. See, for example, the comments on Californians' independence in religion in Ella M. Robinson, *Lighter of Gospel Fires, John N. Loughborough* (Mountain View, Calif.: Pacific Press, 1954), 129. The struggles to organize the state, its legal system, and its government, as well as the battles over land titles, are recounted in any good general history of the state.

33. Janzen, "Transformation," chapter 3; Starr, *California Dream*, 106.

34. Contemporary men's experience was not emphasized in mid-century Anglo-Protestantism; as many recent studies have noted, this was the period of "feminization" in American religion. See especially Ann Douglas, *The Feminization of American Culture* (New York: Alfred A. Knopf, 1977); and Sandra S. Sizer [Frankiel], *Gospel Hymns and Social Religion: The Rhetoric of Nineteenth-Century*

Revivalism (Philadelphia: Temple University Press, 1978), chapter 4. The 1857–58 "businessmen's revival" might be seen as an early attempt to reclaim Christianity for men, but it was not until the Moody revivals with their young men's meetings, and even more Billy Sunday with his sportsman's appeal, that we find specific attention to the male side.

35. Horace Bushnell, on a visit to California in 1856, exhorted Californians to support the churches precisely because they were guardians of order. This was, of course, the disturbing Vigilante period. See Bushnell's *Society and Religion: A Sermon for California* (San Francisco, 1856).

36. On the insanity issue, see the discussion in Crerar Douglas, "The Gold Rush and the Kingdom of God: The Rev. James Woods' Cure of Souls," in *The American West and the Religious Experience*, edited by William M. Kramer (Los Angeles: Will Kramer, 1975).

37. John Higham has argued persuasively that the midcentury years marked a transition from expansiveness to control in his *From Boundlessness to Consolidation: The Transformation of American Culture* (Ann Arbor, Mich.: William L. Clements Library, 1969). In religion, one can certainly observe that movement from open, highly emotional revivals to sentimentalism in Henry Ward Beecher and Dwight L. Moody. I have traced some of this trend in my *Gospel Hymns*. Lawrence Foster has identified similar dynamics in the areas of family and sexuality, in his *Religion and Sexuality: Three American Communal Experiments of the Nineteenth Century* (New York: Oxford University Press, 1981). California, for the reasons of social history I have already presented, was a special case of this broader trend.

38. On interdenominational cooperation in the early years, see *California Christian Advocate*, April 23, 1868, and Kip, *California Pilgrimage*, 27–28. Janzen argues as a primary thesis that the California situation led to Congregationalists becoming nondenominational in ideology; Fleming's *God's Gold* shows the Baptist contrast. The quotation is from the *Occident*, February 13, 1869, 85.

39. Williams, *Pioneer Pastorate*, 119, 193.

40. Josiah Royce, *Race Questions, Provincialism, and Other American Problems* (New York: Macmillan, 1908), 70.

41. For one example among many, see William Ingraham Kip, *Early Days of My Episcopate* (New York: Thomas Whittaker, 1892).

42. James A. Woods, *Recollections of Pioneer Work in California* (San Francisco: Joseph Winterburn, 1878), 47; Joseph J. Mc-Closkey in *Christmas in the Gold Fields, 1849* (San Francisco: California Historical Society, 1959).

43. Starr, *California Dream*, 413; his entire discussion, pp. 374–423, is highly illuminating.

44. See the *California Christian Advocate*, October 17, 1867, for comments on how the Chinese were showing fewer of these bad traits after having been in America.

45. *Pacific*, May 7, 1852.

46. It seems that some clergymen were wont to engage in self-deception about the effects of missions to Asians—or at least to exaggerate them. For example, the *Evangel* (Baptist) printed a letter from a missionary to Japan claiming not only that many Japanese were now looking to Western culture and religion for inspiration but also that "all feel that Bhudisha [*sic*] is a sham" (January 29, 1874). They also assumed, as hinted in the *California Christian Advocate* article cited above, n. 44, that a decrease in the Asian peoples' presumed negative traits meant a greater openness to Christianity.

47. *California Christian Advocate*, October 10, 1851.

48. *New Englander* 60 (1858): 157.

49. *Occident*, February 1, 1868.

50. O. P. Fitzgerald, *California Sketches* (Nashville, Tenn.: Methodist Episcopal Church, South, 1896), 208.

51. There were, of course, Eastern churchmen who were known for their responsiveness to and sermons upon the beauties of nature and the inner meaning of nature. Some were in the dissident liberal tradition, like Theodore Parker and Ralph Waldo Emerson; others were closer to the mainstream, like Henry Ward Beecher. Emerson, of course, became the inspiration for many who were spiritually drawn to nature as well as for people in the alternative metaphysical traditions that we will consider in Chapter 5.

Chapter 2: The Gospel of Unity

1. Thomas Starr King, quoted in Richard Frothingham, *A Tribute to Thomas Starr King* (Boston: Ticknor and Fields, 1865), 200. Among the others pleading the Union cause was another minister, Martin C. Briggs of the Methodist Church (see Anthony, *Methodism*, 34). On the Southern sympathizers in California, see Benjamin

Franklin Gilbert, "The Confederate Minority in California," *California Historical Society Quarterly* 20 (1941). The "Pacific Republic" idea was espoused by Governor Weller and many in the Democratic party. Starr King was careful not to antagonize that element directly by attacking the idea of independence; but he was merciless in his attacks on the South's "treachery." He countered the independence idea indirectly, by appealing to a sense that California's destiny was interrelated with that of the rest of the nation.

2. The phrase is the title of one of King's lectures on Unitarianism; see below.

3. Edwin P. Whipple, Introduction to *Substance and Show, and Other Lectures*, by Thomas Starr King (Boston: James R. Osgood, 1877), xvii.

4. Information about Starr King's life is taken from the (mostly eulogistic) biographies. Notable among them is Arnold Crompton's *Apostle of Liberty: Starr King in California* (Boston, 1950); others include Frothingham's *Tribute*, cited in n. 1; William Day Simonds, *Starr King in California* (San Francisco: P. Elder, 1917); and Charles W. Wendte, *Thomas Starr King, Patriot and Preacher* (Boston, 1921). A critical biography of King is very much needed.

5. Edwin P. Whipple, Introduction to *Christianity and Humanity*, by Thomas Starr King (Boston: James R. Osgood, 1877), xlv.

6. On his nearness to orthodoxy, see the comments in the *Pacific*, January 10, 1861, on his sermon on the Lord's Prayer. The *Pacific* was glad to see him preaching obedience to God's will, since (the editors assumed) that would mean he would advocate the proper worship of Jesus Christ as divine. His admirer Whipple actually claimed (in his Introduction, cited in n. 5) that King was as much an evangelical as Jonathan Edwards, because he believed in the transforming power of the Holy Spirit! King's public attitude to orthodoxy was tolerant, but he wrote privately to a friend that he found among California ministers "the tightest orthodoxy, in connection with a noble large-heartedness among the people" (quoted in Frothingham, *Tribute*, 191).

On his preaching in a conservative church, see Frothingham, *Tribute*, 193. King was also much in demand by reform, philanthropic, and charitable societies; see ibid., 181.

7. King, *Spiritual Christianity* (Boston: American Unitarian Association, n.d.), 5–6.

8. Ibid., 20, 27.

9. King, "Living Water from Lake Tahoe," in *Substance and Show*, 314.

10. Ibid., 316–17.

11. Ibid., 321.

12. Ibid., 323–24.

13. His "comet" and "metallurgy" sermons appear in the same volume, as does "The Earth and the Mechanic Arts" (1861).

14. King, *American Nationality* (San Francisco, 1863), 6.

15. King, "The Privileges and Duties of Patriotism," in *Substance and Show*, 394.

16. King, "Substance and Show," in *Substance and Show*, 3, 8.

17. Ibid., 11.

18. Ibid., 20, 27.

19. On David Starr Jordan, see Starr, *California Dream* 308–309; Widney's reference to King appears in *The Three Americas* (Los Angeles: Pacific Publishing, Times-Mirror Press, 1935), 65.

20. *A Life Sketch of Mrs. E. P. Thorndyke*, edited by L. M. Snow (n.p., 1906).

21. Arnold Crompton in his history of Unitarianism suggests that Hamilton was directly an heir of King's ideas, but I have found no evidence to that effect. Hamilton was the next prominent liberal in the area. He may, of course, have been influenced by King, as he would likely have heard him preach during the Civil War.

Chapter 3: Issues of Death and Life

1. The paper, called *Banner of Progress*, ran for at least two years, until 1868; another, *Light for All*, appeared briefly in 1880. Sources on California Spiritualism and its opponents are scanty and do not justify separate treatment here. Of communities rooted in Spiritualism, the best known is Thomas Lake Harris's Fountaingrove (near Santa Rosa), but judging from the little attention given it by the religious media, it had small impact on the nearby Protestant population. Even when accusations against Harris broke out in 1891, the religious media paid less attention than the secular papers. For the basic story, see Robert V. Hine, *California's Utopian Colonies* (San Marino, Calif.: Huntington Library, 1953).

For samples of orthodox churchpeople's reaction to Spiritualist writings and leaders, see the *Occident*, January 4, 1868 (on Andrew Jackson Davis), and March 28, 1868 (on the Spiritualists' heavenly visitors being in fact spirits on their way to hell). The Methodist M. C. Briggs, besides being a patriot and Sabbatarian crusader, was also known for his anti-Spiritualist lectures. These seem to be no longer extant, but a sharp and witty reply to them, including what appears to be a good summary of Briggs's views, is that of N. I. Underwood, *A Lecture on Spirit Communion* (Sacramento: J. H. Lewis, 1857).

2. See below, Chapter 4, for a fuller description of Adventism in California.

3. See S. D. Simonds, *The Doctrine Concerning God* (San Francisco, 1865), reprinted from the *Methodist Quarterly Review* of July, 1865; on his heresy and reinstatement, see Anthony, *Methodism*, 36, and the *Occident*, June 13, 1868. *California Christian Advocate* issues that would cover Simonds's trial are no longer extant.

4. D. A. Dryden, *Heresy in the California Conference* (San Francisco: John H. Carmany, 1877).

5. Thomas Starr King, quoted in Richard Frothingham, *Tribute*, 191.

6. George H. Shriver, *American Religious Heretics: Formal and Informal Trials* (Nashville, Tenn.: Abingdon Press, 1966).

7. *Pacific Methodist*, Feb. 27, 1869; reports of contemporary sermons in the *Occident* and the *Pacific* confirm that opinion.

8. Universalists were so named because they believed in the universal salvation of all human beings; after death, people might undergo a period of trial or purgation, but ultimately no one would be condemned eternally to hell. Unitarians held no single doctrine on this matter, but most also questioned the theory of eternal punishment. One of the sermons in Starr King's repertoire was on this topic; see "Eternal Punishment," in *Christianity and Humanity*.

9. Elizabeth Stuart Phelps's *The Gates Ajar* (1868) was an immediate best-seller; its sequels *Beyond the Gates* (1883) and *Between the Gates* (1887) were almost as well received. The famous Harriet Beecher Stowe addressed the topic in her popular *The Minister's Wooing* (1859). The American preoccupation with death and the afterlife in this period is treated by Ann Douglas in *The Feminization of American Culture* (New York: Alfred A. Knopf, 1977), chapter 6: "The Domestication of Death: The Posthumous Congregation."

10. This idea was first suggested to me by Michael O'Sullivan, who offers it without much elaboration in his Ph.D. dissertation, "A

Harmony of Worlds: Spiritualism and the Quest for Community in
Nineteenth-Century America" (University of Southern California,
1981).

11. A brief biographical summary appeared in the San Francisco
Evening Bulletin, April 10, 1882, 2.

12. Laurentine Hamilton, *The Future State and Free Discussion:
Four Sermons* (San Francisco: John H. Carmany, 1869). This volume contains all four sermons and his defense before the Presbytery.
The first sermon, "Knowledge of God Eternal Life," is primarily a
critique of revivalism and emotional religion; the third, "Fear the Foe
of Love," returns to the same theme of emotionalism; and the fourth,
"The Uses and Dangers of Skepticism," is a defense of the critical approach Hamilton has taken. Clearly, Hamilton was aware of the radical potentials in the positions he was offering for debate.

13. Hamilton, *Future State*, 44–46.

14. Ibid., 48–49.

15. Ibid., 50–54.

16. Ibid., 12–13.

17. Ibid., 18–20. Later, in his systematic treatise entitled *Reasonable Christianity* (San Francisco: Dewey & Co., 1881), also a
sermon series, he criticized orthodoxy for its awaiting of "special ex-
pedients," as in the "showers" of a revival, and connected this with
a belief in miracles. Hamilton preferred to think of God as operating
within a wholesome natural order, with regularity instead of the
shocks, the ups and downs, of miracles. It seems likely that we are
seeing, in Hamilton's liberalism, the fruits of Bushnell's ideas of an
organic "Christian nurture," possibly carried beyond what Bushnell
would wish. Further, in a funeral sermon published in the *Memorial
to Oscar Lovell Shafter* (San Francisco, 1874), Hamilton criticized
both formalists who demanded adherence to specific religious structures and rites, and pietists who demanded a "mystical" experience.
Mysticism, for him, meant excessive emotionalism. Hamilton thus
was advocating a steadily growing but controlled experience of
religion.

18. See Bishop Thompson's speech to the California Conference,
reprinted in the *California Christian Advocate*, November 18, 1867.

19. The figure of one-half was the *Occident*'s estimate (April 3,
1869), based on observation of the numbers attending the respective
Sunday schools of First Presbyterian and the new Independent Presbyterian Church. It may seem strange that there would be no direct

estimate of the congregation at Hamilton's main service, but then it may have been awkward for an orthodox Presbyterian reporter to show his face near Hamilton's church at the hour he should have been at his own. I have attempted to reconstruct Hamilton's following from membership lists from First Presbyterian before and after the split (there are no extant lists from Independent Presbyterian Church); the church manual lists members and new accessions for 1868 through 1873. Since only about twenty households out of about two hundred remained members of First Presbyterian after the split, I would have guessed a much higher defection, two-thirds or more going with Hamilton. But the membership lists still are uncertain, since there was also a regular high turnover among Oakland churches, probably because of the high mobility of many newcomers as well as some floating among the churches. The church manuals for First Presbyterian Church, Oakland, as well as for First Congregational (1874) are in the Bancroft Library's pamphlet collection (University of California, Berkeley).

20. The *Occident* on February 27 and March 6, 1869, reviewed comments by secular and denominational papers. The March 6 issue also contains a full report of the case. The favorable advertisement appears in the *Directory of the City of Oakland and County of Alameda for the Year 1870* (Oakland, Calif.: Cook and Miller, 1870), 44–46. The same directory, pp. 20–22, gives an interesting summary of the great increase in real estate business in Oakland, mentioning some of the leaders in the business, several of whom were members of either First Congregational or First Presbyterian before the split.

21. See, besides the church manuals and directory cited above, William Warren Ferrier, *Henry Durant, First President of the University of California* (Berkeley: Ferrier, 1942).

22. Sample biographies showing this career pattern appear in James M. Guinn's chronicle, *History of the State of California and Biographical Record of Oakland and Environs* (Los Angeles: Historic Record Co., 1907).

23. Summaries of these thinkers appear in O'Sullivan, "A Harmony of Worlds," cited above, n. 10, and briefly in the more readily available perspective on Spiritualism by R. Laurence Moore, *In Search of White Crows: Spiritualism, Parapsychology, and American Culture* (New York: Oxford University Press, 1977). Both authors emphasize the amorphous nature of spiritualist belief systems, which

makes it difficult to say what any individual Spiritualist believed. The *Banner of Progress* in California, however, seems to have been generally in line with A. J. Davis when it treated metaphysical matters. N. I. Underwood's *Lecture on Spirit Communion*, cited in n. 1, is another example; he cites Davis's theory of creation as more powerful than that of Moses!

24. Moore, *White Crows*, chapters 1–3.

25. Dryden, *Heresy*, 1–10.

26. See Leon L. Loofbourow, *Those Pioneer Wives, What Women!* (San Francisco: Historical Society of the California-Nevada Annual Conference of the Methodist Church, n.d. [ca. 1900]). Issues of the *California Christian Advocate* from 1851 on, when they mention Dryden at all, locate him in a variety of regions around the Bay Area.

27. They were indeed in the vanguard. Most eastern liberals are advancing these views after 1880. See James H. Moorhead, "The Erosion of Postmillenialism in American Religious Thought, 1865–1925," *Church History* 53 (March 1984): 61–77.

28. Most of them also lacked in their theologies any connection with Californians' love of nature, such as Starr King had expressed. Given the later romanticization and sacralization of nature in twentieth-century California, this is surprising. But it is difficult to ascertain how much weight to assign to this feature before, say, 1880. For discussion of John Muir's role in bringing this again to the fore, see Chapter 8.

29. See James White, *The Redeemer and Redeemed: or the Plan of Redemption through Christ* (Oakland: Pacific Press, 1877).

30. *Pacific Methodist*, February 8, 1872; *Evangelist*, October 29, 1872.

31. This assessment is based on a survey of sermons in the Bancroft Library (University of California, Berkeley) under the title, Pamphlets by California Authors on Religion. This small collection is widely ranging enough to be representative, although it is possible that the various sermons were kept by some individual(s) with idiosyncratic tastes before coming into the hands of H. H. Bancroft or other collectors. There are six volumes, comprising ninety-two sermons and essays, most (sixty-four) by mainstream Protestant ministers; some Spiritualist, Unitarian, freethinker, Roman Catholic, and Episcopal documents also appear.

Chapter 4: Sacred Time and Holy
Community

1. Kevin Starr in *California Dream* says that Sabbatarianism and
the linking of the Sabbath to civilization itself was primarily an aspect of the New England enterprise. My research indicates that, on
the contrary, all denominations gathered round the cause, although
the early leaders were of New England origin. Starr is wrong in stating that concern about the Sabbath died out by 1861, as we will see
in this chapter.

2. Even religious people had difficulty in keeping the Sabbath.
One Methodist convert in the 1850s apologized for not observing
the holy day, saying "if he did not *rodeo* [drive] his stock on Sunday,
he would not be able to get help [with the branding]." See Charles
Alexander, *The Life and Times of Cyrus Alexander*, edited by
George Shochat (Los Angeles: Dawson's Bookshop, 1967). Alexander was a late convert, first to Presbyterianism in 1852 at age 47;
shortly after, he donated a farm to the Old School minister James A.
Woods. Later he changed to the Methodist church, for unstated reasons. This change late in his life may have contributed to his difficulty in adopting Sabbath observance.

3. For descriptions, see Rodman Paul, *California Gold: The Beginning of Mining in the Far West* (Cambridge: Harvard University
Press, 1947), 81, and Kenneth Wilson Moore, "Areas of Impact of
Protestantism upon the Cultural Development of Northern California, 1850–1870" (M.A. thesis, Pacific School of Religion, 1970).

4. William Addison Blakely, compiler and annotator, *American
State Papers Bearing on Sunday Legislation*, revised edition (Washington, D.C.: Religious Liberty Association, 1911), 350–53. For another, more popularly written account including a vivid description
of the explosive Fields-Terry relationship, see Warren L. Johns, *Dateline Sunday, U.S.A.* (Mountain View, Calif.: Pacific Press, 1967),
chapter 8. See also William Hanchett, "Blue Law Gospel," 361–68.

5. The early events are chronicled by John Cecil Haussler, "The
History of the Seventh-day Adventist Church in California" (Ph.D.
dissertation, University of Southern California, 1945); Harold O.
McCumber, *The Advent Message of the Golden West* (Mountain
View, Calif.: Pacific Press, 1968), formerly "The Beginnings of the
Seventh Day Adventist Church in California" (Ph.D. dissertation,

University of California, Berkeley, 1934); and Ella M. Robinson, *Lighter of Gospel Fires: John N. Loughborough* (Mountain View, Calif.: Pacific Press, 1954).

6. Clerical examples include M. C. Briggs, *The Sabbath Made for Man* (San Francisco: Methodist Book Depository, 1897); George H. Jenks, *The Lord's Day of the Early Church* (San Francisco: Libby and Swett, 1871); James L. Woods, *Papers* (San Anselmo, Calif.: San Francisco Theological Seminary collection); Theophilus Woodward, *The Sabbath Question* (San Francisco, 1883); Laurentine Hamilton, sermon reprinted in *Occident*, April 1868. Aside from these, the *Pacific* and the *Occident* both contain numerous references to the Sunday question, accounts of legal issues, and reports of ministers' sermons on the subject; the *California Christian Advocate* from the early years onward devoted space to the issue, encouraging the keeping of the Sabbath. Lay treatments include Hiram Plank, "Three Sabbaths: The Jewish Sabbath; the Papal Sabbath; and the Christian Sabbath" (ms., Gilroy, Calif., n.d. [ca. 1890]); Henry Root, "The Question of the Sabbath: Sunday or Saturday?" (San Francisco: scrapbook collection, 1914 [this essay not dated]); and F. Joseph Spencer, *Sunday the Seventh Day* (Fruitvale, Calif., 1904).

7. Accounts of the early Adventists appear in most general histories of American religion. The best recent account of the Whites' rise to prominence and the emergence of positions on various issues is Ronald Numbers, *Prophetess of Health: A Study of Ellen G. White* (New York: Harper & Row, 1976).

8. James White, *The Redeemer and Redeemed: Or, the Plan of Redemption Through Christ* (Oakland: Pacific Press, 1877), 10.

9. Ibid., 46.

10. *The Sunday Law! Enforcement of the 'Christian Sabbath,'* in *Signs of the Times* (Oakland: Pacific Press, 1882).

11. Robinson, *Loughborough*, 130, 131.

12. Briggs, *Sabbath for Man*. While not published in this form until 1897, Briggs's views were well known in Methodist circles much earlier. However, we cannot be sure he was using, in his earlier preaching, all this ammunition from scholarship on the ancient world. We do know that James L. Woods was constructing some similar scheme from the sermons mentioned, but not elaborated, in the reports of his preaching contained in his collected *Papers*.

13. See, for example, Henry Root, "Question of Sabbath." One "researcher," however, claimed that the Sabbath was always Sunday

but in the thirteenth century the Jews changed their observance to Saturday! See F. J. Spencer, *Sunday the Seventh Day.*

14. *Oakland Daily Transcript*, May 12, 1874, 2.

15. Ibid., May 14, 1874, 3.

16. *Banner of Progress*, the Spiritualist paper, regularly commented derogatorily on the Protestant churches' attempts to emphasize the Sabbath; for Spiritualists it was simply an outmoded ritual prescription.

17. *Occident*, March 30, 1881, 4; May 11, 1881, 4.

18. Blakely, *State Papers*, 353.

19. *San Francisco Daily Examiner*, June 20, 1882, 2; June 22, 1882, 3; July 3, 1882, 3.

20. *San Francisco Daily Examiner*, September 5, 1882, 2; *Sacramento Record-Union*, August 31, 1882, 1.

21. Blakely, *State Papers*, 352.

22. *San Francisco Examiner*, September 1, 1882, 2; August 23, 1882, 2.

23. Robinson, *Loughborough*, 160; U.S. Bureau of the Census, *Religious Bodies: 1936*, vol. 1 (Washington, D.C.: Government Printing Office, 1936), 375.

24. Blakely, *State Papers*, 561. For some of the continued Adventist arguments on behalf of religious liberty, see the Sentinel Library collection among the Pamphlet Boxes of Sermons and Religious Papers by Californians (University of California, Berkeley Bancroft Library). Other important sources are the periodicals, the *Review and Herald* and, beginning in California in 1874, the pamphlets issued under the series title *Signs of the Times.*

25. Census reports on religious bodies are not thoroughly reliable because of differing criteria among the churches for what constitutes membership. Nevertheless, it appears that while California Protestant membership sometimes matched that of the urban Northeast (15 to 18 percent of the population), it generally was lower (around 14 percent) and it never compared to that of rural areas in the Midwest or South. Rocky Mountain and Southwestern states also had low Protestant membership. This assessment is based on data from the U.S. Bureau of the Census reports for 1850, 1860, 1870, 1890, and 1906.

26. See Douglas Anderson, "'You Californians.'" We should note, however, that Anglo-Protestant standards had sunk lower in later years. After the 1881 revival the *Occident* commented that

evangelical strength had doubled (adding one to two thousand in the San Francisco area), old members had been reinvigorated, and many others had been reformed "who have not and will not join the churches" (March 23, 1881). The editors were so eager to believe in the efficacy of revivals that they included among their successes people whom they did not expect to make any church commitments at all!

27. See, for example, the *Stockton Independent*, March 29, 1881.

28. *San Francisco Chronicle*, February 7, 1889, 4.

29. *Occident*, November 30, 1898; December 7, 1898. These are representative examples of the general tone at the time. Nor was the lack of church influence confined to the cities. For example, some towns, such as Petaluma, boasted of strong moral and religious sentiment; but in the same county, Sebastopol had only one church to seven saloons and a winery (see Roy P. McLaughlin, "Sebastopol in the 1890s," in *The Carrillo Family in Sonoma County, History and Memories*, by Alma McDaniel Carrillo and Eleanora Carrillo de Haney). A later report cited numerous problems in both city and country churches north of San Francisco Bay, and observed that it was the "small, irresponsible, and unnecessary religious groups" that were "the bane of religious life in California." See Presbyterian Church, in the U.S.A., *A Rural Survey of Marin and Sonoma Counties, California* (New York: Presbyterian Church, 1916), 11. Since the "irresponsible" groups are not named, we do not know whether the church report was referring to the alternative tradition of liberal groups, like Spiritualists or independents, or to evangelically rooted groups like churches of the holiness movement. In northern California the former seems more likely, but additional information must be brought to light before we can be certain.

30. That is not to say that liberal preachers had not been popular in other decades: the two Channings in the 1820s and 1830s, Emerson, and Theodore Parker in the 1850s are obvious examples. In this next wave of liberalism, however, California was definitely a leader.

31. Hiram Plank, "Three Sabbaths."

32. See their publication, *The Gnostic* (1888), of which only one volume is extant. Most such groups appear to have surfaced briefly and enthusiastically for one to three years, but were unable to establish themselves permanently. In the 1890s, longer-lasting organizations appeared.

Chapter 5: Metaphysics in the Southland

1. For accounts of the booms, see Carey McWilliams, *Southern California Country: An Island on the Land* (New York: Duell, Sloan & Pearce, 1946), chapter 7; Robert M. Fogelson, *The Fragmented Metropolis: Los Angeles, 1850–1930* (Cambridge: Harvard University Press, 1967). Charles Nordhoff's *California for Health, Pleasure, and Residence: A Book for Travelers and Settlers*, has recently been reprinted by Ten Speed Press (1975). Nordhoff himself settled in California and died in Coronado (an island off the San Diego coast).

2. Quoted in John Baur, *The Health Seekers of Southern California, 1879–1900* (San Marino, Calif.: Huntington Library, 1959), 19.

3. Walter H. Case, *History of Long Beach and Vicinity* (New York: Arno Press, 1974); see Nordhoff, *California*, for mention of these and other colonies. See also Harland Hogue, "History of Religion in Southern California, 1846–1880" (Ph.D. thesis, Columbia University, 1958). Hogue observes also the Methodist influence in the founding of San Fernando, by, among others, the Reverend Charles Maclay, a businessman and later a legislator, who donated the Maclay School of Theology at the University of Southern California (1887). For a popular account of the Long Beach area, see the *California Independent*, May 27, 1899.

4. See Manuel P. Servin and Iris Higbe Wilson, *Southern California and Its University* (Los Angeles, 1969); Edward Drewry Jervey, "The Methodist Church and the University of Southern California," *Historical Society of Southern California Quarterly* 40 (March 1958).

5. Baur's *Health Seekers*, cited in n. 1, is the best treatment of the health propaganda, health seekers, and health industry in southern California.

6. Gregory H. Singleton, *Religion in the City of Angels: American Protestant Culture and Urbanization, Los Angeles, 1850–1930* (UMI Research Press, 1979).

7. Ibid., chapter 3; also McWilliams, *Southern California*, 134, and Fogelson, *Fragmented Metropolis*.

8. These figures are given in Leland D. Hine, *Baptists in Southern California* (Valley Forge, Pa.: Judson Press, 1966), 121.

9. Singleton's emphasis on traditionalism in Los Angeles is a very important corrective to earlier treatments which, when they touched on religion at all, emphasized mostly the unusual or bizarre. Mc-Williams's *Southern California* is a good example—and he is not always aware of the religious nuances in his sources. For instance, he quotes a woman visitor who wrote, "I am told that the millennium has already begun in Pasadena, and that even now there are more sanctified cranks to the acre than in any other town in America" (p. 249). McWilliams uses this as support for his argument that the region supported many bizarre movements. However, knowing that Pasadena was a temperance town and that the region in general was a strong holiness area, we can be suspicious of his interpretation. Most likely "sanctified cranks" refers to Methodists and other holiness people, not to followers of odd groups; and the reference to the millennium may refer to the issue of pre- or post-millennial attitudes, an argument that many holiness groups brought to the fore.

In response to such interpretive tendencies, Singleton's work is enormously valuable; but it is necessary to examine also the fringe movements that disturbed the apparently placid mainstream, especially those that were much discussed in the pulpit and religious press. An early account supporting Singleton's emphasis (even though it is undoubtedly prejudiced in favor of the main stream of Protestantism) is Rev. Robert J. Burdette's *Greater Los Angeles*, which emphasizes the churches' wealth and their success in promoting temperance. However, Burdette's own sense of the lack of fit appears when he comments on the Los Angeles climate and natural environment: "How can the emblems of the resurrection be very impressive in a land where nature has no symbols of death, but where month answers month, all through the year, in every flower-blossoming cemetery, shaded by fadeless palms and pines, crying, 'Life—everlasting life'!! . . . This is a land of life" (p. 32).

10. On Theosophy, see J. Stillson Judah, *The History and Philosophy of the Metaphysical Movements in America* (Philadelphia: Westminster Press, 1967), and Bruce F. Campbell, *Ancient Wisdom Revived: A History of the Theosophical Movement* (Berkeley and Los Angeles: University of California Press, 1980).

11. The California community is studied in Emmett A. Greenwalt, *The Point Loma Community in California, 1897–1942* (Berkeley and Los Angeles: University of California Press, 1955); see also Robert V. Hine, *California's Utopian Colonies* (San Marino, Calif.:

Huntington Library, 1953). Robert Ellwood and William Miller, in *The Religious Heritage of Southern California: A Bicentennial Survey*, edited by Francis J. Weber (Los Angeles: Interreligious Council, 1976), discuss other theosophical groups and observe (p. 100) that many spiritual teachers in southern California were born and raised at Point Loma.

12. Ralph Waldo Trine, *In Tune with the Infinite* (New York: Thomas Y. Crowell, 1897), 41. On New Thought, see Judah, *Metaphysical Movements*, and Charles S. Braden, *Spirits in Rebellion* (Dallas: Southern Methodist University Press, 1963).

13. For interpretations of the derivation of Eddy's ideas, see Stephen Gottschalk, *The Emergence of Christian Science in American Religious Life* (Berkeley and Los Angeles: University of California Press, 1973); Robert Peel, *Christian Science: Its Encounter with American Culture* (New York: Holt, 1958); and *Mary Baker Eddy: The Years of Discovery* (New York: Holt, Rinehart & Winston, 1966), the first of three volumes of biography.

14. To grasp Eddy's thought, it is necessary to read her *Science and Health with Key to the Scriptures*, preferably in several editions (I have used the 1889, 1898, and 1906 editions as reference points), and her *Retrospect and Prospect* (1912). Problems in interpreting her work, due to the many changes in the basic texts, are numerous, but for our purposes I have tried simply to describe the most general and stable of her ideas. For interpretation, Gottschalk's work, cited in n. 13, is the most incisive and comprehensive. Another helpful work, though marred by some hostility to the movements, is Gail Thain Parker's *Mind Cure in New England: From the Civil War to World War I* (Hanover, N.H.: University Press of New England, 1973); it includes New Thought as well as Christian Science.

15. Joseph Adams, quoted in Gottschalk, *Emergence*, 114–15.

16. Baur, *Health Seekers*, 93–94; Los Angeles Directory, 1893 and 1910–11.

17. See George Wharton James, "The Christian Science Architecture of California," *Out West* n.s. 4 (August 1912): 71–79.

18. The estimates are Parker's in *Mind Cure*: she believes they have national application. Our only supporting information, with no numerical data, comes from the Unity School of Christianity library (Kansas City, Mo.: miscellaneous files, 1891–1910). Unity publicized its work in California as beginning in the north with Malinda Cramer's energetic proselytizing in 1891. At that time a group

was formed called Silent Unity, based on metaphysical principles of harmony with the true Spirit. Later, however, Cramer's work was organized separately as Divine Science, based in Denver. The Los Angeles Unity church in 1893 may have been the first California center after Cramer's. By 1910 Unity had eleven groups in the south and twelve in the north, with a few more in the inland towns. Clearly, metaphysical religions were operating in the north as well as the south; our present focus on the southern area is intended to show that the new movements could prosper even in a heavily traditional area. One cannot explain them simply by reference to a previous liberal tradition, as one might in the north.

19. McWilliams, *Southern California*, 256–58.

20. Malinda Cramer, *Basic Statements and Health Treatment of Truth*, 2d edition (San Francisco, 1893), 11.

21. Karl Holl, "Der Szientismus," in *Gesammelte Aufsätze zur Kirchengeschichte*, vol. 3 (Tübingen: J. C. B. Mohr, 1921–28 [orig. 1918]), 460–79.

22. Figures are derived from the U.S. Bureau of the Census, *Religious Bodies: 1916* (Washington, D.C.: 1916). The census reports 2753 Scientists in California in 1906—probably a low figure, as there were at least thirty-two chartered churches then, of which at least six were building a second or larger building, indicating probable memberships of three hundred or more. Los Angeles churches must have had 1200 members; if the other twenty-odd churches had only fifty members apiece, there would have been at least four thousand Scientists in the state. The published census figures for Los Angeles do not count the Scientists separately, indicating that their membership was less than 1 percent of the population (less than 1,227 out of 122,697). But if so, it must have been just barely less. In 1909 the city of Los Angeles proper had four churches, one of which was building a church to accommodate 1200, while two of the other three were meeting in large halls—an auditorium seating about five hundred and a symphony hall (seatings unknown, but probably three hundred or more). These are estimated from the article, "The Scientists' New Churches," *Los Angeles Times*, July 25, 1909, V, 16–17. If in 1909 there were sittings for over two thousand people, it seems quite likely that in 1906 there could have been about 1200 members.

23. Singleton, *City of Angels*, Appendix I, 193.

24. Fogelson, *Fragmented Metropolis*, discusses this whole pattern in considerable detail.

25. McWilliams, *Southern California*, 105, 107.

26. Ibid., 107–110.

27. Nordhoff, *California*, 181.

28. Nathaniel West, cited in Fogelson, *Fragmented Metropolis*, 197.

29. The health literature is probably the best source for both the paradisal view of California and the warnings about taking care of one's nerves. See, for example, William A. Edwards and Beatrice Harraden, *Two Health Seekers in Southern California* (Philadelphia: J. B. Lippincott, 1897), 22 and 29–36; Emma H. Adams, *To and Fro in Southern California* (Cincinnati: W.M.B.C. Press, 1887), 73–85, 278–79; Joseph Weed, *A View of California As It Is* (San Francisco: Bynon & Wight, 1874), 165–67, 176–77. The latter is also an excellent example of a later version of the California mythology discussed in Chapter 1.

30. Joseph Boskin, "Associations and Picnics as Stabilizing Forces in Southern California," *California Historical Society Quarterly* 44 (1965): 17–26.

31. Quoted in Hine, *Baptists*, 11.

32. Singleton, *City of Angels*, 54.

33. McWilliams, *Southern California*, 70–82, has an excellent discussion of the romanticizing tradition, while Starr, *California Dream*, discusses its emergence among intellectuals (365–414). For the Mediterranean architecture, see Starr, ibid., and Fogelson, *Fragmented Metropolis*, 157–58. These discussions are so excellent that I have not attempted to reproduce the details here.

34. Clara Burdette, *The Rainbow and the Pot of Gold* (Pasadena, Calif.: Clara Vista Press, 1908), 2.

35. Estimates range from half to four-fifths not joining a church; attendance is seldom remarked upon, and difficult to estimate. See McWilliams, *Southern California*, 270–72; Fogelson, *Fragmented Metropolis*, 193–94. Singleton's work suggests that commitments were higher; nevertheless, the data are ambivalent. Between 1900 and 1910 the "voluntaristic Protestant" proportion of the Los Angeles population dropped from 17.6 to 10.6 percent (after two decades of steady increase), then between 1910 and 1920 rose sharply again, to sixteen percent. Each decade saw migrations of over two

hundred thousand people into Los Angeles. The 1910–1920 period saw the beginning of more migration from the South, which might explain at least part of the rise in that period; a close examination of churches established between 1910 and 1920 is needed, but is outside the scope of the present study. The sharp decrease between 1900 and 1910 is another issue. Other than the ferment caused by the metaphysical movements and their attraction (at least temporarily) of new members, I have found no other religious explanation for this change.

Whatever the ultimate explanations of these changes, my estimates of the metaphysical movements suggest that for every eight people joining a traditional Protestant denomination, one joined one of the metaphysical religions. A much larger number of the Anglo-Protestant segment had some involvement, at least through reading literature, with one of the movements. The impact on many congregations would be significant; on the more liberal denominations, like the Congregationalists, it would be quite disturbing.

36. We find indeed that the Scientists' churches, more than any other group, followed the areas of most desirable settlement. Not only did most of the substantial early settlements have Christian Science churches within five or ten years, but as the population grew, new ones quickly established themselves. While the first three Scientist churches were within the original city (the Third Church having obtained a prestigious site a block away from First Congregational), the fourth church was established in Highland Park (annexed to the city in 1895), the fifth in Hollywood (annexed 1910), and the sixth not far from the University of Southern California, a citadel of Methodist influence and, of course, home to many of the city's most intellectual personages. Unity School was less fortunate; its three centers in 1910 were still in the downtown area—not unfavorable, because they were easily accessible to many, but not in the newer residential areas, either. Nonetheless, Unity also had three centers in Long Beach, two in Pasadena, and another three in outlying towns.

37. Malinda E. Cramer, "Christ Method of Healing, or Thought-Transference—Which?" *Harmony* 12 (May 1900), 237. *Harmony* was the magazine of Divine Science; another important New Thought journal in California was *Now: A Journal of Affirmation*, which began publication in 1900 and continued until 1928.

Chapter 6: Mainstream Churches
and the New Mysticism

1. *Occident*, November 6, 1889. One occasionally finds evangelists in the field encountering Christian Scientists; see, for example, Lizzie Miller, *The True Way* (Los Angeles: author, 1895), 209–11.

2. *Occident*, June 28, 1899. An August 10, 1881 article in the *Occident* is the earliest reference I have found to non-western religions or philosophies as potential competitors with Protestantism (setting aside, that is, the derogatory stereotypes that recur throughout our period). There are extensive criticisms of the new movements in the *California Christian Advocate* from 1905 to 1909. The editors of this paper lumped all the new movements together in one comment (November 12, 1908):

> We are living in a great religious movement; we may add, a great religio-psychological movement, the Christian Science, the theosophy, mental healings of innumerable kinds, the alleged miraculous speaking with tongues, the holy rollers, the holy jumpers, and a vast deal of phenomena we cannot understand, and for that very reason the greatest care should be taken to hold onto the truth.

They went on to say that the subconscious mind "has the charm of the mystical and wierd [*sic*] power of hypnotism, and it is dangerous to introduce it into personal religious problems."

3. Robert V. Hine, *California's Utopian Colonies*, 51.

4. Ibid., 44, on Otis; and see the *Occident*, June 28, 1899.

5. Clara Burdette, *Robert Burdette and His Message* (Philadelphia: John C. Winston/Clara Vista Press, 1922).

6. See Raymond J. Cunningham, "From Holiness to Healing: The Faith Cure in America 1872–1892," *Church History* 43 (1974): 499–513. Cunningham identifies healing as the most prominent expression of holiness, before glossolalia emerged as the "sign" of Pentecost. He traces the development from the Boston homeopath Charles Cullis, who in 1862 received the "second blessing" of holiness and was called to his "Faith Work," a home for consumptives on Beacon Hill. His actual faith healing began after 1870, and in 1874 he started summer Faith Conventions—holiness camp meetings with at least one healing service. At the 1881 convention Albert B. Simpson was convinced of the new practice and incorporated di-

vine healing into his program in a New York City Presbyterian church. The Baptist holiness preacher, Adironam Judson Gordon of Boston, became a trustee of Cullis's Faith Work; his influence on the holiness movement is well known. Cullis's *Faith Cures* (1879) and A. J. Gordon's *Ministry of Healing* (1882) were highly instrumental in spreading news of the work. John Dowie's "Divine Healing," a slightly different approach, received a hearing in California for eight months in 1888; see his *American First Fruits* (San Francisco: Leaves of Healing, 1889).

7. Pond, *Gospel Pioneering*, 179. For an account of Protestant responses to Christian Science nationwide, see Raymond J. Cunningham, "The Impact of Christian Science on the American Churches, 1880–1910," *American Historical Review* 72 (April 1967): 885–905.

8. I will not deal here with those who entirely left the traditional denominations, but one example is worth mentioning: Fenwicke Holmes, brother of the Ernest Holmes who founded the Church of Religious Science in Los Angeles in 1917. Fenwicke was founder and pastor of a Congregational church in Venice, then a rather wealthy beach community near Los Angeles. He ministered there for six years beginning in 1911. During that time he became more interested in New Thought and related philosophies and gradually introduced the new ideas into his ministry. Finally he decided it would be more appropriate for him to leave the traditional pastorate, so he became a New Thought lecturer, first in California, then in the East. The significance of this example is that, as Fenwicke admits, his parishioners were being exposed to New Thought whether he acknowledged it to them or not, while he was doing traditional preaching and supervising church activities. How common this sort of development might have been is difficult to ascertain, as most ministers left no such records. See the biographical material in Fenwicke Holmes, *Ernest Holmes: His Life and Times* (New York: Dodd, Mead & Company, 1970).

9. Charles Edward Locke, "Eddyism: Is It Christian? Is It Scientific? How Long Will It Last?," *West Coast Magazine* 9 (March 1911), 483–98, and 10 (April, May, June 1911), 53–64, 177–92, 305–20. The magazine published a reply in July (vol. 10, pp. 433–44) by a local Scientist, Edward W. Dickey: "Christian Science: The Truth About It." Locke seems to be stating and expanding every negative comment made about the Scientists. Most writings content

themselves with brief disparaging remarks; see, for example, Eliza M. Otis, "Lay Sermons," in *California "Where Sets the Sun"* (Los Angeles: Times-Mirror, 1905), 165.

10. Locke, "Eddyism," 312.

11. Ibid., 487.

12. Charles Reynolds Brown, *My Own Yesterdays* (Boston: 1931); in this memoir he does not mention his encounter with Christian Science.

13. Brown was a liberal in that he accepted biblical criticism and the Social Gospel, but still held to the divinity of Christ—more like Beecher or Brooks in theology, rather than Unitarian in tendencies.

14. Brown, *Faith and Health* (New York: Thomas Y. Crowell, 1910), 56, 71–85, 188; the quotation is from p. 85.

15. Ibid., 59–61.

16. Ibid., 194–95.

17. Ibid., 141–67. The Emmanuel Movement, founded by a minister and a doctor in Boston, had introduced some psychological practices in the form of counseling and suggestion into the program of an Episcopal church. The movement was a response to Christian Science's healing appeal; but unlike the Scientists, Emmanuel's practitioners worked closely with regular physicians and would not take any patients without medical recommendations. For an overview, see John Gardner Greene, "The Emmanuel Movement, 1906–1929," *New England Quarterly* 7 (1934): 494–532.

18. Ibid., 105.

19. Ibid., 106, 108, 112, 178–93.

20. Ibid., 122–23.

21. Ibid., 125–26.

22. James M. Campbell, *What Christian Science Means and What We Can Learn From It* (New York: Abingdon Press, 1920), 69.

23. Ibid., 109.

24. James M. Campbell, *New Thought Christianized* (New York: Thomas Y. Crowell, 1917), 74.

25. Ibid., 96, 100.

26. Parker, *Mind Cure*, passim.

27. James M. Campbell, *The Presence* (New York: Eaton and Mains, 1911), 171.

28. Ibid., 30.

29. Campbell, *Christian Science*, 46.

30. See Benjamin Fay Mills, "Why I Became a Liberal in Reli-

gion" (Oct. 9, 1898), *Twentieth Century Religion*, vol. 1 (Boston: Morris Lefcowitch, 1898), no. 2. For examples of his earlier work, see *Victory Through Surrender: Plain Suggestions Concerning Entire Consecration* (Chicago: Fleming H. Revell, 1892), and *God's World and Other Sermons* (Chicago: Fleming H. Revell, 1894). The volume *Victory Through Surrender* appears to have been mildly influenced by holiness ideas.

31. See the brief account in George William Haskell, "Formative Factors in the Life and Thought of Southern California Congregationalism, 1850–1908" (Ph.D. dissertation, University of Southern California, 1947), 154–55.

32. H. H. Bell, *A Modern Task, or the Story of the Religious Activities of the Committee of One Hundred* (San Francisco, 1916), 59–60.

33. Among these, the *Twentieth Century Religion* series printed in Boston stands out (it should not be confused with the later Oakland series under the same title).

34. In one sermon, "What is Theosophy?", *Twentieth Century Religion* (Oakland [1902?]), Mills states that "My mental and spiritual indebtedness to Theosophy is a considerable one" (20). His treatment of Theosophy is quite extensive and shows considerable study.

35. Benjamin Fay Mills, *The Divine Adventure* (Los Angeles, 1907), 170–71.

36. Ibid., 119; see the continuing discussion, 121–27.

37. "The Problem of Evil" (Dec. 5, 1898), *Twentieth Century Religion*, vol. 1 (Boston), no. 10, p. 5.

38. Mills, *Divine Adventure*, 193–95.

39. Mills, "The Divinity of Man," *Twentieth Century Religion* (Oakland), 16.

40. Mills, *Divine Adventure*, 208. For example, he says in his analysis of "The Model Prayer" that "May Thy Kingdom come" means "*May the ideal become actual; May we bring the God within into perfect harmony with the God without*" (ibid., 199).

41. Ibid., 9–13.

42. See the brief account in "Builders of the Commonwealth," *Touring Topics* 24 (May 1932): 17. Widney's own descriptions of his life can be found in *The Three Americas: Their Racial Past and the Dominant Racial Factors of Their Future* (Los Angeles: Pacific Publishing, Times-Mirror Press, 1935), 56–86, supplemented by mate-

rial in *Race Life and Race Religions: Modern Light on Their Growth, Their Shaping and Their Future* (Los Angeles: Pacific Publishing, 1936). The only biography to date is Carl W. Rand's *Joseph Pomeroy Widney: Physician and Mystic*, edited by Doris Sanders (Los Angeles: University of Southern California School of Medicine, 1970).

43. Rand, *Widney*, 52–53.

44. City Mission in 1921 merged with Newman Methodist Church to become the Church of All Nations. It is unclear whether Widney remained an active participant in the new organization. See Edward Drewry Jervey, *The History of Methodism in Southern California and Arizona* (Nashville, Tenn.: Parthenon Press, 1960), 113.

45. Rand, *Widney*, 75.

46. Joseph P. Widney, *The Way of Life; Holiness Unto the Lord; The Indwelling Spirit; The Baptism of the Holy Ghost* (Los Angeles, 1900). The faith cure essay has remained unavailable to me; its existence is mentioned briefly by Rand, *Widney*, 59–60. Despite Widney's criticism of faith cures, he was very much interested in health issues—as a physician, he would be—and wrote in cooperation with other authors about the healthful geography, climate, and natural advantages of the Los Angeles area.

47. Joseph P. Widney, *Race Life of the Aryan Peoples*, 2 vols. (New York: Funk and Wagnalls, 1907); vol. 2, *The New World*, especially 296–305. On the Scots-Irish, see 106–8. Cf. *Three Americas*, 32–45.

48. Joseph P. Widney, *The Faith that Has Come to Me* (Los Angeles: Pacific Publishing, 1932), 94, 132–37.

49. Widney, *Aryan Peoples*, vol. 2, 109. His otherwise glowing account of the Scots-Irish is dampened only when he notes their tendency to hold onto Calvinism. Methodism, he said, with its "hopeful hymns and scant theology" was a better way. Nevertheless, ecclesiasticism was growing even in the Methodist church. "But," he declared firmly, "the current of Teutonic spiritual life is going the other way" (ibid., 107–8).

50. The phrase is in Rand, *Widney*, 107.

51. Widney, *Faith*, 157; *Aryan Peoples*, vol. 2, 350.

52. Widney, *Faith*, 237, 239, 256, 346.

53. Widney, *Three Americas*, 65.

54. Joseph P. Widney, *The Genesis and Evolution of Islam and Judeo-Christianity* (Los Angeles: Pacific Publishing, 1932).

55. E.g., Widney, *Aryan Peoples*, vol. 2, 104; *Faith*, 163. Widney claimed that a distant forebear of his, from the late Middle Ages, was Jewish; and he spoke out against anti-Semitism and for the Jew (though in a rather condescending way) in *Faith*, 228–33. In *Genesis*, he argued that the desert breeds monotheism, while the diversity of the plains and the coast breeds polytheism (17–18).

Chapter 7: Holiness in California

1. The account that follows is based primarily on the following works: Charles Edwin Jones, *Perfectionist Persuasion: The Holiness Movement and American Methodism 1867–1936*, ATLA Monograph Series, no. 5 (Metuchen, N.J.: Scarecrow Press, 1974); Melvin Easterday Dieter, *The Holiness Revival of the Nineteenth Century*, Studies in Evangelicalism, no. 1, edited by Kenneth E. Rowe and Donald W. Dayton (Metuchen, N.J.: Scarecrow Press, 1980); and Timothy L. Smith, *Called unto Holiness: The Story of the Nazarenes: The Formative Years* (Kansas City, Mo.: Nazarene Publishing House, 1962).

2. Jesse T. Peck, *The Central Idea of Christianity* (Boston: Henry V. Deger, 1858), 52.

3. See, for example, A. J. Gordon, *The Ministry of the Spirit* (Philadelphia: American Baptist Publication Society, 1894), 113–15.

4. For an account of the developing controversy between Keswickians and Wesleyans, see George M. Marsden, *Fundamentalism and American Culture: The Shaping of Twentieth-Century Evangelicalism: 1870–1925* (New York: Oxford University Press, 1980), 75–80, 93–101.

5. Vinson Synan argued for a connection between populism and holiness in *The Holiness-Pentecostal Movement in the United States* (Grand Rapids, Mich.: William B. Eerdmans, 1971).

6. Marsden suggests that the holiness people were lower middle-class or lower class, but not of the poorest strata like the Pentecostals; see *Fundamentalism*, 256–57, n. 17.

7. Phineas F. Bresee, "After Pentecost," in *The Certainties of Faith: Ten Sermons by the Founder of the Church of the Nazarene*, introduced by Timothy L. Smith (Kansas City, Mo.: Nazarene Publishing House, 1958), 42. These sermons are all from 1903; other published ones are undated.

8. Bresee's sermons include two on the temperance issue, in the

volume *Sermons on Isaiah* (Kansas City, Mo.: Nazarene Publishing House, 1926). Two other sermons in the same collection allude to war: "War and Conflict" and "The Conquering Word." One may suspect they were preached at some time when war was on the minds of Bresee's audiences (perhaps 1914?). In each case, however, Bresee dismisses the topic rather abruptly, saying that earthly conflicts are of meager significance compared to the great Christian warfare of sin versus holiness. In short, aside from the temperance cause, he did not address social concerns at all in the published sermons.

9. "To Know Him," *Certainties*, 84–88; "The Continued Message," ibid., 46. Cf. "The Baptism with Fire," in *Isaiah*, 36.

10. "The Atmosphere of the Divine Presence," *Certainties*, 91–93.

11. "The Verities of Salvation," *Isaiah*, 105–6. Sometimes Bresee used a more corporate image of God showing himself in transformed humanity: holy people, taken together, are God's self-revelation. Thus in "The Perpetual Servant" (ibid., 155) he said:

> The Servant was a *people*, then a *remnant* of people. . . . then a Person, the ripe fruitage of the people, in whom dwelt all the fullness of God. The Servant became the people, made after the image of the Person, a further incarnation of God. . . . It is in transformed humanity that God is seen.

In other words, the Holy Ghost united with human beings is the latter-day incarnation of God, in the image of Jesus Christ, continuing his life and ministry. This is of course connected to a traditional idea of the church, but put in a context that is both more mystical and broader. Compare H. Orton Wiley's understanding of the work of the Logos, discussed in the text below.

12. Phineas Bresee, "The Eye of the Soul," in *Sermons from Matthew's Gospel* (Kansas City, Mo.: Nazarene Publishing House, n.d.).

13. "The Passion That Absorbs," *Isaiah*, 160.

14. "The Poor in Spirit," *Matthew's Gospel*, 65.

15. "Danger Points," *Matthew's Gospel*, 163–64. It is notable that this same proverb was used by Charles Reynolds Brown in defending his use of the techniques of suggestion.

16. "The Eye of the Soul," *Matthew's Gospel*, 143, 144–45. Cf. "The Master Passion of the Soul," ibid., 151, where Bresee speaks of how the presence of Jesus enlarges human powers:

Christ puts our love so under the delightful, heavenly pressure of His
own love that it must continuously enlarge. There is such a pressure
upon thought, of the clear, vast, mighty thought of Christ, that thought
must continuously throb with mightier force.

17. A. B. Simpson, *The Holy Spirit, or Power from on High*, 2
vols. (New York: Christian Alliance Publishing, 1895), part 1, 21–
22.

18. Marsden, *Fundamentalism*, 80.

19. Simpson, *Holy Spirit*, vol. 1, 142–43; Gordon, *Ministry of
Spirit*, 93.

20. Bresee, "The Rest Giver," *Matthew's Gospel*, 197.

21. "The Poor in Spirit," *Matthew's Gospel*, 64.

22. "Pentecost," *Matthew's Gospel*, 40.

23. H. Orton Wiley, *Christian Theology*, 3 vols. (Kansas City,
Mo.: Nazarene Publishing House, 1940). This work was intended as
a teaching text for Nazarene students, and as a result it contains a
great deal of the history of theology and doctrine common to all
Protestants. The section on the Holy Spirit and the experience of
sanctification is the only specifically Nazarene section, and even here
one does not find the distinct emphases of Wiley's thesis. He does,
however, consider and reject the Keswickian and Plymouth Brethren
conceptions of holiness.

24. H. Orton Wiley, "The Logos Doctrine in the Prologue of the
Fourth Gospel" (M.S.T. thesis, Pacific School of Religion, 1917),
2–5.

25. Ibid., 16–25.

26. Ibid., 32. In Wiley's other major work, *Epistle to the Hebrews* (Kansas City, Mo.: Nazarene Publishing House, 1934), we
find some of this large sense of the spirit. Wiley taught Hebrews and
developed his commentary on it while teaching in schools and summer camps, possibly not long after Bresee's death. He writes that
while studying the epistle at one point, he received a new understanding of it that came "like a sunburst," showing him that the central point of the epistle was not the symbolic understanding of the
tabernacle, as he had previously thought, but the Melchizedek priest-
hood of Christ. This he understood newly as the manifestation by
which Christ pours out blessings continuously and forever on humanity. Christ's work under the "symbol of Melchisedec" referred to
the "eternal increase of life and love," going beyond mere cleansing

from sin "to make our hearts His divine presence chambers, where His glory shall be revealed more and more" (239–40). Here we find echoes of Wiley's "Logos Doctrine," which emphasized the fullness of blessing and the continual movement toward completion, fullness, and perfection in humanity as a whole.

27. Non-Catholic bodies grew by slightly under 200 percent in this period; the Nazarenes' 280 percent in the state is comparatively small for a new sect at the peak of its growth period elsewhere. For figures, see U.S. Bureau of the Census, *Religious Bodies: 1936*, 385.

28. See T. L. Smith, *Called*, 273. The infighting among the Nazarenes was one of the reasons California lost its own "native" leadership: John W. Goodwin of California, one of the newly elected general superintendents after Bresee's death, was called to another region and E. F. Walker was brought in from outside.

29. For substantiation, see Robert Mapes Anderson, *Vision of the Disinherited: The Making of American Pentecostalism* (New York: Oxford University Press, 1979).

30. We should be aware that census reports of Pentecostal bodies nationwide were very incomplete. Most Pentecostal church members were not counted until 1926 or 1936. Even so, the largest Pentecostal group in 1916, the Assemblies of God, was reported as having nearly seven thousand members nationwide and only 286 members in California. (We also know that nationally the two major periodicals of the Pentecostal movement had, by 1915, over twenty-five thousand subscribers—a number that may better approximate the number of members and church attenders. By the same token, California Pentecostals might number three or four times their reported membership; but that would still leave only one thousand Pentecostals in the region.) That state of affairs changed dramatically in the 1920s. By 1926 the California members of the Assemblies of God numbered about eight thousand, while the Church of God (Tomlinson) numbered 1,700, and Aimee Semple McPherson had attracted several thousand to her International Church of the Foursquare Gospel (not reported till 1936, but then numbering seven thousand).

As for holiness churches other than the Nazarenes, California in 1916 was reported to have about five thousand members in other holiness or holiness-related groups, including primarily the Christian Missionary Alliance, the Free Methodists, and the Salvation Army. For the data, see U.S. Bureau of the Census, *Religious Bodies: 1936*.

Chapter 8: Into the Sierras

1. John Muir, *The Life and Letters of John Muir*, vol. 1, edited by William Frederic Bade; vol. 9 of *The Writings of John Muir* (Boston: Houghton Mifflin, 1923), 155.

2. Ibid., 164–65.

3. Ibid., 167.

4. Ibid., 179.

5. John Muir, *John of the Mountains*, edited by Linnie Marsh Wolfe (Boston: Houghton Mifflin, 1938), 77.

6. Muir, *Life and Letters*, vol. 2, 333–34.

7. Ibid., vol. 1, 218.

8. Ibid., 251–52.

9. Starr, *California Dream*, 187. Starr puts John Muir in a category with Henry George and Josiah Royce, as Californians who picked up various strands of the California mentality, all of them having a deep feeling for the land and a sense of place. I have not dealt with these here, for George's social criticism and Royce's philosophy were distant from the development of Anglo-Protestantism in California, whereas Muir's impact was direct and local.

Bibliography

Newspapers

Banner of Progress. (Spiritualist.)
California Christian Advocate. (Methodist.)
California Independent. (Interdenominational.)
Evangel. (Baptist.)
Evangelist. (Baptist.)
Gnostic. (Theosophical.)
Harmony. (Divine Science.)
Herald of Truth. (Baptist.)
Los Angeles Times.
Light for All. (Spiritualist.)
Metropolitan Banner. (Independent Baptist.)
Now: A Journal of Affirmation. (New Thought.)
Oakland Daily Transcript.
Occident. (Presbyterian.)
Pacific. (Congregational.)
Pacific Methodist. (Methodist, South.)
Petaluma Daily Crescent.
Petaluma Journal and Argus.
Sacramento Record-Union.
San Diego Union.
San Francisco Daily Examiner.
San Francisco Chronicle.
San Francisco Evening Bulletin.
Sonoma County Journal.
Sonoma Democrat.
Stockton Independent.

Primary Sources

Adams, Emma H. *To and Fro in Southern California.* Cincinnati: W.M.B.C. Press, 1887.

Alexander, Charles. *The Life and Times of Cyrus Alexander*. Edited by George Shochat. Los Angeles: Dawson's Bookshop, 1967.

Anthony, C. V. *Fifty Years of Methodism*. San Francisco: Methodist Book Concern, 1901.

Bancroft Library, University of California, Berkeley. Pamphlets by California Authors on Religion. 6 vols.

———. Pamphlet Boxes of Sermons and Religious Papers by Californians. 11 vols.

Benton, Joseph A. *California As She Was: As She Is: As She Is To Be*. Sacramento, 1850.

———. *Some of the Problems of Empire*. San Francisco: Excelsior Press, 1868.

Bell, H. H. *A Modern Task, or the Story of the Religious Activities of the Committee of One Hundred*. San Francisco, 1916.

Blakely, William Anderson, compiler and annotator. *American State Papers Bearing on Sunday Legislation*. Revised edition by Willard Allen Colcord. Washington, D.C.: Religious Liberty Association, 1911.

Bresee, Phineas F. *The Certainties of Faith: Ten Sermons by the Founder of the Church of the Nazarene*. Introduction by Timothy L. Smith. Kansas City, Mo.: Nazarene Publishing House, 1958.

———. *Sermons from Matthew's Gospel*. Kansas City, Mo.: Nazarene Publishing House, n.d.

———. *Sermons on Isaiah*. Kansas City, Mo.: Nazarene Publishing House, 1926.

Briggs, Ellen [Green]. *Our Pioneer Ministers' Wives*. California Annual Conference of the Methodist Episcopal Church, 1908.

Briggs, M. C. *The Sabbath Made for Man*. San Francisco: Methodist Book Depository, 1897.

Brown, Charles Reynolds. *Faith and Health*. New York: Thomas Y. Crowell, 1910.

———. *My Own Yesterdays*. Boston, 1931.

Burbank, Luther. *My Beliefs*. New York: Avondale Press, n.d.

Burdette, Clara B. *The Rainbow and the Pot of Gold*. Pasadena, Calif.: Clara Vista Press, 1908.

———. *Robert J. Burdette: His Message*. Philadelphia: John C. Winston and Clara Vista Press, 1922.

Bushnell, Horace. "California: Its Characteristics and Prospects." In S. Willey, *California Miscellany*. San Francisco, 1858.

———. *Society and Religion: A Sermon for California*. San Francisco: Sterett, 1856.

Campbell, James M. *New Thought Christianized*. New York: Thomas Y. Crowell, 1917.

———. *The Presence*. New York: Eaton and Mains, 1911.

———. *What Christian Science Means, and What We Can Learn From It*. New York: Abingdon, 1920.

Cook, Mabel Collins. *Light on the Path*. Pasadena, Calif.: Theosophical University Press, 1968 (orig. 1888).

Coues, Elliott. "Theosophy: What It Is Not." *Californian Illustrated* 1 (February 1892): 133–37.

Cramer, Malinda E. *Basic Statements and Health Treatment of Truth: A System of Instruction in Divine Science Treatment*. 2d edition. San Francisco, 1893.

———. "Method of Healing, or Thought-Transference—Which?" *Harmony* 12 (May 1900).

Dickey, Edward W. "Christian Science: The Truth About It." *West Coast Magazine* 10 (July 1911): 433–44.

Dowie, John Alexander. *American First Fruits, Being a Brief Record of Eight Months Divine Healing Missions in the State of California*. San Francisco: Leaves of Healing, 1889.

Dryden, D. A. *Heresy in the California Conference*. San Francisco: John H. Carmany, 1877.

Eddy, Mary Baker. *Retrospect and Prospect*. Boston, 1912.

———. *Science and Health with Key to the Scriptures*. Boston, 1889, 1898, 1906.

Edwards, William A., and Beatrice Harraden. *Two Health Seekers in California*. Philadelphia: J. B. Lippincott, 1897.

Farley, Charles A. "The Moral Aspect of California: A Thanksgiving Sermon of 1850." Introduction by Clifford Merrill Drury. *California Historical Society Quarterly* 19 (December 1940): 299–307.

Fitzgerald, O. P. *California Sketches*. Nashville, Tenn.: Methodist Episcopal Church, South, 1896.

Fleming, Sandford. "Selected Letters of Osgood Church Wheeler." *California Historical Society Quarterly* 27 (1948): 9–18, 123–31, 229–36, 301–9.

Gibbs, Mifflin Wister. *Shadow and Light: An Autobiography*. Washington, D.C., 1902.

Gordon, A. J. *The Ministry of the Spirit*. Philadelphia: American Baptist Publication Society, 1894.

"The Gregson Memoirs." *California Historical Society Quarterly* 19 (June 1940): 112–43.

Hamilton, Laurentine. *The Future State and Free Discussion: Four Sermons*. San Francisco: John H. Carmany, 1869.

——. *A Reasonable Christianity*. San Francisco: Dewey, 1881.

Hazen, Edward Adams. *Salvation to the Uttermost*. Lansing, Mich.: Darius D. Thorp, 1892.

H[ertslet], E. M. *Ranch Life in California*. London: W. H. Allen, 1886.

Holmes, Fenwicke L. *Ernest Holmes: His Life and Times*. New York: Dodd, Mead, 1970.

James, George Wharton. "The Christian Science Architecture of California." *Out West* n.s. 4 (August 1912): 71–79.

Jenks, George H. *The Lord's Day of the Early Church*. San Francisco: Libby and Swett, 1871.

Jewell, Frank F. *Crown "Jewells."* San Jose: First Methodist Episcopal Church, 1892.

Johnston, N. R. *Looking Back from the Sunset Land, or People Worth Knowing*. Oakland, 1898.

King, Thomas Starr. *American Nationality*. San Francisco, 1863.

——. *Christianity and Humanity*. Boston: James R. Osgood, 1877.

——. *Eternal Punishment*. Boston: American Unitarian Association, n.d.

——. *Spiritual Christianity*. Boston: American Unitarian Association, n.d.

——. *Substance and Show, and Other Lectures*. Boston: James R. Osgood, 1877.

Kip, William Ingraham. *A California Pilgrimage*. Fresno, Calif., 1921.

——. *The Early Days of My Episcopate*. New York: Thomas Whittaker, 1892.

Locke, Charles Edward. "Eddyism: Is It Christian? Is It Scientific? How Long Will It Last?" *The West Coast Magazine* 9 (March 1911): 483–98, and 10 (April, May, June 1911): 53–64, 177–92, 305–320.

McCloskey, Joseph J., and Hermann J. Sharmann. *Christmas in the Gold Fields, 1849*. San Francisco: California Historical Society, 1959.

Mackenzie, Robert. *Miracles: Their Nature and Possibility*. San Francisco: Occident Printing House, 1889.

——. "Presbyterianism in California." *Californian Illustrated* (April 1892): 426–42.

Miller, Lizzie. *The True Way*. Los Angeles: author, 1895.

Mills, Benjamin Fay. *The Divine Adventure*. Los Angeles, 1907.

———. *God's World and Other Sermons*. Chicago: Fleming H. Revell, 1894.

———. *Twentieth Century Religion*. Boston: Morris Lefcowitch, 1898.

———. *Twentieth Century Religion*. Oakland, Calif. [1902?].

———. *Victory Through Surrender*. Chicago: Fleming H. Revell, 1892.

Minton, Henry C. *The Parliament of Religions: Its Results Reviewed*. San Francisco, 1894.

Muir, John. *The Writings of John Muir*. 10 vols. Boston: Houghton Mifflin, 1923.

———. *John of the Mountains: The Unpublished Journals of John Muir*. Edited by Linnie Marsh Wolfe. Boston: Houghton Mifflin, 1938.

Nordhoff, Charles. *California for Health, Pleasure, and Residence: A Book for Travelers and Settlers*. New York: Ten Speed Press, 1973 (orig. 1873).

Oakland. *Directory of the City of Oakland and County of Alameda for the Year 1870*. Oakland, Calif.: Cook and Miller, 1870.

Otis, Eliza M. *California "Where Sets the Sun."* Los Angeles: Times–Mirror, 1905.

Peck, Jesse T. *The Central Idea of Christianity*. Boston: Henry V. Deger, 1858.

Phelps, Philo F. *The Relief Signal in the Hour of Need*. San Francisco, 1880.

Phillips, Grace Darling. *Seventy-Five Romantic Years*. Hollywood-Beverly Christian Church, 1963.

Pierce, Robert. *Apples of Gold: or, Words Fitly Spoken*. Introduction by P. F. Bresee. Los Angeles: Pentecostal Church of the Nazarene, 1907.

Plank, Hiram. "Three Sabbaths: The Jewish Sabbath; The Papal Sabbath; and the Christian Sabbath." Manuscript, State Historical Society. Gilroy, Calif., n.d. [ca. 1895].

Pond, William C. *Gospel Pioneering: Reminiscences of Early Congregationalism in California, 1833–1920*. Oberlin, Oh., 1921.

Presbyterian Church in the U.S.A. Board of Home Missions. *A Rural Survey of Marin and Sonoma Counties, California*. New York: Presbyterian Church, 1916.

Root, Henry. *The Question of the Sabbath: Saturday or Sunday?* San Francisco, 1914.

Royce, Josiah. *California: From the Conquest in 1846 to the Second Vigilance Committee in San Francisco: A Study of American Character.* New York: Alfred A. Knopf, 1948.

———. *Race Questions, Provincialism, and Other American Problems.* New York: Macmillan, 1908.

Shipley, William Chapman. *Tales of Sonoma County.* Santa Rosa, Calif.: Sonoma County Historical Society, 1965.

Shuck, Oscar T., comp. *The California Scrap Book.* San Francisco: H. H. Bancroft, 1869.

Simmons, J. C. *Thirtieth Anniversary of a California Pastor.* San Francisco: Winterburn, 1882.

———. *My Trip to the Orient.* San Francisco: Whitaker and Ray, 1902.

Simpson, A. B. *The Holy Spirit, or Power from on High.* 2 vols. New York: Christian Alliance, 1895.

Simonds, S. D. *The Doctrine Concerning God.* San Francisco, 1865.

Snow, L. M. *A Life Sketch of Mrs. E. P. Thorndyke.* N.p., 1906.

Speer, William. *China and California: Their Relations, Past and Present.* San Francisco, 1853.

Spencer, F. Joseph. *Sunday the Seventh Day: Its History and Origin.* Fruitvale, Calif., 1904.

Stokes, Darius. *A Lecture upon the Moral and Religious Elevation of the People of California.* San Francisco, 1853.

Stone, A. L. *Leaves from a Finished Pastorate.* New York and San Francisco, 1882.

"The Sunday Law! Enforcement of the 'Christian Sabbath.'" *Signs of the Times.* Oakland, Calif.: Pacific Press, 1882.

Taylor, William A. *Seven Years Street Preaching in San Francisco.* New York, 1856.

Trine, Ralph Waldo. *In Tune with the Infinite.* New York: Thomas Y. Crowell, 1897.

Underwood, N. I. *A Lecture on Spirit Communion: Being a Review of Rev. M. C. Briggs' Recent Lectures on Spiritism.* Sacramento: J. H. Lewis, 1857.

Waugh, Lorenzo. *Autobiography.* 3d, enlarged edition. San Francisco: S. P. Taylor, 1885.

Weed, Joseph. *A View of California As It Is.* San Francisco: Bynon & Wight, 1874.

White, James. *The Redeemer and Redeemed: Or, the Plan of Redemption through Christ*. Oakland, Calif.: Pacific Press, 1877.

Widney, Joseph P. *The Faith That Has Come to Me*. Los Angeles: Pacific Publishing, 1932.

———. *The Genesis and Evolution of Islam and Judeo-Christianity*. Los Angeles: Pacific Publishing, 1932.

———. *Race Life of the Aryan Peoples*. 2 vols. New York: Funk & Wagnalls, 1907.

———. *The Three Americas: Their Racial Past and the Dominant Social Factors of Their Future*. Los Angeles: Pacific Publishing, 1935.

———. *The Way of Life; Holiness Unto the Lord; The Indwelling Spirit*. Los Angeles, 1900.

———. *Whither Away? The Problem of Death and the Hereafter*. Los Angeles: Pacific Publishing, 1934.

Wiley, H. Orton. *Christian Theology*. 3 vols. Kansas City, Mo.: Nazarene Publishing House, 1940.

———. *Epistle to the Hebrews*. Kansas City, Mo.: Nazarene Publishing House, 1934.

———. "The Logos Doctrine in the Prologue of the Fourth Gospel." M.S.T. Thesis, Pacific School of Religion, 1917.

Williams, Albert. *A Pioneer Pastorate and Times*. San Francisco: Wallace & Hassett, 1879.

Woods, James A. *Recollections of Pioneer Work in California*. San Francisco: Joseph Winterburn, 1878.

———. *A Sermon at the Dedication of the Presbyterian Church of Stockton, California, May 5, 1850*. Barre: Patriot Press, 1851.

Woods, James L. Papers. San Francisco Theological Seminary Collections, San Anselmo.

Woodward, Theophilus. *The Sabbath Question*. San Francisco, 1883.

Secondary Sources

Anderson, Douglas F. "Give Up Strong Drink, Go to Work, and Become a Man: William Taylor in Gold Rush San Francisco." Paper for the American Academy of Religion, Western Region, March 1982.

———. "'You Californians': San Francisco Evangelicalism, Re-

gional Religious Identity, and the Revivalism of D. L. Moody."
Fides et Historia 15 (Spring/Summer 1983): 44–66.

Anderson, Robert Mapes. *Vision of the Disinherited: The Making of American Pentecostalism.* New York: Oxford University Press, 1979.

Bohme, Frederick G. "Episcopal Beginnings in Southern California." *Southern California Quarterly* 47 (1965): 171–90.

Boskin, Joseph. "Associations and Picnics as Stabilizing Forces in Southern California." *California Historical Society Quarterly* 44 (1965): 17–26.

Braden, Charles S. *Spirits in Rebellion: The Rise and Development of New Thought.* Dallas: Southern Methodist University Press, 1963.

Buckham, John Wright, and Charles Suner Nash, editors. *Religious Progress on the Pacific Slope.* Boston: Pilgrim Press, 1917.

"Builders of the Commonwealth." *Touring Topics* 24 (May 1932): 17.

Campbell, Bruce F. *Ancient Wisdom Revived: A History of the Theosophical Movement.* Berkeley and Los Angeles: University of California Press, 1980.

Case, Walter H. *History of Long Beach and Vicinity.* New York: Arno Press, 1974.

Caughey, John, and Laree Caughey. *Los Angeles: Biography of a City.* Berkeley and Los Angeles: University of California Press, 1976.

Cole, Clifford A. *The Christian Churches of Southern California: A History.* [St. Louis], 1959.

Crompton, Arnold. *Unitarianism on the Pacific Coast: The First Sixty Years.* Boston: Beacon Press, 1957.

Cunningham, Raymond J. "From Holiness to Healing: The Faith Cure in America, 1872–1892." *Church History* 43 (1979): 499–513.

———. "The Impact of Christian Science on the American Churches, 1880–1910." *American Historical Review* 72 (April 1967): 885–905.

Daniels, Douglas Henry. *Pioneer Urbanites.* Philadelphia: Temple University Press, 1980.

Dieter, Melvin Easterday. *The Holiness Revival of the Nineteenth Century.* Studies in Evangelicalism, no. 1, edited by Kenneth E.

Rowe and Donald W. Dayton. Metuchen, N.J.: Scarecrow Press, 1980.

Douglas, Crerar. "The Gold Rush and the Kingdom of God: The Rev. James Woods' Cure of Souls." In *The American West and the Religious Experience*, edited by William M. Kramer, Western American Study Series. Los Angeles: Will Kramer, 1975.

Douglass, Ann. *The Feminization of American Culture*. New York: Alfred A. Knopf, 1977.

Drury, Clifford M. "The Beginnings of the Presbyterian Church on the Pacific Coast." *Pacific Historical Review* 9 (June 1940): 195–204.

———. *The Centennial of the Synod of California*. Presbyterian Synod of California, 1951.

———. *A Chronology of Protestant Beginnings in California*. Northern California–Western Nevada Council of Churches, n.d.

———. "Church-Sponsored Schools in Early California." *Pacific Historian* 20 (1976): 158–66.

———. *Historical Sketch*. First Presbyterian Church, Stockton, California, 1940.

Ferrier, William Warren. *Henry Durant, First President of the University of California*. Berkeley: author, 1942.

———. "The Origins and Growth of the Protestant Church on the Pacific Coast." In *Religious Progress*, edited by Buckham and Nash.

Fleming, Sandford. *God's Gold: The Story of Baptist Beginnings in California, 1849–1860*. Philadelphia: Judson Press, 1949.

Fogelson, Robert M. *The Fragmented Metropolis: Los Angeles, 1850–1930*. Cambridge: Harvard University Press, 1967.

Frothingham, Richard. *A Tribute to Thomas Starr King*. Boston: Ticknor and Fields, 1865.

Gilbert, Benjamin Franklin. "The Confederate Minority in California." *California Historical Society Quarterly* 20 (1941): 154–67.

Goodykoontz, Colin B. "Protestant Home Missions and Education in the Trans-Mississippi West, 1835–1860." In *The Trans-Mississippi West*, edited by James F. Willard and Colin B. Goodykoontz. Boulder, Colo.: University of Colorado, 1930.

Gottschalk, Stephen. *The Emergence of Christian Science in American Religious Life*. Berkeley and Los Angeles: University of California Press, 1973.

Greene, Charles S. *Magazine Publishing in California*. San Francisco: Library Association of California, 1898.

Greene, John Gardner. "The Emmanuel Movement, 1906–1929." *New England Quarterly* 7 (1934): 494–532.

Greenwalt, Emmett A. *The Point Loma Community in California, 1897–1942*. Berkeley and Los Angeles: University of California Press, 1955.

Grivas, Theodore. "A History of the Los Angeles Young Men's Christian Association: The First Twenty Years." *California Historical Society Quarterly* 44 (1965): 205–27.

Guarneri, Carl, and David Alvarez, editors. *Religion and Society in the American West*. Lanham, Md.: University Press of America, forthcoming.

Guinn, James M. *History of the State of California and Biographical Record of Oakland and Environs*. Los Angeles: Historic Record, 1907.

Hanchett, William. "The Question of Religion and the Taming of California, 1849–1854." *California Historical Society Quarterly* 32 (1953): 49–56, 119–44.

———. "The Blue Law Gospel in Gold Rush California." *Pacific Historical Review* 24 (1955): 361–68.

Hansen, Harvey J., and Jeanne Thurlow Miller. *Wild Oats in Eden: Sonoma County in the Nineteenth Century*. Santa Rosa, Calif.: Hooper, 1962.

Haskell, George William. "Formative Factors in the Life and Thought of Southern California Congregationalism, 1850–1908." Ph.D. dissertation, University of Southern California, 1947.

Haussler, John Cecil. "The History of the Seventh-day Adventist Church in California." Ph.D. dissertation, University of Southern California, 1945.

Higham, John. *From Boundlessness to Consolidation: The Transformation of American Culture*. Ann Arbor, Mich.: William Clements Library, 1969.

Hine, Leland D. *Baptists in Southern California*. Valley Forge, Pa.: Judson Press, 1966.

Hine, Robert V. *California's Utopian Colonies*. San Marino, Calif.: Huntington Library, 1953. Reprinted Berkeley and Los Angeles: University of California Press, 1983.

Hogue, Harland. "History of Religion in Southern California 1846–1880." Ph.D. dissertation, Columbia University, 1958.

Holl, Karl. "Der Szientismus." In *Gesammelte Aufsätze zur Kirchengeschichte*, vol. 3. Tübingen: J. C. B. Mohr, 1921–28(orig. 1918).

Hutchison, William R. *The Modernist Impulse in American Protestantism*. Cambridge: Harvard University Press, 1976.

Janzen, Kenneth L. "The Transformation of the New England Tradition in California, 1849–1860." Ph.D. dissertation, Claremont Graduate School, 1964.

Jervey, Edward Drewry. *The History of Methodism in Southern California and Arizona*. Nashville, Tenn.: Parthenon Press, 1960.

———. "The Methodist Church and the University of Southern California." *Historical Society of Southern California Quarterly* 40 (1958): 59–69.

Johansen, Dorothy O. "A Working Hypothesis for the Study of Migrations." *Pacific Historical Review* 36 (1967): 1–12.

Johns, Warren L. *Dateline Sunday, U.S.A.: The Story of Three and a Half Centuries of Sunday-law Battles in America*. Mountain View, Calif.: Pacific Press, 1967.

Jones, Charles Edwin. *Perfectionist Persuasion. The Holiness Movement and American Methodism, 1867–1936*. ATLA Monograph Series no. 5. Metuchen, N.J.: Scarecrow Press, 1974.

Judah, J. Stillson. *The History and Philosophy of the Metaphysical Movements in America*. Philadelphia: Westminster, 1967.

Larsen, Lawrence H. *The Urban West at the End of the Frontier*. Lawrence: Regents Press of Kansas, 1978.

Layne, J. Gregg. "Annals of Los Angeles." *California Historical Society Quarterly* 13 (1934): 315–34.

Loofbourow, Leon L. *Those Pioneer Wives, What Women!* San Francisco: Historical Society of the California-Nevada Annual Conference of the Methodist Church, n.d.

Looney, Floyd. *History of California Southern Baptists*. Fresno, Calif., 1954.

McCumber, Harold O. *The Advent Message of the Golden West*. Mountain View, Calif.: Pacific Press, 1968.

McDonald, William, and John E. Searles. *The Life of Rev. John S. Inskip*. Boston: McDonald & Gill, 1885.

McLaughlin, Roy P. "Sebastopol in the 1890s." In *The Carrillo Fam-*

ily in Sonoma County, History and Memories, by Alma McDaniel Carrillo and Eleanora Carrillo de Haney. San Francisco, 1930.

McWilliams, Carey. *Southern California Country: An Island on the Land.* New York: Duell, Sloan & Pearce, 1946.

Marsden, George M. *Fundamentalism in American Culture: The Shaping of Twentieth Century Evangelicalism.* New York: Oxford University Press, 1980.

Montesano, Philip M. "San Francisco Black Churches in the Early 1860s: Political Pressure Group." *California Historical Society Quarterly* 52 (1973): 145–52.

Moore, Kenneth Wilson. "Areas of Impact of Protestantism upon the Cultural Development of Northern California, 1850–1870." M.A. thesis, Pacific School of Religion, 1970.

Moore, R. Laurence. *In Search of White Crows: Spiritualism, Parapsychology, and American Culture.* New York: Oxford University Press, 1977.

Moorhead, James H. "The Erosion of Postmillenialism in American Religious Thought, 1865–1925." *Church History* 53 (March 1984).

Numbers, Ronald. *Prophetess of Health: A Study of Ellen G. White.* New York: Harper & Row, 1976.

Nunis, Doyce B., Jr. "California, Why We Come: Myth or Reality." *California Historical Society Quarterly* 44 (1963): 123–38.

———. *Los Angeles Bibliography.* Los Angeles: Ward Ritchie Press, 1973.

O'Sullivan, Michael. "A Harmony of Worlds: Spiritualism and the Quest for Community in Nineteenth-Century America." Ph.D. dissertation, University of Southern California, 1981.

Ostrander, Gilman M. *The Prohibition Movement in California, 1848–1933.* Berkeley and Los Angeles: University of California Press, 1957.

Parker, Gail Thain. *Mind Cure in New England: From the Civil War to World War I.* Hanover, N.H.: University Press of New England, 1973.

Paul, Rodman Wilson. *California Gold: The Beginning of Mining in the Far West.* Cambridge: Harvard University Press, 1947.

———. *The California Gold Discovery: Sources, Documents, Accounts, and Memories Relating to the Discovery of Gold at Sutter's Mill.* Georgetown, Calif.: Talisman Press, 1967.

————. *Mining Frontiers of the Far West 1848–1880.* New York: Holt, Rinehart & Winston, 1963.

————. "Patterns of Culture in the American West." *Alaska Review* 3 (1967–68): 137–50.

Peel, Robert. *Christian Science: Its Encounter with American Culture.* New York: Holt, 1958.

————. *Mary Baker Eddy: The Years of Discovery.* New York: Holt, Rinehart & Winston, 1966.

Pomeroy, Earl. *The Pacific Slope: A History of California, Oregon, Washington, Idaho, Utah, and Nevada.* New York: Alfred A. Knopf, 1966.

————. "Toward a Reorientation of Western History: Continuity and Environment." *Mississippi Valley Historical Review* 41 (1954–55): 579–600.

Power, Richard Lyle. "A Crusade to Extend Yankee Culture." *New England Quarterly* 13 (1940): 638–53.

Rand, Carl W. *Joseph Pomeroy Widney: Physician and Mystic.* Edited by Doris Sanders. Los Angeles: University of Southern California School of Medicine, 1970.

Rand, Christopher. *Los Angeles: The Ultimate City.* New York: Oxford University Press, 1967.

Rischin, Moses. "Immigration, Migration and Minorities in California." In *Essays and Assays: California History Reappraised*, edited by George H. Knoles. Los Angeles: Ward Ritchie Press/California Historical Society, 1973.

Robinson, Ella M. *Lighter of Gospel Fires, John N. Loughborough.* Mountain View, Calif.: Pacific Press, 1954.

Robinson, W. W. *Los Angeles: A Profile.* Norman: University of Oklahoma Press, 1968.

Seager, Robert, II. "Some Denominational Reactions to Chinese Immigration to California, 1856–1892." *Pacific Historical Review* 28 (1954): 49–66.

Servin, Manuel P., and Iris Higbe Wilson. *Southern California and Its University.* Los Angeles, 1969.

Shriver, George H. *American Religious Heretics: Formal and Informal Trials.* Nashville, Tenn.: Abingdon Press, 1966.

Simonds, William Day. *Starr King in California.* San Francisco: P. Elder, 1917.

Singleton, Gregory H. *Religion in the City of Angels: American*

Protestant Culture and Urbanization, Los Angeles, 1850–1930.
UMI Research Press, 1979.

Sizer [Frankiel], Sandra S. *Gospel Hymns and Social Religion: The Rhetoric of Nineteenth Century Revivalism.* Philadelphia: Temple University Press, 1978.

Smith, Timothy L. *Called unto Holiness: The Story of the Nazarenes: The Formative Years.* Kansas City, Mo.: Nazarene Publishing House, 1962.

Starr, Kevin. *Americans and the California Dream, 1850–1915.* New York: Oxford University Press, 1973.

Synan, Vinson. *The Holiness-Pentecostal Movement in the United States.* Grand Rapids, Mich.: William B. Eerdmans, 1971.

U.S. Bureau of the Census. *Historical Statistics of the U.S., Colonial Times to 1970.* Part 1. Bicentennial Edition. Washington, D.C.: Census Bureau, 1975.

———. *Religious Bodies: 1936.* Washington, D.C.: Government Printing Office, 1941.

Ware, E. B. *History of the Disciples of Christ in California.* Healdsburg, Calif., 1916.

Weber, Francis J., ed. *The Religious Heritage of Southern California: A Bicentennial Survey.* Los Angeles: Interreligious Council of Southern California, 1976.

Wendte, Charles. *Thomas Starr King, Patriot and Preacher.* Boston, 1921.

Wesley, Norton. "'Like a Thousand Preachers Flying': Religious Newspapers on the Pacific Coast to 1865." *California Historical Society Quarterly* 56 (1977): 194–209.

West, W. B., Jr. "Origin and Growth of the Churches of Christ in California." M.A. thesis, University of Southern California, 1936.

Wicher, Edward Arthur. *A Summary of the History of San Francisco Theological Seminary.* San Anselmo, Calif., 1921.

Wright, Doris Marion. "The Making of Cosmopolitan California, 1840–1870: An Analysis of Immigration." *California Historical Society Quarterly* 20 (1941): 65–79.

Young, Nellie May. *William Stewart Young, 1859–1937.* Glendale, Calif.: Arthur H. Clark, 1967.

Index

Eternal punishment, doctrine of, 33–37.
  See also Afterlife, views of
Ethnic groups, xiii, 2, 7, 14, 62, 126–27
Evangelicalism, ix–x, 126; institutions
  of, ix; and roots of holiness move-
  ment, 103, 116
Evans, Warren Felt, 64

Ferguson, T. P. and Manie, 106–7
Fields, Stephen (Justice), 48
Finney, Charles Grandison, 103
Fitzgerald, O. P., 15–16

Gold Rush, 9, 12
Gordon, Adironam Judson, 156n6

Hamilton, Laurentine, 30, 32–42, 52,
  71
Harris, Thomas Lake, 140n1
Health issues: important in California,
  59–60; and faith healing, 80, 155–
  56n6; in the metaphysical religions,
  79–80, 84–88, 124; in Widney's
  thought, 99
Hellman, Isaias, 60
Heresies, 32–34. *See also* Dryden,
  D. A.; Hamilton, Laurentine
Hinduism: criticism of, 79; preparation
  for, 129
Holiness movement, xiii, 62, 116–18,
  150n9; and Bresee, 109–14, 116–18;
  and faith healing, 80, 96; history of,
  103–5; language of, 112
Holiness Church, 106
Holmes, Ernest and Fenwicke, 156n8
Hough, C. A., 48

Inskip, John S., 104

Jesus, views of, 24, 41, 50, 66, 70, 82,
  90, 93–95, 98
Jordan, David Starr, 30, 125
Judge, William Q., 63, 69

Keswickians: conferences, 105; attitudes, 109, 112

King, Thomas Starr, xii, 18–30, 43, 52,
  71, 98–99, 120, 124
Krishnamurti, 63

Liberalism, xii, 10, 21, 30–33, 52, 62,
  71, 80, 90
Locke, Charles Edward, 80–83
Loomis, A. W., 14
Los Angeles, religious development of,
  60–62, 69–76, 91
Loughborough, J. N., 48, 50

Mahan, Asa, 103
McKee, S. B., 38
Maclay, Charles, 149
McClure, D., 38
McIntyre, Robert, 91
McPherson, Aimee Semple, 117–18,
  129
Materialism in California, 7–8, 29,
  126, 135n28
Mental healing. *See* Health issues
Metaphysical religions, xii–xiii, 63–68,
  70–71; appeal of, 77; compared with
  Muir, 124; criticism of, 79–83, 88–
  89
Methodist Church, ix, 2–4, 6, 9, 15,
  41–42; and holiness movement, 103–
  7, 109, 150n9; heretics in, 32, 37;
  Widney's connection to, 96
Methodist Church, South, 7, 15, 54
Mexican heritage in California, 8, 13,
  47–48, 75–76
Mills, Benjamin Fay, 81, 90–95
Moody, D. L., 53, 135n23, 137n34
Mormons, 10, 60
Muir, John, xiii, 121–25
Mysticism: as part of alternative tradi-
  tion, xi–xiv, 70, 80, 90, 128; in meta-
  physical religions, 64, 87; in the
  thought of Bresee, 109, 113, 118; in
  King, xii, 22–24; in Mills, 94–95; in
  Muir, 124–25; in Widney, 98–100;
  in Wiley, 115–16; criticized by Ham-
  ilton, 142n17

National Camp Meeting Association
  for the Promotion of Holiness, 105

Compositor:	Wilsted and Taylor
Text:	10/12 Sabon
Display:	Sabon
Printer:	Braun-Brumfield, Inc.
Binder:	Braun-Brumfield, Inc.